SEAFOOD LOVER'S
CHESAPEAKE BAY

Restaurants, Markets,
Recipes & Traditions

FIRST EDITION

Mary Lou Baker with Holly Smith

gpp

Guilford, Connecticut

An imprint of Rowman & Littlefield
Distributed by NATIONAL BOOK NETWORK

Copyright © 2015 by Rowman & Littlefield

Maps: Alena Joy Pearce © Rowman & Littlefield

Profiles of Old Salty's and Suicide Bridge Restaurant contributed by Andrea Vernot and Brent Burkhardt

British Library Cataloguing-in-Publication Information Available

Library of Congress Cataloging-in-Publication Data

Baker, Mary Lou, 1946-
  Seafood lover's Chesapeake Bay : restaurants, markets, recipes & traditions / Mary Lou Baker with Holly Smith. — First edition.
     pages cm
  Includes index.
   ISBN 978-1-4930-0153-8 (paperback)
 1. Restaurants—Chesapeake Bay Region (Md. and Va.)—Guidebooks. 2. Cooking (Seafood)—Chesapeake Bay Region (Md. and Va.) 3. Chesapeake Bay Region (Md. and Va.)—Guidebooks. I. Smith, Holly, 1970- II. Title.
   TX907.3.C47B35 2015
   641.6'920975518—dc23

                                                                    2014038274

♾️™ The paper used in this publication meets the minimum requirements of American National Standard for Information Sciences—Permanence of Paper for Printed Library Materials, ANSI/NISO Z39.48-1992.

All the information in this guidebook is subject to change. We recommend that you call ahead to obtain current information before traveling.

Contents

About the Authors

Mary Lou Baker has been a food and travel writer since the 1980s, first as a restaurant reviewer and weekly travel columnist for the *Capital Gazette* newspaper in Annapolis and later as food and wine editor at *Baltimore Magazine*. She has traveled to London, Ireland, France, and Italy on food-centered excursions, served as the restaurant reviewer for *Chesapeake Life*, *Annapolis Lifestyle*, and *Shore Living* magazines and is the coauthor with Bonnie Rapoport of *Dining In Baltimore*. This native New Englander has lived in Annapolis for many years with her husband, raising four children and a series of Labrador retrievers and cooking with joy for family and friends who insist on being in the kitchen to watch while she bangs those pots and pans.

Holly Smith is managing editor of the nonprofit Washington Independent Review of Books in Washington, DC, and a longtime freelance writer. Her work has appeared in the *Washington Post, More Mirth of a Nation, USA Today* Travel's 10Best, CNBC.com, *Maryland Life, Brain, Child*, and many other publications. She blogs at HollySmithWrites.com and spends her free time hiding from her four kids. Wait, she doesn't have any free time . . .

Acknowledgments

As Holly and I came to the end of our seafood-centered treasure hunt on Maryland's Eastern and Western shores, we began another task: thanking folks who helped out along the way. First, of course, are the chefs and restaurant owners who came through with recipes to share. Granted, we had to be as persistent and pesky as summertime mosquitoes, but most of them stepped up—and we thank them all for their time and interest.

There are several generous "donors" deserving of thanks for their contributions to the book. One is Eastern Shore artist Nancy Hammond, known nationally as well as locally for her vibrant bay-themed creations. She authored a humorous "recipe" to accompany her *Chesapeake Bay Dinner* woodcut. And we are delighted to include John Payne's painting *Clear Skies*, courtesy of the McBride Gallery in Annapolis.

We thank the Maryland Office of Tourism for letting us use their detailed map of the Chesapeake Bay; Andrea Vernot and Brent Burkhardt, for their descriptions of Suicide Bridge and Old Salty's restaurants; author and chef John Shields of Gertrude's Restaurant at the Baltimore Museum of Art and noted food writer John Mariani for their encouragement along the way; Peter Lesher of the Chesapeake Bay Maritime Museum for sharing his knowledge of the bay's history; and Steve Vilnit of the Maryland Department of Natural Resources for his guidance on the state's seafood sources. We also thank the many tourism officials from the counties surrounding the bay; their input helped immensely.

But most of all, I want to acknowledge the invaluable contributions of Holly Smith, the organizational force and unofficial "left brain" behind this book. Holly was managing editor of *Maryland Life* magazine before it succumbed to the changing times and agreed to "help out" when I first signed up for this project. Neither of us was prepared for what lay ahead, but suffice it to say that Holly is now the official coauthor of *Seafood Lover's Chesapeake Bay* and, despite some rough waters, we remain fast friends.

Finally, we are both grateful to Globe Pequot editor Tracee Williams for her support and patience throughout the process and for her unfailing optimism that *Seafood Lover's Chesapeake Bay* would be a worthy addition to a series that also includes foodie tomes centered on New England and the Pacific Northwest. "You're only as good as your editor," goes a saying in the publishing world. We hope we've done Tracee proud.

—Mary Lou Baker

Introduction

Maryland's nickname may be the Free State, but it could just as aptly be dubbed the Seafood State. With nearly half its 23 counties hugging the Chesapeake Bay, Marylanders' access to fresh fish and other underwater delicacies must surely make their Mid-Atlantic neighbors jealous. And as any seafood lover worth his or her tartar sauce knows, the blue crab reigns supreme among these delicacies.

Often the star of crab cakes and soft-shell sandwiches—imagine two lightly battered claws poking out from between slices of white bread—blue crabs truly take center stage during that Maryland mainstay, the crab feast. Picture a dozen or so hungry friends sitting around a paper-covered table piled high with just-boiled crabs. Mallet in hand, each diner grabs one of the still-steaming crustaceans, gives it a solid whack, and starts picking out the sweet white flesh. Now picture several pitchers of beer and stacks of hand wipes scattered around. They're important parts of a crab feast, too.

Of course, sea-foodies can't live on crab alone. And in Maryland's Chesapeake Bay region, they don't have to. Another prized bay offering—the oyster—is fresh and plentiful here, at least during months with an "R" in them (that's when they're in season). Many Free State eateries get creative with the critters, going way beyond "served on the half shell" by tempting diners with everything from messy, delicious oyster po' boys to the more highfalutin oyster flatbread. But whether served dredged and deep-fried or glistening and raw, they'll satisfy even the pickiest bivalve buffs.

For anyone whose ideal seafood spread requires all things gilled and finned, the region delivers with its array of native fish, including catfish, American shad, Atlantic croaker, eel, and summer flounder. It's Maryland's official state fish, the rockfish, though, that usually gets top billing among diners. Also known as striped bass, rockfish is the star of many maritime munchies around the Chesapeake. Blackened and broiled or diced up appetizer-style, it deserves a place of honor on any undersea platter.

So there it is: Maryland's stellar seafood lineup in a clamshell, er, nutshell. Any state with an official fish *and* an official crustacean (the blue crab, naturally) must take its seafood seriously, and Maryland does. Read on to find out more about the bay's culinary offerings and the best Free State locales for sampling them. And remember: After a visit to the Chesapeake Bay region, you'll leave with a newfound love of the area, but there's not a chance you'll leave hungry.

The Chesapeake Bay: An Overview

Formed approximately 10,000 years ago when rising waters from the last ice age flooded the Susquehanna River Valley, the Chesapeake Bay—whose name comes from the Powhatan Indian word "chesepiooc," which means "great shellfish bays"—runs from the top of eastern Maryland to the bottom and plays a major role in the state's geography, economy, and way of life. Here are several key facts about this vital body of water:

- The bay is one of the largest estuaries (a body of water where fresh water and salt water mix) in the US.

- It is 200 miles long, stretching from Havre de Grace, Maryland, to the Atlantic Ocean.

- At its widest point, the bay spans 30 miles; at its narrowest, it spans just under 4 miles.

- The average depth of the bay (including all its tributaries) is 21 feet, although several troughs run nearly 9 times that deep.

- It holds more than 18 trillion gallons of water, half of which come from the Atlantic Ocean.

- The bulk of the bay's fresh water is supplied by the Potomac, Susquehanna, and James Rivers.

- Each day, roughly 51 billion gallons of water flow into the bay from its tributaries.

- Counting its tributaries, the bay has 11,684 miles of shoreline and 4,480 square miles of surface area.

- The bay is part of the Intracoastal Waterway, connecting the Chesapeake and Delaware Canal (which links the bay to the Delaware River) with the Albemarle and Chesapeake Canal (which links the bay to Virginia's Elizabeth River and North Carolina's Albemarle Sound beyond).

- The bay remains an active, important shipping channel for large container vessels entering or leaving the Port of Baltimore.

- The bay is home to 2,700-plus species of plants and animals, 521 of which are finfish or shellfish.

- Approximately 500 million pounds of seafood are harvested from the bay's waters every year.

- One-third of the Atlantic coast's entire migratory bird population winters on the bay.

- Molting blue crabs seek shelter from predators in bay grass, more than 80,000 acres of which grow in shallow areas of the bay and its tributaries.

Although several seafaring explorers reached the area before him, it's famed British captain John Smith who first mapped the Chesapeake Bay region, a 2-year project begun in 1607. Less than 30 years later, in 1634, Lord Baltimore established the first English colony in Maryland, known then (and now) as St. Mary's City.

Over the next two centuries, the bay area witnessed its share of growth—and conflict. Site of the Revolutionary War's Battle of the Chesapeake (wherein a French fleet crushed the Royal Navy near the mouth of the bay in Virginia), the estuary played an even more decisive role in the War of 1812. Not only did the "rockets' red glare" from a skirmish at Ft. McHenry in Baltimore Harbor inspire Francis Scott Key to pen "The

"From the earliest days of American colonialism, the Chesapeake first kept alive, then nourished, generations of settlers for whom the bounty of the bay was limitless, enduring, and among the finest seafood regions of the world. If today the Chesapeake itself needs nourishing, it is still a gleaming symbol of the excellence of American marine life and a rich source of lore for so many food cultures, from Native Americans to the immigrants who came after them."
—John Mariani, author of *The Encyclopedia of American Food and Drink*

Clear Skies—oil painting (18 x 26) by John Payne of fishermen at Assateague Island National Seashore, courtesy of McBride Gallery, Annapolis MD; giclee print available.

Star-Spangled Banner," but British troops used the waterway as a quick route to Washington, DC, which they promptly overran and burned.

The Chesapeake Bay's more recent history has involved far fewer battles, but just as many fights. The so-called Oyster Wars, which took place from 1865 until 1959, consisted of licensed, legal fishermen perpetually duking it out with "oyster pirates" over who had rightful claim to harvest the bay's bounty. (An ill-conceived Maryland Oyster Navy was formed in 1868 to patrol the waters; no match for the heavily armed pirates, it was ultimately disbanded.)

While the Oyster Wars eventually petered out, the plight of the oysters themselves (as well as that of blue crabs, rockfish, other fish, and plants) took a dramatic turn for the worse. By the 1970s, pollution, algae blooms, disease, and overfishing led to serious oxygen depletion and, soon after, to the Chesapeake's dubious distinction as one of the world's first "marine dead zones." As the bay withered, so did the number of men and women whose livelihoods depended on the water.

Today, thanks to intensive conservation efforts, harvesting regulations, and repopulation programs, the bay is beginning once again to flourish. Although it's unlikely the Chesapeake will ever return to its original glory days—when there were enough oysters to filter the entire bay in just 3.3 days, a feat that now takes roughly a year—groups like the Chesapeake Bay Foundation and the Oyster Recovery Partnership are making strides toward reinvigorating the region's most essential body of water and the treasure trove of seafood swimming within it.

Maryland's Seafood Traditions

Backyard barbecues. Crab feasts. Boat lunches. Bull roasts. Hunt breakfasts. Oyster suppers. Raw bars. Crab cakes. Soft-shell crab sandwiches. Broiled rockfish. Planked bluefish. Fried clams. Steamed mussels. Maryland crab soup. Cream of crab soup. Sweet potato pie. Corn chowder. Clam chowder. Eggplant fritters. Stuffed Smithfield ham. Strawberry pie. Apple cobbler. Fried green Eastern Shore tomatoes. Silver Queen corn. Crab imperial. Venison stew. Sauerkraut. Fried chicken. Clam pie. Terrapin soup. Beaten biscuits. Roast duck. Venison kebabs. Shad roe. Spring lamb. Smith Island cake.

Maryland sets a bountiful table, groaning under the weight of regional specialties inspired by the abundance of the Chesapeake Bay and its fertile farmlands and fruit orchards. While traditional Maryland cooking can trace its origins to its Native American settlers and Colonial times, those who have come more recently to this hospitable land of pleasant living have made their own ethnic contributions, creating a cuisine as varied and abundant as anywhere in the world.

If, as a recent travel survey shows, people rank the food of a region high on their list when selecting a vacation destination, Maryland is a gustatory shoo-in. From a growing number of upscale restaurants to colorful crab houses, the Chesapeake Bay region offers an endless variety of delectable choices and hospitable settings.

As "armchair tourists," set out with us for a trip in search of regional specialties and some of the cooks who are working hard to make diners happy. Space and stamina limit the number of "stops" we can make on our odyssey, and we apologize upfront for overlooking many worthy destinations.

One need look no further than the home cook for a taste of typical Maryland cooking. The addition of sauerkraut to the traditional turkey dinner is widespread, a quirky twist that raises the eyebrows of out-of-state guests visiting for the holidays. Steamed crabs are a Maryland staple that also befuddles visitors, mostly because the art of picking a crab has a certain barbaric quality that is alien to the inlander. Isn't it true that there is a level of unholy glee associated with introducing them to the ritual of the Crab Feast—complete with newspapers on the table, wooden mallets and knives in place of cutlery, and paper towels instead of napkins?

Cantler's, a family-owned crab and seafood restaurant on a creek outside of Annapolis, has entertained more than its share of first-time crab-pickers. Several years back, Dan Cantler was invited to stage a Maryland crab feast at the prestigious James Beard House in Manhattan. When he arrived with his brown paper "tablecloths," mallets, and knives, he was shown into a dining room set with fine china, silver, and crystal. Cantler diplomatically asked that the room be reset in proper "crab-feast style" and quickly saved the day by transforming the setting from Big City to Maryland Style.

INSIDER TIPS
Crab Feasts 101

About to attend your first crab feast? You're in for a treat! (Assuming you can get over the shock of seeing grown people zealously pound piles of crustaceans with little wooden hammers.)

Before heading to the big event, keep in mind that crab feasts are:

- **Messy.** This is no time to go all genteel and pompous. You're going to get your hands—and, quite possibly, your clothes and your hair—dirty. So relax. It's part of the fun.

- **Communal.** There's no ordering off the a la carte menu at a crab feast. Expect to be served big platters of steamed crabs and corn on the cob, along with such sides as coleslaw and boiled potatoes. Condiment-wise, look for Old Bay Seasoning, lemon wedges, and maybe some tartar or cocktail sauce.

- **Primal.** You may be self-conscious about breaking crab claws in half to dig out the meat, or about bashing the shell with a mallet, but don't be. There's no elegant way to eat a whole crab, so don't bother trying. Miss Manners will understand.

Another anecdote involves the late (and lamented) iconic Obrycki's restaurant in Baltimore, operated for years by the Cernak family. Among their many guests were the owners of several upscale New York City restaurants, who so enjoyed their "crab initiation" at Obrycki's that they invited the Cernaks to stage a series of crab feasts at Rockefeller Plaza. They were wildly successful and inspired an enterprising New Yorker to open a Maryland-style crab house in his city.

An example of yet another "Maryland export," this one overseas, is the fried chicken with gravy listed on the menu of a popular bistro in Paris. The late William Taylor, a Southern Maryland caterer who earned a national reputation as the guru of Chesapeake cuisine, happened upon the bistro and asked the chef for the recipe.

- **Simple.** Don't expect linen napkins or a wine list. Crab feasts demand newspaper-covered tables, hand wipes, cold beer, soda, and little else.

- **A lot of fun.** Even if you aren't a seafood lover, it's hard not to get caught up in the playful atmosphere at a crab feast. How can you take things too seriously when bits of shell are flying and the brews are flowing?

ILLUSTRATION COURTESY OF THE CRAB CLAW IN ST. MICHAELS, MARYLAND

"Deep-fry the chicken, then make the gravy by adding flour and milk to the grease," he was told. Ever the Southern gentleman, Taylor restrained himself and thanked the chef. "I found that, in Europe, if the bird is fried, they call it Maryland chicken," said Taylor, who made a name for himself as "the dinner designer" for guests at the historic Sotterley Plantation in Southern Maryland.

Southern Maryland, site of the state's first capital in St. Mary's City, is also the cradle of typical Maryland cuisine. Its regional specialties have changed little since Colonial days, with kale and cabbage creating a green layer in slices of pale pink stuffed Smithfield hams that appear on springtime tables. We recently attended a "how-to-stuff-a-ham" workshop at the Historic St. Mary's City Museum, watching as the senior-citizen demonstrators carried on the traditions of their ancestors by using a fish-boning knife to make crescent-shaped gashes in the ham, filling them with piles of leafy greens, and tying up the meat with fishing twine. The technique, we were told, was originally used by slaves and passed along through the years by their descendants.

Moving north, a stop in Annapolis should include a step back in time at the historic Maryland Inn, where the kitchen remains a bastion of Maryland cuisine. Here you will find specialties such as Maryland-raised lamb, rockfish simply broiled or crowned with crab imperial, and perhaps a Colonial-style trifle layered with fresh local berries. If icy oysters and clams on the half shell are your preference, try the raw bars at Blackwall Hitch in Eastport and McGarvey's across from the City Market in Annapolis, or down an oyster shooter at the Middleton Tavern next door to McGarvey's.

For a view of the Annapolis Harbor while feasting on crabs, climb the steps to Phillips Crab Deck, where you can watch the staff counting out the crustaceans and shucking the oysters. Or take the free ferry from the City Dock for a quick trip to Carrol's Creek Cafe in Eastport, where seafood of all kinds is a specialty and the waterside setting is another plus.

Cantler's, a rustic crab house and seafood restaurant, is another worthy stop, but be sure to get directions before wending your way over a backcountry road to get there. You will notice a parking lot full of cars with out-of-state plates at this popular destination, but once inside, there's breezy service by a young waitstaff and crabs fresh out of the water. Wander down to the creek and see crustaceans moving in the holding tubs as they await their fate.

Maryland's Eastern Shore seems to have become a magnet for graduates of well-known cooking schools. Three of them are Eastern Shore natives, who, after graduation, worked at some of the best restaurants on both coasts before "going home" to open their own places. Jordan Lloyd, chef-owner of the Bartlett Pear Inn in Easton, and Ian Campbell, chef-owner of Bistro Poplar in Cambridge, are graduates of the Culinary Institute of America in Hyde Park. Doug Potts, a Cordon Bleu graduate, is the chef at the Peacock Restaurant at the Inn at 202 Dover in Easton. Jim Hughes, chef-owner of Restaurant 213 in the tiny town of Fruitland, has international credentials in the culinary stratosphere. Each of these chefs likes to add a Maryland-style twist to their menus in terms of style and ingredients.

In Baltimore the long-reigning queen of Maryland cookery is Nancy Longo, the chef-owner of Pierpoint in the city's Fell's Point neighborhood. Known for her emphasis on regional cooking since opening in the 1980s, Longo at one time would smoke the just-caught game of a hunter, custom-create a spring symphony of fresh asparagus and shad roe, and improvise a "Maryland-style cioppino" by adding rockfish, clams, scallops, and oysters to her original "soup crabs" stock. Fed by her Baltimore roots and her extensive research into the origins of Maryland cooking, Longo brings her passion into the present, calling her style both "new-wavey and nontraditional."

Maryland cuisine has come a long way from its 17th-century origins. Today's chefs might stuff their ravioli with oysters, fry cattail shoots from an Eastern Shore marsh to use as garnish, sauté soft crabs in a crust of chopped walnuts and cornflakes, make a crab timbale with spaghetti squash, or use flecks of Smithfield ham to enliven a beurre blanc sauce.

Our research has taken us to the Eastern and Western shores of the Chesapeake region, and we are grateful to the restaurants who so generously shared their recipes with us—and with our readers. Many are simple enough for the home cook, though several are pretty advanced. And, by the way, we never did find that "perfect crab cake" in our travels. Maybe it exists only in the minds of its maker. Guess it's up to our readers to take up the hunt.

How to Use This Guide

Although Maryland is small, it has unrivaled access to fresh seafood; more than half its counties ring the Chesapeake Bay, giving the Free State unlimited undersea offerings. Since each area lining the Chesapeake Bay is distinct—with its own unique foodie draws—we've divided this book into regions: the Upper Bay, the Eastern Shore, the Western Shore, and Southern Maryland. Broken out by county are some of the best seafood restaurants. These are the places that serve authentic Chesapeake Bay seafood in settings ranging from upscale to down-home. Some are newish, others are elder statesmen, but they're all terrific.

Within these regions, you'll also find information on:

Maritime Must-Sees. A list of the captivating lighthouses, public piers, museums, and other nautical draws that make the region special.

Cherishing the Chesapeake. A peek at the programs and initiatives aimed at returning the bay to its former glory.

Colorful Characters. A look at some of the interesting people who live near, work on, promote, or simply love the Chesapeake Bay.

Insider Tips. Whether it's how to hold a crab mallet or where to find the region's sweetest oysters, these tips will have you looking (and eating) like a local in no time.

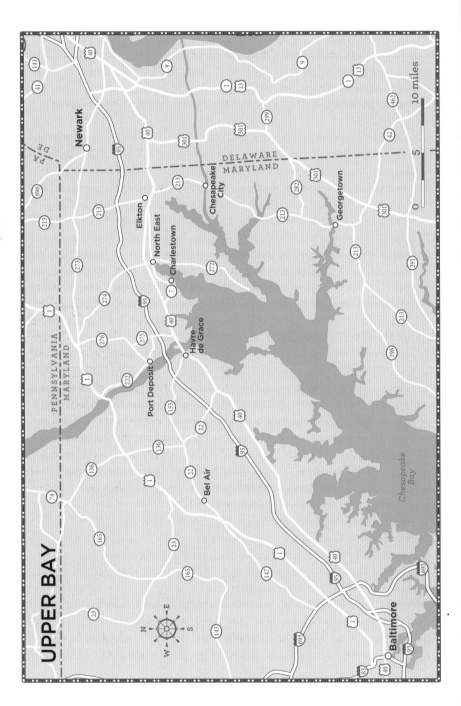

THE UPPER BAY

Capping the Chesapeake's headwaters, Cecil and Harford Counties make up Maryland's Upper Bay region. Cecil lies in the state's northeast corner, right along the Pennsylvania and Delaware borders. With several beautiful rivers—including the Susquehanna, Elk, and North East—flowing through it and into the bay, the county was once an important shipping port. Today, it lures visitors with historic towns like Port Deposit and South Chesapeake City, as well as with draws like the Turkey Point Lighthouse and the Conowingo Dam. It's also a must-visit stop on any seafood lover's tour of the state.

The same can be said of Harford County, whose quaint towns—including historic Havre de Grace, which unfolds along the banks of the Susquehanna and boasts some of the area's finest waterfront views—offer endless opportunities to explore, shop, and (most importantly) eat. After touring the county's Decoy Museum, the Concord Point Lighthouse, the Havre de Grace Maritime Museum, and the Skipjack *Martha Lewis*, hungry visitors' challenge won't be deciding what to eat (seafood, of course!), but where to eat it.

Casual noshers hoping to dine alfresco won't be disappointed by the Upper Bay's crab houses. As long as the seasons (summer and fall) and seasoning (Old Bay) are at hand, eateries along the rivers and bay offer the perfect place to grab a mallet—and a beer—and get cracking (literally!). Higher-end culinarians can opt for a more upscale establishment, where the tablecloths are white and the catch of the day is likely to include a wine pairing. (Just don't be afraid to eat with your hands; certain seafood dishes, no matter how high-brow, somehow taste better when you forgo the fork.)

Cecil County

Backfin Blues Bar and Grill, 19 S. Main St., Port Deposit, MD 21904; (410) 378-2722; backfinblues.com. Bob Steele, chef-owner of this seafood-themed eatery in the tiny town of Port Deposit (population 653), loves his job. "Otherwise, I wouldn't do it," says the veteran restaurateur and passionate cook, who features three different seafood dishes every weekend. And while his crab dishes are made with Maryland blue crab, he uses a reliable supplier as a source for South African lobster tails, Chilean sea bass, Coho salmon, New England scallops, barramundi, wahoo, swordfish, and Washington State sole. Steele is known for his creativity in the kitchen, saucing a savory appetizer of Crab Louis with his own brown-butter-brandy blend, using a red pepper base to color and flavor a deliciously different lobster bisque, and dressing up calamari fried in cornmeal with his own garlic-infused tomato sauce. Finfish specials are sauced in a variety of ways, depending on the chef's whim. Backfin Blues, with a reputation as a "gourmet casual" restaurant, does not offer hard crabs on its menu. Rather, it is known for crab cakes made with "colossal lump crab," cream of crab soup, and Chef Bob's special crab imperial. In addition to seafood, Backfin Blues is known as the place to go for first-rate beef entrees and for its well-priced and well-chosen wine list. Ask about its Wine Club. Townhomes block what was once a full view of the Susquehanna River, now only partially visible from the two seasonal outdoor spaces (a deck and a side porch seating 60) and the 75-seat dining room. Count on friendly service and super seafood at Chef Bob's place. Note: Backfin Blues serves dinner from 5 p.m. Wed through Sat and Sun brunch 10 a.m. to 4 p.m.

Bayard House, 11 Bohemia Ave., Chesapeake City, MD 21915; (410) 885-5040; bayardhouse.com. We were delighted to discover Wernfried Wiesnegger, chef-owner of the beautiful Bayard House in the pretty 19th-century shipping village of Chesapeake City. Idyllically situated on the shores of the scenic Chesapeake and Delaware Canal, his property includes an upscale restaurant, as well as the quirky Hole-in-the-Wall Bar and an adorable cottage straight out of a storybook. Wiesnegger has his own story—although his innate modesty veils his considerable talents and culinary background. A native of Austria, he studied at the same culinary school of which Wolfgang Puck is an alumnus and orchestrates a kitchen that rivals the best in the state. A perusal of the Bayard House menu reflects Wiesnegger's classical training, evident in the use of sauces in such special treats as his signature "Tournedos Baltimore"—a pairing of twin beef filets with a lobster cake finished with a seafood Champagne sauce and a crab cake napped with a lovely Madeira cream sauce. Peruse the lunch or dinner menus as you enjoy the bucolic scenery from the outdoor patio, in one of the two enclosed porches or in a comfortable inside dining room. Seafood has a starring role on the Bayard House bill of fare—blending the best of Eastern Shore specialties with the chef's European flair. An appetizer of clams steamed in a garlicky white wine broth comes with a toasted French baguette to mop up the savory sauce; mussels Provençal live up to expectations, steamed in a drinkable broth flecked with tomatoes, shallots, and fresh herbs; a crab and artichoke dip is worth the calories. Top-notch crab cakes are enhanced with a lemon beurre blanc; the chef's seafood stew (aka cioppino) features scallops, clams, shrimp, mussels, and chunks of fish in a vibrant tomato broth; a unique entree featuring Anaheim peppers filled with lobster, crab, and shrimp, doused with a green chili sauce and cheddar cheese, then baked and topped with sour cream is a popular item at both lunch and dinner. Chef Weisnegger takes good care of carnivores with grilled lamb chops enhanced with a Madeira demi-glace and parmesan risotto and a 12-ounce rib eye crowned with caramelized onions. Bayard House is a thoroughly delightful destination—and guests can even overnight in the adjoining cottage and wander down the street in the morning for breakfast at the Bohemia Cafe and Bakery, another of Chef Weisnegger's "gifts" to Chesapeake City.

Captain Chris' Crab Shack, 1701 Turkey Point Rd., North East, MD 21901; (410) 287-7070; captainscrabs.com. If you're looking for a combined crab feast and beach party, think about this super-casual crab shack in Cecil County, about 0.5 mile from the North East River. Owned and operated by Captain Chris Shelton since 2008, it has become a popular spot for visitors to the nearby Elk Neck State Park and the outdoor-themed North Bay recreation center, as well as locals and tourists longing for that sweet taste of Maryland blue crabs. Come prepared to get sandy as you join the crowds at picnic tables that seat about 200 on a replica of an ocean beach. While the biggest attraction is the seasonal All-You-Can-Eat Crabs and Sweet Corn Feast for $24.95, another is the selection of steamed-to-order seafood, including jumbo peel-and-eat shrimp flecked with onions and green peppers; wild-caught littleneck clams properly escorted with natural broth freshened with garlic and melted "real" butter; a pound of Prince Edward Island mussels with the same accompaniments; and Louisiana "crawdads" billed as "Maryland meets Louisiana" in tribute to Captain Chris' secret seasoning recipe. Leashed and well-mannered Fidos are welcome, although management jokingly warns that rowdy kids could be used as crab bait. Despite that dire threat, kids' meals include fries or chips and a beverage for $4.95. Note: Captain Chris' Crab Shack is open every day but Tues from late Apr until late Oct.

CHERISH THE CHESAPEAKE
Area Restaurants Embrace the
"True Blue Crabs" Campaign

Steve Vilnit is picky about the crabmeat he eats. "Locally harvested or none at all" is the mantra of this cheerleader for Maryland's signature seafood—the blue crab. Responding to the surge of crabmeat imported from elsewhere, Vilnit, director of seafood marketing at the Maryland Department of Natural Resources (DNR), launched the "Maryland True Blue Crabs" campaign in 2012. He originally enlisted five local restaurants to pledge their allegiance to "the real thing"—a number that has grown to nearly 200 supporters statewide,

PHOTO COURTESY OF JAY FLEMING

including restaurants, caterers, retailers, schools, and even some hospital food service providers.

Vilnit and his colleagues at DNR also cast their nets to lure some 500 chefs to experience firsthand what it takes to bring Chesapeake Bay seafood to their tables. Chefs from Maryland, Virginia, Philadelphia, Delaware, and Washington, DC, have been treated to boat trips on the bay and its tributaries, meeting Maryland watermen and witnessing firsthand their labor-intensive work.

While 2012 marked a banner year for blue crabs, unseasonably cold weather in 2013 and 2014 meant that the crustaceans extended their hibernation period, slept late in their bay-bottom beds, and shortened their reproductive cycle. This catch-22 of limited supply and undiminished demand translates into higher prices for consumers. While males have long been favored as superior in size to the females, 2014 saw a reversal in roles as females outweighed their counterparts. A debate about a possible temporary moratorium on crab harvesting is troubling to both watermen and restaurant owners.

For those who demand the sweet taste of Maryland blue crabs, look for the Maryland True Blue Crabs logo on restaurant windows—and tell them Steve Vilnit sent you.

PHOTO COURTESY OF THE MARYLAND DEPARTMENT OF NATURAL RESOURCES

The Granary, 100 George St., Georgetown, MD 21930; (410) 275-1603; granary.biz. Splendidly situated on the Sassafras River, The Granary site has been a local landmark in one iteration or other since the 1800s—first as a storage location for corn and grain, then a yacht club, and then a restaurant opened in the 1940s. Fire destroyed the original building in 1985, leaving behind only the hand-hewn beams in the "new" Granary that reopened in 2013 and is going strong under the direction of Owner David Anderson, a graduate of the Culinary Institute of America with years of experience as an executive chef at several Delaware restaurants. His establishment is multifaceted, offering breakfast, lunch, dinner, and carryout or dockside pickup in its casual Sassafras Grill as well as lunch and dinner in the more "dressed up" inside tables of The Granary. Chef Jess Burress is a talented chef who devotes a good part of the restaurant's menu to seafood, buying local when he can and providing fresh in-season produce from area farms. His style, honed by 12 years at Harry's Savoy Grill in Delaware, shows some innovative twists that add interest to The Granary's menu. This is evident in his original scallop dish, featuring dry-boat biggies served with a mélange of pickled jalapeño, red onion, arugula, and feta cheese sparked with a lemon-orange dressing and sprinkled with a balsamic vinegar reduction. We liked such little amenities as his version of the oyster po' boy, lightly battered seafood bedded on good French bread; meaty Maryland crab cakes sided in-season with fresh corn and lima bean succotash; a casserole of macaroni and cheese with crab, andouille sausage, corn, and roasted red peppers with a surprise touch of tomato fondue; and the option of partnering tomato-based Maryland crab with the creamy version on top. This may be the only restaurant serving Sassafras River Fries—dressed up with crabmeat and cheese sauce seasoned with Old Bay. You have to taste it to believe it. Everyone is glad to have The Granary back in business. Friendly service, a prime location, and a variety of options from dockside carryout to romantic dining seem to ensure its success.

Mick's Crab House, 902 E. Pulaski Hwy., Elkton, MD 21921; (443) 485-6007; mickscrabhouse.net. If you get a craving for crabs as soon as you cross the Maryland line on Route 95, you are only 5 minutes away from Mick's Crab House in Elkton. Crab-hungry customers come from New Jersey, Philly, and Delaware, according to Owner Michael ("Mick") McNeal, who bought the popular seafood spot in 2010. Crab is king at his place, which cannot claim a water view despite a sand-covered outside patio, which is pleasant in cool weather but not so in the summer. The big draw is that Mick's Crab House is open year-round and has a year-round all-you-can-eat (AYCE) crab policy that in-season features Maryland blue crabs. Otherwise, McNeal looks to Louisiana, Georgia, and the Carolinas for supplies. A unique feature of his restaurant is a daily online posting on the restaurant's website giving sizes and market prices for the much-in-demand crustaceans. Crabs may account for a big chunk of the business at this 200-seat restaurant, but there are lots of other seafood options on the menu. Steamed shrimp, mussels, and clams are popular, as are oysters, scallops, and salmon prepared down-home style by a team of cooks in the kitchen. "We don't have chefs here—but we do have good cooks," says McNeal. He buys his produce locally and loves the season when Maryland corn and tomatoes are available.

Nauti Goose, 100 Cherry St., North East, MD 21901; (410) 287-7880; nautigoose.net. Gotta love the name—a provocative ID that Nauti Goose has used to good advantage since opening in 2001. Situated at the mouth of the scenic North East River on the Upper Chesapeake Bay, this attractive multilevel restaurant has the seasonal advantages of waterfront docking and waterfront dining on its deck or terrace, as well as a sheltered, more formal dining room. Just coming in for a drink and maybe light fare? You have your choice of five bar areas where there's a lot of happy talk going on and probably some lively music. Nauti Goose has a full menu of choices, and appetizers are a good way to start. Chunks of breaded and fried rockfish come with a tangy barbecue sauce, an excellent crab dip comes with toasted flatbread for dipping, and seared ahi tuna is brightened with segments of mandarin oranges and mayonnaise hottened with sriracha sauce. Nauti Goose can be proud of its lump crab cake sandwich, the cake crusted from a quick sear and bedded on a brioche-style roll with a smear of garlic aioli. Another winning sandwich is grilled rockfish that picks up the spicy flavor of its dry rub and is sweetened with homemade mango salsa. Seafood entrees include a buttery seafood scampi featuring shrimp, scallops, and mussels piled on pasta brightened with spinach and baby tomatoes; and a creamy old-fashioned baked crab imperial. We're guessing that some folks just come for drinks and for the Nauti Goose's famous desserts: a rich fudge cake soaked in either coffee liqueur or raspberry brandy and filled with chocolate mousse or cheesecake with raspberry puree. They may be Nauti—but they're so very good.

The River Shack at the Wellwood, 523 Water St., Charlestown, MD 21914; (410) 287-6666; wellwoodclub.com/RiverShack; @ TheWellwood. The Wellwood is an historic site on the North East River in Cecil County. Dating back to the late 1800s as a private club for "optimists and humanitarians . . . to promote the 'happy habit' . . . and discourage strife and promote good fellowship," it thrives today as a beautiful destination for upscale dining in the main building or for casual crab feasts in a separate venue called River Shack on the edge of a sandy beach. Over the years, visitors to the Wellwood included presidents Theodore Roosevelt and Calvin Coolidge, remembered with a hand-carved bar said to be donated by President Roosevelt after his visit. Today, these and other antiques add elegance to the Wellwood's warren of dining rooms, where seafood starters include shrimp steamed with a dose of Old Bay, mussels in a spicy marina sauce served with good French bread for "mopping" purposes, blackened ahi tuna sided with a hot wasabi sauce and a cool-down cucumber salad, and fried "lobster bites" accompanied by the kitchen's original honey-jalapeño sauce. Seafood entrees feature a fun "Select Your Fish" option (flounder, salmon, tuna, rockfish, and fish of the day) broiled or blackened, with a choice of toppings (lobster cream, bruschetta, crab imperial) and sauces (wild berry, Dijon mustard-caper, lemon-herb). Cold-water lobster tails, crab cakes, Dungeness and snow crab legs, scallops, and oysters round out the menu. In season, the Wellwood's River Shack is a favorite place for boaters who dock at the establishment's slips to enjoy a crab feast at picnic tables set up on a sandy strip outdoors—or order carryout food or beverages. Steamed hard crabs are a specialty (subject to availability), but there are other seafood options, such as oysters on the half shell, steamed shrimp and clams, mussels in a red sauce, and a fish sandwich. The River Shack's sherried crab bisque and tomato-based Maryland crab, each made from family recipes, are outstanding. Owned since 1958 by the Metz family, the Wellwood and its River Shack are well-run operations that make patrons happy to be there.

Schaefer's Canal House, 208 Bank St., Chesapeake City, MD 21915; (410) 885-7200; schaeferscanalhouse.com; @Schaefers Marina. Watercraft large and small parade in front of Schaefer's Canal

House beside the Chesapeake & Delaware Canal, a busy thoroughfare for trade and travel. The sprawling restaurant, with an outdoor Lighthouse Bar and dining decks on two levels, is a tried-and-true favorite of boaters who like the convenience of pulling into the adjacent deep water marina for food, fuel, and friendly service. Landlubbers like it, too. Schaefer's goes back a ways, the property held by the Schaefer family from 1907 until 1973. The restaurant started with a beer garden in 1935 and has evolved through several owners to become the showplace it is today. But it still retains an old-fashioned charm despite a total makeover that is nothing short of stunning. And seafood remains the big draw, whether it's the restaurant's delicious crab dip (lump crabmeat topped with bacon and chopped scallions), a bountiful fried seafood platter of panko-battered jumbo shrimp and oysters, the kitchen's top-notch crab cake; or a heavenly combination of meaty scallops bedded on sautéed wild mushrooms and a fluffy risotto dressed up with white truffle oil. Other options are the kitchen's knock-out "C&D Jambalaya"—big shrimp and scallops, clams, mussels, lobster, and andouille sausage in a creole sauce mixed with saffron-tinged rice. Lobster tails are broiled and served with drawn butter, fresh mahimahi gets crusted with Parmesan cheese, and grilled salmon comes with basil-lemon butter. Take just about any seat at one of Schaefer's tables and you can watch a real live "boat show" while enjoying good food and attentive service. And on weekends, there is music to go along with it all—everything from reggae to blues to jazz.

The Tap Room, 201 Bohemia Ave., Chesapeake City, MD 21915; (410) 885-2344; taproomcrabhouse.com. If a restaurant celebrates its 34th year in business, as The Tap Room Restaurant did in 2014, the owner must be doing something right. That's the way it is with Chef-Owner Joe Montesusco, whose Italian mother's kitchen was his cooking school. His most spectacular seafood special is The Tap Room's garlic crabs, an original preparation that involves removing the shell and innards of the crabs and simmering them in a butter-and-garlic sauce with Montesusco's special spices. A friend who lives in Chesapeake City told me about them, and I thank her. The restaurant, about a block away from the Chesapeake and Delaware Canal, is convenient for boaters, who can "park" at the nearby marina. Decor is nautical rustic, with sailboats on the curtains and brown paper-covered tables at the ready for the messy business of picking crabs. Aided in the kitchen by longtime assistant Sandy, Montesusco is also at the ready to doctor up his homemade linguini with a pair of jumbo lump crab cakes or (in season) whale soft shells, mussels, shrimp, clams, or "all of the above" in The Tap Room's legendary Seafood Pescatore. Diners have a choice of the chef's homemade sauces—marinara, tomato, or a light wine-butter blend. Home-cooked food, friendly service, and those garlic crabs make a visit to The Tap Room special. But remember—this place is so homey that neither credit cards nor personal checks are accepted.

Woody's Crab House, 29 S. Main St., North East, MD 21901; (410) 287-3541; woodyscrabhouse.com. If you're looking for the "real deal" crab house, Woody's is the place to go. You can "meet" Woody online by going to his restaurant's website, where he stars in two videos—one preparing a down-home crab cake dinner in his own kitchen and the other offering tips on how to eat a hard-shell crab. Chances are he will remind you of your favorite uncle—or maybe your husband. Woody has slowed down a bit recently, but his daughter Rachel and son-in-law Chip are keeping things just the way Woody would. Crabs are still the focus—Maryland hard-shells for picking and exceptionally great crab cakes—more than 2 million sold since Woody's Crab House opened in 1993. It started small, with seating for about 100, and has expanded into 3 buildings that can accommodate 300 inside and another 150 on the tiki bar deck. The crowds come for simple reasons: The food is good and the service is friendly. While Woody's is not on the water, the nautical theme is set at an entrance marked with pilings and boat rope, and the atmosphere is decidedly casual. "If it's on the table today, it was sleeping in the bay or the ocean last night" promises the kitchen about the selection of fresh fish that changes daily and can be ordered broiled, baked, or fried. There's a light and lovely lump crab salad, a rich trio of crab cakes, crab gratin, and crab imperial broiled in a casserole and served with fresh seasonal vegetables. And if you are secretly wishing for a Maine lobster instead of a Maryland crab, Woody's might just have one for you. The cream of crab and Maryland crab soups are made from family recipes—and Woody's has his very own creation on the menu: tea sandwiches made with thinly sliced cucumbers. Gotta love that guy.

Harford County

Laurrapin Grille, 209 N. Washington St., Havre de Grace, MD 21078; (410) 939-4956; laurrapin.com; @laurrapin. Curious about the name? Laurrapin is a folksy old Southern expression for "tasty po' folks food," says Bruce Clarke, chef and co-owner with his wife, Sherifa, of this exceptional eatery in scenic Havre de Grace. The couple chose the town for its closeness to both bay and farmland, and since opening in 2004 have stayed true to their "green" vision by relying almost exclusively on local farmers and watermen as suppliers for their seasonally dictated menus and adhering to environmentally aware practices. A visit to Laurrapin is a revelation of what an imaginative team can achieve in the kitchen as well as at tables seating 140 in the restaurant's bar and two dining rooms. Take the menu, for instance, where the ubiquitous shrimp and grits combo benefits from a blackening of the seafood and the addition of Tasso ham to its creamy homemade companion, and pan-seared diver scallops (a seasonal specialty) arrive garnished with segments of scarlet grapefruit, a confit of fennel and arugula, and a swirl of grapefruit veloute. A sweet Maryland crab salad lightly dressed with a white (yes!) balsamic rides on an avocado shell; char-grilled oysters from local suppliers are kissed with a bacon-anchovy butter, barely pan-seared ahi tuna rests on a bed of seaweed moistened with a pineapple-flecked soy mustard. Chef Clarke makes his own *fazzoletti* (square-shaped pasta) as a foil for a delicious seafood dish featuring sea scallops, gulf shrimp, asparagus tips, and baby tomatoes in the house pesto, topped with pine nuts and fresh mozzarella. Clarke follows recommendations for his sustainable fish of the day (either wild-caught or farm-raised) and favors simple preparations. One of Laurrapin's outstanding seafood entrees is Chesapeake Bay rockfish served over blue crab, slivers of Smithfield ham and sweet potato hash, and finished with a wonderful Meyer lemon butter sauce and grilled asparagus. Pretty close to the perfect "state dish" for Maryland. PS: When you go, check out the whimsical art work by local talent, including a mural of downtown Havre de Grace by Ezra Berger.

MacGregor's Restaurant, 331 St. John St., Havre de Grace, MD 21078; (410) 939-3303; macgregorsrestaurant.com. The old maxim "Don't judge a book by its cover" applies to first impressions of MacGregor's from the outside. The restaurant, open since 1987, sits shyly on a corner in the quiet town of Havre de Grace, giving no indication that once through the front door you will find a wonderful outdoor space at the rear of the building. The Pearl Deck is a gem, overlooking the waters of the Susquehanna River and the bridge above it. MacGregor's food has always had good press, and its seafood offerings cover the waterfront. Its signature dish is "Harbor of Mercy Rockfish," a combination of a thick fillet served over garlic Yukon mashed potatoes, asparagus, sweet corn, marinated tomatoes, and sauced with a cracked mustard lemon beurre blanc. The chef

MARITIME MUST-SEES
Can't-Miss Attractions in the Upper Bay

Concord Point Lighthouse: Built in 1827 at the confluence of the Susquehanna River and the Chesapeake Bay, the beautiful Concord Point Lighthouse continues standing sentry over the water, its Fresnel lens and 100-watt bulb illuminating the waves around it. One of the East Coast's oldest continually operating lighthouses, Concord Point enjoys a spot on the National Register of Historic Places. Open to the public on weekends from Apr through Oct, the lighthouse and its restored keeper's quarters are as impressive now as ever. *The Concord Point Lighthouse, corner of Concord and Lafayette Streets, Havre de Grace, MD 21078; (410) 939-3213; concord pointlighthouse.org.*

Conowingo Dam: A few miles north of Havre de Grace, the Conowingo Dam—a hydroelectric dam that supports a 9,000-acre reservoir—is a fantastic place to observe native wildlife. Especially favored by bird watchers—the area is home to an estimated 100 species of birds, including great blue herons, osprey, and terns—are the gulls and bald eagles that reside here en masse. (Use the fisherman's catwalk across the front of the dam for an up-close view of feeding birds.) Anglers holding a valid freshwater-fishing license can cast for walleye, bass, perch, shad, muskie, and catfish. For safety's sake, call ahead (410-457-4076) to see when the dam is planning its next water release; stay on dry land until the levels even back out. Conowingo Dam sits on the border between Cecil and Harford Counties, about 5 miles from the Pennsylvania state line.

Elk Neck State Park: A fantastic vantage point from which to soak up the beauty of the Elk River, North East River, and Chesapeake Bay, the 2,188-acre Elk Neck State Park offers hiking trails, marshland, sandy beaches, swimming, and wooded bluffs. Look out over the waves, and you'll be vividly reminded why the Chesapeake region has wooed poets and sailors for centuries. (When visiting, don't miss the on-site Turkey Point Lighthouse, located at the southern tip of the park.) *Elk Neck State Park, 4395 Turkey Point Rd., North East, MD 21901; (410) 287-5333; dnr2.maryland.gov.*

Havre de Grace Decoy Museum: Established in 1986 as a private, nonprofit institution, the Havre de Grace Decoy Museum seeks "to preserve the historical and cultural legacy of waterfowling and decoy making on the Chesapeake Bay." Boasting more than 2,700 objects, including decoys and decorative carvings by masters of the craft, the museum celebrates this unique American folk art that helped earn Havre de Grace the title "Decoy Capital of the World." One visit and you'll have a newfound appreciation for carved ducks! *The Havre de Grace Decoy Museum, 215 Giles St., Havre de Grace, MD 21078; (410) 939-3739; decoymuseum.com.*

Havre de Grace Maritime Museum: Like its name suggests, the Havre de Grace Maritime Museum honors the region's rich seafaring history. True to its mission to "collect, document, preserve, and interpret the maritime skills and cultural heritage of the Lower Susquehanna River and Upper Chesapeake Bay region," the museum's permanent exhibits include "Beyond Jamestown: Life 400 Years Ago," "Working on the Bay," "Recreation on the Chesapeake," and "Ships' Life-Saving Equipment." Special events include an annual Wetland Clean-Up Day and a free ongoing summer concert series. *The Havre de Grace Maritime Museum, 100 Lafayette St., Havre de Grace, MD 21078; (410) 939-4800; hdgmaritime museum.org.*

Historic Chesapeake City: Considered a "hidden treasure of the Chesapeake," Chesapeake City has a long and varied maritime history. Having sprung up around the 14-mile Chesapeake & Delaware Canal, the city enjoyed an extended heyday from the mid-1800s to the early 1900s. That all changed in 1927, when the canal was dredged to sea level, and ships no longer had to idle in Chesapeake City's locks; other financial and structural hurdles further tested the place's mettle. Today, as Maryland's only town still situated on a working canal, Chesapeake City is enjoying a resurgence—and a coveted spot on the National Register of Historic Places. Spend a day strolling the restored downtown, perusing the exhibits at the Canal Museum, touring the replica lighthouse, and admiring the many ocean-going vessels sailing by. It's everything a day in the Chesapeake Bay region is supposed to be. *chesapeake city.com*.

Historic Port Deposit: What tiny Port Deposit—just 2.3 square miles in area—lacks in size, it more than makes up for in character. Tucked between granite cliffs along the banks of the Susquehanna River, the town (listed on the National Register of Historic Places) saw its first recorded European visitor, Capt. John Smith, in the early 17th century. For the next 200 years or so, Port Deposit was a place where shipping, quarrying, and fishing magnates made their fortunes. Today, the restored downtown—boasting 19th-century architecture, excellent restaurants, and unique shops—makes for a perfect waterfront day trip. And anglers, take note: There are endless places from which to cast a line. *(410) 378-2121; ccgov.org*.

The Promenade in Havre de Grace: Stroll along this scenic ¾-mile boardwalk running along the Susquehanna River and take in the beautiful waterfront views. Open daily from sunrise to sunset, the Promenade is an excellent jumping-off point for exploring some of Havre de Grace's other must-sees, including Tydings Park, the Concord Point Lighthouse, and the Havre de Grace Maritime Museum. Interpretive signage along the Promenade will fill you in on the area's flora, fauna, and history. *Commerce Street, Havre de Grace, MD 21078; hdg tourism.com*.

Skipjack *Martha Lewis*: One of the few remaining working dredge boats of its kind, the skipjack *Martha Lewis* represents the one-time hundreds of vessels in the Chesapeake Bay oyster fleet. Built in 1955 and restored in 1994, the 8-ton *Martha Lewis* harks back to an era when ships were king and the bay provided unlimited bounty. Owned and operated by the Chesapeake Heritage Conservancy and docked at the Havre de Grace City Yacht Basin, the *Martha Lewis* today is a "floating classroom" dedicated to keeping the region's unique heritage alive. Private and group tours and excursions are available. *The Skipjack* Martha Lewis*, Havre de Grace City Yacht Basin, 352 Commerce St., Havre de Grace, MD 21078; (410) 939-4078; skipjackmarthalewis.org.*

Susquehanna Museum at the Lock House: Considered one of Havre de Grace's most important landmarks, the Lock House is a living, breathing example of times past, when the local economy depended on the Susquehanna and Tidewater Canal (1840–1890s). Now listed on the National Register of Historic Places, the Lock House (and on-site museum) today greets visitors with a snapshot of the past in the form of a replica 1800s kitchen, a toll collector's office, a mid-1800s bedroom, other rotating exhibits, and numerous maritime artifacts. A visit here is like a journey back to the 19th century! *The Susquehanna Museum at the Lock House, 817 Conesteo St., Havre de Grace, MD 21078; (410) 939-5780; thelockhouse museum.org.*

Turkey Point Lighthouse: Once tasked with guiding mariners transitioning from the Chesapeake Bay to the Elk River en route to the C&D Canal and Delaware Bay beyond, the Turkey Point Lighthouse has stood sentry over these waters since 1833 (officially decommissioned in 2000, it again illuminates the bay under the auspices of the nonprofit Turkey Point Light Station). Located at the southern end of Elk Neck State Park and famous for its long history of female lighthouse keepers, Turkey Point today is a must-see stop on any lighthouse lover's tour of the bay region. (Note: The lighthouse is open seasonally; during weekends from Apr to Nov, visitors may ascend the steps of the 35-foot-tall tower and check out the amazing view from the top.) *Turkey Point Lighthouse, Elk Neck State Park, 4395 Turkey Point Rd., North East, MD 21901; lighthousefriends.com.*

graciously agreed to share this special recipe in our book. The kitchen at MacGregor's is creative. Sushi-grade ahi tuna is served over purple sticky rice (Asian style) and topped with an Asian slaw, pickled ginger, and a soy vinaigrette—then garnished with the restaurant's delicious coconut shrimp. Wild-caught Atlantic salmon bedded on a blend of spinach and rice gets a sweet and savory apricot-chipotle glaze. Mediterranean mahimahi is dressed up with artichoke hearts, tomatoes, and fresh basil and paired with garlicky spinach and mashed potatoes. The chef's imagination is at work again with "Rockfish Popsicles" (Corona beer-battered and fried seafood strips on a skewer), bay scallops glistening with barbecue sauce and scattered with bacon and a lovely avocado and crab cake salad colored with diced tomatoes and corn kernels. Out on the Pearl Bar, you'll find a nice selection of oysters, as well as Prince Edward Island mussels steamed in either a Belgian beer with garlic, shallots, blue cheese, bacon, and herbs or a traditional white-wine broth. Both come with garlic toast—a thoughtful touch. Service is thoughtful as well, and a visit here makes you wish MacGregor's was in your own neighborhood.

Main Street Oyster House, 119 Main St., Bel Air, MD 21014; (443) 371-7993; mainstreetoysterhouse.com; @MainStOyster. There's lots of oyster talk at the bar of the Main Street Oyster House, a new restaurant

in an old building in Bel Air. The whole town's talkin' about this new
upscale seafood restaurant in a county that doesn't have many such establishments. Ticking off the members of the restaurant's "Oyster Honor Roll"
may make lovers of this bivalve feel like making a beeline for the place.
There they'll find Salt Ponds from Judith Point, Rhode Island, with a "salty
ocean finish"; Chesapeake Golds from Maryland's Hoopers Island—"mildly
salty with a pure clean finish"; House from Tom's Cove—harvested exclusively for the Main Street Oyster House; plump Long Island Sound Blue
Points—"medium salty finish"; Prince Edward Island's Cook's Cove—"plump
and salty"; Cape May Salts from the Delaware Bay—"firm, with clean ocean
finish"; Shooting Point Salts from Virginia's Hog Island—"sweet, plump,
pure brine finish"; and the Chesapeake Bay's Nassawadox Salts—"salty,
sweet, Chesapeake Bay taste." On the fence? The $16 House Sampler lets
you try one of each. But oysters are not the only attraction here. You may
also order steamed clams, pickled herring, or lobster claws from the raw

bar or choose from an appealing menu that reflects the skills of Chef Ryan Kaplin. His grilled swordfish with smoked scallops and dried cherry ravioli in a Madeira sauce is superb; a bouillabaisse is a top-notch rendition of this seafood classic; and we love that his specialties (a 5-pound Maine lobster stuffed with scallops, shrimp, and crabs; a wonderful lobster pie; and a New England clam bake) serve 4 to 6 people. (Be sure to call 2 days in advance to order these special feasts.) Just passing through? It's well worth a stop for some special treats: a delicious Maine lobster roll; a clam roll that is the real thing (not strips, but bellies); the chef's wonderful oysters Rockefeller

INSIDER TIPS
The Maryland Lighthouse Challenge

Are you up for a bit of competitive nautical fun? Then sign up for the Maryland Lighthouse Challenge! It's an outstanding way to see some of the state's finest maritime beacons. Held each fall, the event spans one weekend and requires entrants to:

- Visit all (or as many as possible) of the participating lighthouses.*

- Collect the special commemorative souvenir from each lighthouse visited.

- Complete the visits within the hours of 8 a.m. to 6 p.m.

- Sign the Challenge Completion Sheet.

What do lighthouse-hoppers get for their trouble? Besides bragging rights, that is? Well, they receive a cool "completion" souvenir for one thing. But even better, they'll come away having explored some of the Free State's truly spectacular lighthouses. It's an only-in-the-Chesapeake-Bay-region experience!

For more information on the Maryland Lighthouse Challenge, visit cheslights.org.

*Past participants include the Choptank River, Concord Point, Hooper Strait, Cove Point, Drum Point, Seven Foot Knoll, and Piney Point lighthouses.

or house-smoked trout pate. Maine Street Oyster House is a stellar addition to Maryland's roster of seafood restaurants. PS: Check out the spectacular mural on the side of the building.

Tidewater Grille, 300 Franklin St., Havre de Grace, MD 21078; (410) 939-3313; thetidewatergrille.com. Free docking at a 90-foot dock. Great view. Good reputation as seafood destination. Tidewater Grille in the picturesque town of Havre de Grace is a longtime favorite among locals and travelers who can take a quick detour off Route 50 en route to points east, west, north, or south or steer their boats into the restaurant's 90-foot dock on the Susquehanna River at the headwaters of the Chesapeake Bay. The establishment is gorgeous, with colorful umbrella tables on the rambling outdoor decks, sheltered dining on a year-round porch, and a cozy dining room with wood-beamed ceilings or a handsome bar. The curved windowed walls separating inside from outside make stopping here for lunch or dinner a lovely experience—and guess what? Well-behaved dogs are welcome. About the seafood? For starters, there's a "healthy" crab dip served with celery and carrots; steamed littleneck clams in either a garlicky white wine sauce or house-made marinara; baby versions of the kitchen's good crab cakes; a small seafood sampler of steamed shrimp, clams, and Prince Edward Island mussels served with garlic toast for dipping in the savory broth; marinated and then fried catfish strips that are surprisingly good accompanied by a relish of black bean and corn salsa with the kitchen's homemade remoulade sauce. The "Seafood Market" section of Tidewater Grille's menu features crab cakes, a broiled crab cake and 12-ounce cold-water lobster tail, and a combo platter of broiled crab cake, fillet of salmon, Gulf shrimp, and sea scallops. They come with fresh seasonal vegetables and a choice of rice pilaf, baked potato, or whipped garlic potatoes. Want something different? The kitchen does a winning scallops marsala with mushrooms, Tasso ham, and shallots tossed with linguini and a seafood mac-and-cheese studded with jumbo lump crab, shrimp, and lobster. Lighter fare is available for smaller appetites, with good choices that include the Tidewater's signature sandwich of two small crab cakes with grilled Black Forest ham, tomato, and Hollandaise on a split croissant. Watch the boat and bridge traffic from most any seat in the house at a restaurant that has earned a reputation for consistently good food and service—in addition to its idyllic waterfront location.

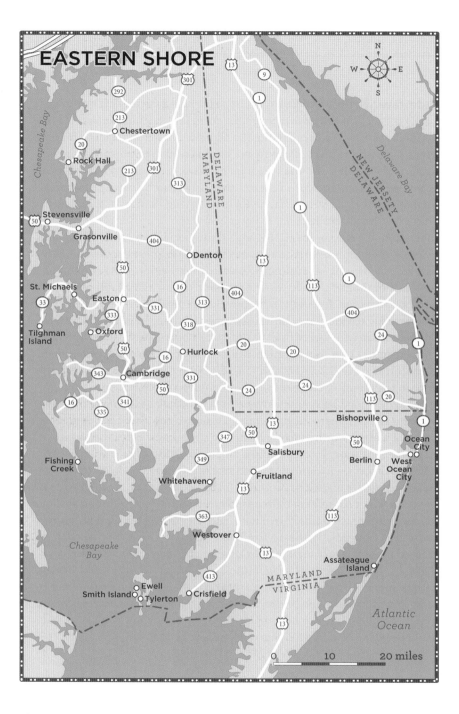

EASTERN SHORE

THE EASTERN SHORE

What many people think of when they think of maritime Maryland, the Eastern Shore is straight out of central casting (there's a reason movies like *The Runaway Bride* and *Wedding Crashers* were filmed here). Picture marinas filled with sailboats and other craft; tumbledown crab shacks; genteel town squares; authentic fishing villages; expansive swaths of unspoiled land; and spectacular sunsets. That's what awaits visitors to Queen Anne's, Kent, Caroline, Talbot, Dorchester, Somerset, Wicomico, and Worcester Counties.

As are other Chesapeake regions, the Eastern Shore and the bay are fully intertwined. Essentially cut off from the Western Shore, the Eastern Shore was once better connected to Philadelphia (via overland railroad routes) than it was to Baltimore. This changed in the 1800s, when steamships became commonplace, and trips between the "mainland" and the shore became less arduous. A century later, in 1952, the first span of the iconic William Preston Lane Jr. Memorial Bridge (aka the Bay Bridge) opened, finally offering motorists a direct route between the Western and Eastern shores. (Although it's not always a quick one; just ask any driver heading east on a warm weekend. *Any* warm weekend.)

Throughout its history—both before the building of the Bay Bridge and since—the Eastern Shore has been synonymous with fresh seafood and destination-worthy travel. Ocean City, Maryland's most popular beachfront getaway, hosts scores of visitors who head "down the ocean" for sun, fun, and one too many funnel cakes. A few miles away, the unspoiled Assateague Island National Seashore is home to herds of wild ponies who, to this day, trot along its wide shores while ignoring the strange two-legged creatures snapping pictures of them. And across the Eastern Shore, towns from St. Michaels, Cambridge, and Easton to Chestertown, Rock Hall, and Crisfield lure guests with their mix of good looks, good people, and good food.

MARITIME MUST-SEES
The Chesapeake Bay Maritime Museum

A visit to St. Michaels, a charming town on Maryland's Eastern Shore, is not complete without spending time (the more you have, the better) at the world-renowned Chesapeake Bay Maritime Museum. One of the many friendly features of the CBMM is that paid admission is good all day long, so you can break for lunch at one of the town's many restaurants—and then come back for more!

Set on 18 waterfront acres, the campus is dotted with 12 buildings that include a working boatyard, where you can watch shipwrights restore and build wooden boats; the Hooper Strait Lighthouse, which you can climb to the top like a lighthouse keeper of old; a cavernous shed that once housed a cannery and today features an authentic interior of a long-defunct crab-picking plant; the Point Lookout Tower that once guided boats into the Potomac River; and an amazing mini-museum called "At Play on the Bay" that features a wealth of interactive exhibits.

Its "sound-scape" reproduces the sights and sounds of activities on the Chesapeake Bay, chitchat between two guys in an eerily realistic stage set of an old tackle shop, and conversations among oystermen onboard an antique oyster boat. Its "see-scape" features videos of sailors racing sailing log canoes and a mock seafood restaurant where antique menus show how affordable dining out was "back in the day."

The museum's collection of authentic Chesapeake Bay watercraft is the largest in existence. Lovingly restored and maintained by the museum's master shipwrights and their apprenticeships, nine of the collection's largest boats are floating at the museum's docks. The latest addition to the floating fleet is the *Winnie Estelle*, a 1920 buy boat that will carry up to 45 passengers for cruises on the Miles River on weekdays.

Buy boats, as the name implies, bought the catch of watermen in remote parts of the Chesapeake and brought it directly to city markets and packing houses. The *Winnie Estelle* joins a fleet that includes the recently restored 1955 skipjack *Rosie Parks*, an 1889 nine-log bugeye, a 1912 river tug, a 1909 seven-log crab dredger, a 1934 dovetail, a 1931 Potomac River dory boat, and a 1961 Jackson-built Pot Pie skiff.

It's all about "getting real" at the CBMM, and what could be more so than what goes on at Waterman's Wharf at the far end of the campus. Here we came upon barefoot children experiencing the thrill of catching crabs with nets and bait, supplied courtesy of the museum. They were too engrossed being "watermen" to notice us—but it is likely they will not forget their experience at this special place.

I was fortunate to be escorted on a private tour of the museum by Senior Curator Peter Lesher, who summered as a child on the Eastern Shore. Upon completing his doctorate in 1992, Lesher began his career at the CBMM and has made major contributions to the museum's mission of preserving the legacy of the Chesapeake Bay and the history of its residents.

Note: The Chesapeake Bay Maritime Museum Store is a treasure trove, stocking everything from wooden mallets to children's books (kids love *My Life As An Oyster*), a fascinating oral portrait of Eastern Shore crab picking based on interviews with the people who made their living in the industry, and the Tilly Hats favored by travel writers. Staffed by some of the museum's 250 volunteers, it is a friendly place to browse while learning more about the history of Maryland, the Chesapeake Bay, and the museum that so passionately curates its legacy.

The CBMM is open daily except for Thanksgiving, Christmas, and New Year's. For more information, visit its website at cbmm.org or call (410) 745-2916. Children under 6 are free; ages 6–17, $6; seniors and students $12, adults $15. Group rates and guided tours available.

Directions: By land, take Rte. 50 to Easton. Exit onto Rte. 322. From Rte. 322, take Rte. 33 to St. Michaels. Go through St. Michaels and turn right at museum entrance. Parking is free in the museum lot. By water: On the Miles River off Eastern Bay, a tributary of the Chesapeake Bay. Limited day dockage available. Call the dockmaster on VHS 16 for more information.

Harry's on the Green, 4 S. 1st St., Denton, MD 21629; (410) 479-1919; harrysonthegreen.com. Jeri and Harry Wyre loved the country inn they owned in Maine for many years, but 20 years ago, they migrated to Maryland to be closer to family. They bought an historic house in Caroline County, gutted it (Harry's hobby is restoring historic buildings), and opened an inn-cum-restaurant that enjoyed a successful run until 2010, when they moved to the current site of Harry's on the Green in the small town of Denton. Harry once again orchestrated a complete re-do of another historic property, which today sits next to the town library

PHOTOS COURTESY OF HARRY'S ON THE GREEN

and across from the courthouse. Chef Jeri says her style of cooking is influenced by the many trips the couple took to France, where they made friends with five well-known chefs who agreed to a unique Chef Exchange Program: Each chef changed places with Jeri for a month—she spending time in their kitchens while they were "guest chefs" at Harry's. "That's where I got my classical training," says Jeri, whose divine entree of scallops and lobster in champagne sauce deliciously proves the point. She is a versatile and creative cook, incorporating local ingredients in a Maryland-inspired dish of oven-roasted halibut on a bed of corn chowder flecked with tomatoes, Cajun-spiced scallops and shrimp over pasta, Scottish oysters (a recipe brought back from Scotland), multiple preparations of local rockfish, and a celebratory call-ahead combination of Maine lobster, a petit filet, and veal Ermanthal. Harry's creative talents are apparent in the charming restoration of the property, featuring wraparound porches, two dining rooms seating 25 each, a tavern-style bar, and a rear patio. Music is part of the package here, with weekend performers on rotation. The Wyres' daughter Jeanine, who also trained in France, is Jeri's teammate in the kitchen and has a particular passion for pastry. Hint: Harry's signature dessert is an ice-cream-filled cream puff smothered in Jeanine's house-made fudge sauce.

Dorchester County

Bistro Poplar, 535 Poplar St., Cambridge, MD 21613; (410) 228-4884; bistropoplar.com. Chef-Owner Ian Campbell is a wunderkind who knew at a tender age he wanted a career in cooking. A graduate of the Culinary Institute of America who was influenced by California celebrity chef Thomas Keller, he returned to his Eastern Shore roots in 2007 to open this charming little bistro in the heart of Cambridge. Bistro Poplar has succeeded in bringing authentic French country cuisine to the local scene, earning personal popularity and professional accolades from the Maryland Restaurant Association as well as *Zagat* and *Fodor*'s. Seafood makes up 50 percent of the restaurant's menu, which changes with the seasons. You may find monkfish, salmon, flounder, or striped bass featured alongside imaginative preparations of oysters, mussels, crab, and shrimp. The menu is small but appealing and the wine list well-chosen. An in-house pastry chef makes delicious desserts (try the profiteroles) and on Sunday the kitchen turns out an assortment of tasty tapas for about $5 each. Campbell has been known to prepare oysters 14 different ways! Note: Dinner Thurs through Mon; lunch Sat, in season.

Blue Point Provision Company, Hyatt Regency Chesapeake Bay Golf Resort, Spa and Marina, 100 Heron Blvd./Rte. 50, Cambridge, MD 21613; (410) 901-6410; chesapeakebay.hyatt.com. Eastern Shore seafood specialties are the focal point of Blue Point Provision Company, a casual waterfront restaurant that is part of the lush Hyatt Regency Chesapeake Bay Golf Resort, Spa and Marina. Overseen by Executive Chef Thomas Olson, Blue Point's menu features signature regional favorites such as Maryland crab cakes, Eastern Shore mac-and-cheese, and Maryland crab dip. "Really Fresh Fish" is the chef's daily offering of three of the freshest catches from fish markets up and down the Eastern Shore. Be sure to enjoy some of the restaurant's famous namesake Blue Point oysters and enjoy one of the kitchen's favorite dishes—whimsically christened "Drunken Dancing Prawns" and singing with Asian flavors. Blue Point's modern nautical theme speaks of the Chesapeake region, and the adjoining deck offers panoramic views of the Choptank River and glimpses of waterfowl in their natural habitat. The resort itself is situated on 400 acres of Eastern Shore landscape and features a spa, a championship golf course, and full-service marina. Relax in Michener's Library with an after-dinner drink and explore the premises of this stellar addition to Maryland's hospitality options.

PHOTO COURTESY OF THE HYATT REGENCY CHESAPEAKE BAY GOLF RESORT, SPA AND MARINA

The High Spot, 305 High St., Cambridge, MD 21613; (410) 228-7420; thehighspotgastropub.com; @TheHighSpot. Gastropubs seem to be replacing bistros as the favored formula for trendy places to eat and drink in a casual setting. Proof is the popularity of The High Spot in Cambridge, where beer is king and the fare ranges from simple to sophisticated. Chef and Co-owner Patrick Fanning (with Brett and Janie Summers) has outpaced the competition from other such Eastern Shore establishments during its 2-year lifespan. Proof for us came in the form of many recommendations from area residents who rave about this place and recommended its inclusion in this book. What makes it so special? Surely not the bare-bones decor of this recently renovated property, which features a front room dominated by a functional bar and TV set and a rear dining room functionally furnished with cafeteria-style tables and chairs. Rather it is the restaurant's remarkably diverse selection of domestic and international craft beers and an imaginative menu skillfully orchestrated by Chef Fanning. We arrived at the restaurant one evening just as a beer festival was winding down in front of High Spot. Every inside table was filled, so we were seated at one of the outdoor sidewalk cafe tables—not one of the best places to be unless you like flies. Making up for the uncomfortable setting was the warm welcome from Caitlin, our server, and the parade of tasty treats that followed. Beer is big here, strutting its stuff on a list featuring 18 imported craft varieties and 22 domestics. They are much pricier and exotic than the popular brands, also on tap. We had fun sipping from a flight of the day's six featured beers, listed on two enormous blackboards. Attractively presented in shot glasses, each had a distinctive personality, with flavors ranging from a fruity Canadian Ephemere Cassis to a hoppy Indian Pale Ale and a Mana Wheat Ale brewed with Maui Gold pineapple—both from the Maui Brewing Company in Hawaii. It was then time to move on to the food options on a menu offering an expansive selection of appetizers, soups, salads, supper, and sandwiches on the menu. Buffalo oysters were a tasty starter—a half-dozen meaty specimens in a crusty coating arranged in a circle around a pool of hot sauce and house-made ranch dressing on a chiffonier of crisp romaine lettuce. Fish tacos here are another of the chef's original creations—a mélange of seafood bathed in lemon butter and served in a big bowl scattered with shards of crisp taco shells. Both starters deserved high marks for flavor, freshness, and presentation. Chef Fanning takes pride in patronizing local suppliers who provide fresh produce as well as seafood. We were pleasantly surprised to see monkfish (sometimes called "poor man's lobster") and halibut among his daily specials on the evening of our visit. The chef, whose signature talent is his ability to tweak traditional preparations, used a ribbon of bacon to encircle the monkfish and lend it a subtle smoky flavor. Paired with a corn-flecked risotto and fresh asparagus, it is a happy marriage. Halibut, a highly regarded and expensive fish, needs nothing but a gentle butter poach to taste delicious. Desserts get special attention. In season, you may enjoy an old-fashioned strawberry shortcake featuring sweet biscuits layered with fresh berries and real whipped cream; off-season, a house-made chocolate cake frosted with ganache, layered with buttercream, and tasting like a Dove bar.

Ocean Odyssey, 316 Sunburst Hwy./Rte. 50, Cambridge, MD 21613; (410) 228-8633; toddseafood.com; @OceanOdysseyMD. Don't bypass this modest restaurant on Route 50 in Cambridge on Maryland's Eastern Shore. Ocean Odyssey has a solid reputation for fine fresh seafood, a tradition started by the Todd family in 1947. Originally a seafood packing plant, the site has evolved from its simple beginnings to a popular restaurant, complete with a new beer garden, where the kitchen puts out fresh local crabs, oysters and clams, and sustainable finfish as well as anyone around. Grandson Travis Todd is a vocal supporter of Eastern Shore watermen and walks the talk by offering a wide range of seafood selections

PHOTO COURTESY OF OCEAN ODYSSEY

at Ocean Odyssey. "We're a no-fuss place with a lot of pride," he says, adding that he only uses Maryland crab—handpicked on the premises. The Virginia Tech graduate was called back to manage (and sometimes cook for) his family's restaurant and has earned recognition on Food Network and PBS. You will find a fine selection of sustainable fish on his flexible menu. In addition to local crabs, oysters from the Choptank Boys James Parker and Bubba, rockfish, wild blue catfish, and the occasional noninvasive snakehead (tastes like a mild catfish), you may find wild Atlantic salmon, mahimahi, and other species bought from one of his several suppliers. The new outdoor deck (complete with a play area for children) is a popular place for crab feasts, and when there is music, a younger crowd shows up. Note: The restaurant closes from Thanksgiving Day until mid-Apr, when the crab season starts.

Old Salty's, 2560 Hoopers Island Rd., Fishing Creek, MD 21634; (410) 397-3752; oldsaltys.com. Driving to Old Salty's in Dorchester County (an area the locals call "Down Below") is a step back in time for the Chesapeake adventurer. Wind past the windswept 28,000-acre Blackwater National Wildlife Refuge to the southwestern edge of this heart-shaped county. As you enter Fishing Creek, the Hooper's Island village where the restaurant is situated, you'll park near dozens of "buy" boats used by

watermen for fishing, crabbing, and oystering. Old Salty's is located in the Island's historic schoolhouse where the former gym is now an event space. Set on a spit of land surrounded by the Chesapeake Bay on one side and the Honga River on the other, the restaurant serves Chesapeake specialties fresh from the nearby waters, including Maryland crab in dozens of dishes—crab cakes, balls, soup, imperial, stuffed in mushrooms, atop oysters and fish, soft and hard shell. Also available are rockfish, flounder, and oysters, including premium bivalves available year-round from the Island's oyster farming operations. Make room for the homemade rolls and desserts baked on the premises. No trip to Old Salty's is complete without a taste of their famous "Crab Bites," soft-shell crabs (in season) fried, cut in half, and served piping hot with spicy cocktail sauce. While some menu items are seasonal, Old Salty's world-famous crab cakes made exclusively with Maryland back fin and lump crabmeat are always available thanks to pasteurizing. Make time to hang with the locals in the small bar separating the dining room from the "gym" or visit their country store packed with antiques, local crafts, and books. Note: Call ahead before making the trip, as the restaurant has seasonal hours.

Suicide Bridge Restaurant, 6304 Suicide Bridge Rd., Hurlock, MD 21643; (410) 943-4689; suicide-bridge-restaurant.com. Enter Suicide Bridge Restaurant and its oyster shell-encrusted walls any Friday evening, and you'll quickly discover the mouthwatering Chesapeake Bay seafood buffet that's been drawing Eastern Shore residents for 2 decades. Teeming with fresh-shucked oysters on the half shell; broiled, baked, and grilled fish; and scallops, shrimp, and crab specials deliciously prepared by the chef, the buffet is a signature event. Located 10 miles north of Route 50 in Dorchester County, the restaurant with the funny name looks over the bridge where there is a unique history of suicides and foul play. Waterman Dave Nickerson purchased the former seafood shack in 1979 because he needed a place to prepare his catch. It has grown into one of the Shore's premier dining destinations. Area boaters enjoy arriving at Suicide Bridge

from Cabin Creek off the Choptank River and docking at one of the many slips reserved for the restaurant. Whether you bike, boat, or drive here, the seafood-rich menu is stuffed with soups, appetizers, sandwiches, salads, and entrees featuring crabs, fish, oysters, clams, and shrimp. House specialties include crab-stuffed rock and flounder, oysters Rockefeller, linguini with clams, and crab anyway you can imagine. For casual or late-night fare, climb the steps to the Light House Lounge overlooking the marina. Warm weather welcomes outdoor diners with two decks and a waterside patio where you can watch the restaurant's two stern wheel paddleboats take

visitors out for river cruises. The restaurant and surrounding gardens are a showcase for renowned local metal artist Paul Lockhart. From the steel Striped Bass sign suspended high over the parking lot, to the gigantic cooper crabs scaling the lobby, to contemporary herons standing sentry over the paddleboat docks, Lockhart's art is as much a fixture at this Chesapeake dining destination as the restaurant's signature seafood dishes. Note: Open May through Dec, Tues through Sun; Jan through Apr, Thurs through Sun.

PHOTO COURTESY OF SUICIDE BRIDGE RESTAURANT

MARITIME MUST-SEES
Can't-Miss Attractions on the Eastern Shore

Assateague Island National Seashore: Unspoiled, gorgeous, and free of hotels, restaurants, and other man-made clutter, Assateague Island National Seashore doesn't just offer spectacular Atlantic Ocean beaches and an unhurried vibe; it also boasts a herd of wild ponies that roams the island unfettered (don't get too close—they bite!). Spend a day here splashing in the waves, casting a line in the water, or simply sitting back and watching the beautiful ponies as they trot along (and sometimes roll in) the sand and surf. Assateague Island National Seashore is located just outside of Ocean City, MD. *assateagueisland.com.*

Choptank River Heritage Center: Now home to the Caroline Office of Tourism, the Choptank River Heritage Center is a replica of the 1883 Maryland Steamboat Company's Denton Wharf. Among other things, it features a re-created passenger waiting room, a warehouse, and a steamship agent's office. Harking back to a time when West Denton was a thriving maritime hub, the center brings to life an era when the Chesapeake Bay—and its endless bounty—formed the backbone of this community. *The Choptank River Heritage Center, 10219 River Landing Rd., West Denton, MD 21629; (410) 479-0655 to schedule a tour.*

Choptank River Lighthouse: Owned by the city of Cambridge, this replica screwpile lighthouse, completed in 2012, is the Chesapeake Bay's newest. More than just a re-created beacon to passing ships, the lighthouse also houses a small museum and the Cambridge Municipal Yacht Basin dockmaster's offices. From May through Oct, the lighthouse is open daily for free, self-guided tours. In the off-season, it is open by appointment. *The Choptank River Lighthouse, Long Wharf Park, at the intersection of High and Water Streets, Cambridge, MD 21613; (410) 228-4031; choptankriverlighthouse.org.*

Crisfield City Dock: Situated on the Chesapeake Bay just off Tangier Sound—and known as the "Crab Capital of the World"—Crisfield (a waterfront town whose municipal wharf was literally built on a foundation of crushed oyster shells) is a must-see destination for any serious seafood lover. And one of its finest sites is its City Dock. Enjoying a protected harbor, the City Dock is the landing point for many oystermen and crabbers bringing in their daily catch. It's also an excellent jumping-off point from which to explore the rest of this tiny, splendidly nautical town. *Crisfield City Dock, 1300 W. Main St., Crisfield, MD 21817; crisfieldchamber.com.*

Delmarva Discovery Center: The 16,000-square-foot Delmarva Discovery Center on the Pocomoke River celebrates the fascinating history of the Delmarva (Delaware, Maryland, and Virginia) Peninsula. Filled with exhibits on river ecology, Native Americans, indigenous flora and fauna, Colonial life, and much more (including aquariums filled with live animals), the center is an excellent place to get a feel for what's so special about this region. *The Delmarva Discovery Center, 2 Market St., Pocomoke City, MD 21851; (410) 957-9933; delmarva discoverycenter.org.*

Eastern Neck National Wildlife Refuge: Sprawled across 2,285 acres at the confluence of the Chester River and the Chesapeake Bay, the Eastern Neck National Wildlife Refuge is home to more than 100,000 swans, ducks, geese, and other migrating waterfowl. Songbirds, shorebirds, and bald eagles also call Eastern Neck home, as do countless fish and crabs (all just waiting to be caught!). Gorgeous views of the bay and a universally accessible waterside trail make the park a fantastic place to soak up the beauty of the region. *Eastern Neck National Wildlife Refuge, 1730 Eastern Neck Rd., Rock Hall, MD 21661; (410) 639-7056; fws.gov.*

Harriet Tubman Museum and Educational Center: Dorchester County's most famous daughter is honored in this small, simple museum that pays homage to her heroism. Tubman, whose Underground Railroad led countless slaves to freedom, was herself born into bondage just a few miles from where the facility stands today. Tours of the surrounding area are available by appointment. *The Harriet Tubman Museum and Educational Center, 424 Race St., Cambridge, MD 21613; (410) 228-0401; htorganization.blogspot.com.*

Harriet Tubman Underground Railroad Byway: Escaped slaves journeyed along the Underground Railroad to freedom in the North. All along the Harriet Tubman Underground Railroad Byway—some of which runs through Caroline County—are sites where the famed Tubman guided them to safety, always at great peril. Important stops along the trail include Poplar Neck; the Jacob Leverton Dwelling, a private residence that is the only documented stop on the Underground Railroad remaining on the Eastern Shore; the Courthouse Square in Denton; and Hillsboro, the place where Frederick Douglass' family was broken up and sold off. *Call (410) 479-0655 or visit harriettubmanbyway.com for more information, or to request a copy of the "Finding the Way to Freedom" map, which outlines various sites along the byway.*

Janes Island State Park: Enjoy miles of unspoiled, isolated shoreline and marshes, not to mention endless opportunities to go crabbing and fishing at this gorgeous, ADA-compliant park. Boasting more than 100 campsites, plus cabins, bath houses, a conference center, canoe/kayak and bike rentals, a boat launch, a fish-cleaning station, and more, Janes Island (part of which is accessible only by boat) is the perfect place to soak up the rustic beauty of the Chesapeake Bay region. *Janes Island State Park, 26280 Alfred Lawson Dr., Crisfield, MD 21817; (410) 968-1565; dnr.state.md.us.*

Nathan of Dorchester: A true labor of love, the skipjack *Nathan* of Dorchester—commissioned on the Fourth of July in 1994—was funded by donors and built entirely by volunteers. The project's goal? To preserve the boat-building technology once integral to the region. Today, the *Nathan* serves to show visitors the Choptank River and the Chesapeake Bay from a truly unique vantage point—the deck of an authentic skipjack. The vessel offers public sails every weekend; private charters are also available. *The* Nathan of Dorchester, *Long Wharf (at the end of High Street), Cambridge, MD 21613; (410) 228-7141; skipjack-nathan.org.*

Schooner *Sultana*: Maintained by the Sultana Education Foundation, the schooner *Sultana* is a reproduction of a Boston-built merchant vessel used by the British Royal Navy from 1768 to 1772 to enforce the Townsend Act (aka "Tea Taxes"). Available today for educational excursions and public sails along the Chester River, the schooner offers guests a unique vantage point from which to experience the region's rich maritime heritage. *The Sultana Education Foundation, 105 S. Cross St., Chestertown, MD 21620; (410) 778-5954; visit sultanaeducation.org.*

Smith Island Cultural Center: Paying homage to a way of life as much as to a place, the Smith Island Cultural Center preserves the history of this unique, only-in-Maryland maritime community. Through exhibits and artifacts and other educational materials, the center offers visitors a glimpse of the place's past; a tour of Smith Island (which guests should tackle on their own afterward) gives a poignant account of its present. (Note: Smith Island is accessible only by boat; several charters depart from the city dock in Crisfield, MD.) *The Smith Island Cultural Center, 20846 Caleb Jones Rd., Ewell, MD 21824; (410) 425-3351; smithisland.org.*

The Stevensville Historic District: A visit to Stevensville is like a trip back in time to an era when this quaint town prospered because of its prime Chesapeake Bay steamboat-shipping-route location. Today, the Stevensville Historic District enjoys a spot on the National Register of Historic Places; visitors will enjoy the blast-from-the-past experience of touring one of Maryland's authentic waterfront towns. Sites not to miss include the Cray House, Stevensville Train Depot, Old Stevensville Post Office, and Old Christ Church and Broad Creek Cemetery. *The Stevensville Historic District, Stevensville, MD 21666; historicqac.org.*

Ward Museum of Wildfowl Art: Seafood isn't the Chesapeake Bay region's only famous fauna. Its waterfowl are legendary, too, and they're spotlighted at this one-of-a-kind museum filled with masterfully carved decoys, paintings, sculptures, jewelry, books, gifts, and other collectibles. Outdoors, it boasts a lovely nature trail, an observation deck overlooking Schumaker Pond, and a large picnic area. *The Ward Museum of Wildfowl Art, 909 S. Schumaker Dr., Salisbury, MD 21804; (410) 742-4988; wardmuseum.org.*

The Waterman's Museum: Filled with exhibits on oystering, fishing, and crabbing; historical photos and artifacts; carvings by local artisans; boats; and a reproduction shanty house, the Waterman's Museum pays simple, straightforward homage to Rock Hall's seafaring past. *Waterman's Museum, 20880 Rock Hall Ave., Rock Hall, MD 21661; (410) 778-6697.*

Fenwick Island, DE

Nantuckets, 601 Coastal Hwy., Fenwick Island, DE; (302) 539-2607; nantucketsrestaurant.com. Nantucket is a name associated with a magical island and good seafood, each of which applies to this restaurant in a charming New England-y cottage, lovingly operated by Owners David and Janet Twining. In its 10-year history, its reputation among locals and travelers has been burnished, thanks to the cozy yet elegant interior and a sociable 4–7 p.m. happy hour daily in the Tap Room. You can spoon its delicious Quahog "Chowdah" while you sip. David was reluctant to part with the recipe, but eventually was gracious enough to share in this

PHOTO COURTESY OF NANTUCKETS

book's recipe section. There are lots of other good things to eat at this popular gathering spot for local residents and summertime tourists. Long-time Executive Chef Michael Priola never seems to miss the mark on an expansive menu that hits all the right buttons for seafood seekers. Jumbo day boat scallops are pan-seared to perfection and sauced with the chef's whim-of-the-day; steamed clams are there for the drowning in drawn butter; the house bouillabaisse is a multi-feast of scallops, mussels, shrimp, and a local fish swimming in a tomato broth kissed with saffron; Maryland crab makes the crab cakes special; and the chef does a delicious variation on shepherd's pie—sautéeing a 6-ounce Canadian lobster tail with wild mushrooms, spinach, and a whisper of Chardonnay and bedding the savory mix on a mound of garlic smashed potatoes. Nantuckets has a beguiling personality—a blend of traditional and modern sensibilities that make it a most comfortable place to enjoy good food, good wine, and good company.

Kent County

Blue Heron Cafe, 36 Cannon St., Chestertown, MD 21611; (410) 778-0188; blueheroncafe.com. Cornell School of Hospitality graduate Paul Hanley opened this little gem in 1997 on a side street in picturesque Chestertown a block away from the town park. Open for dinner only, the cozy restaurant has a loyal following, due in large part to the talents of longtime Chef Eugene Bathel and the eight crew members whose combined services total 70 years. Parents of students at Washington College know the Blue Heron Cafe as a perfect place to take their families for a special dinner—and many wish it was still open for lunch. An appealing array of appetizers includes the chef's famous oyster fritters, baked Chesapeake oysters with a lemony sauce, crab-stuffed shrimp with artichoke hearts and a fresh pineapple sauce—all in the $10 range. Stand-out main courses include Bathel's festive cioppino (lobster, mussels, clams, crabmeat, and a local finfish) and local rockfish prepared according to the chef's whim. The wine list is well-priced, with by-the-glass at $7.50 per and about 20 bottles with familiar names like Fetzer, Stags Leap, Ecco Domani, and Mumm's Cordon Rouge (a bargain $45).

Fish Whistle, 98 Cannon St., Chestertown, MD 21620; (410) 778-3566; fishandwhistle.com. Waterfront restaurants often put view before vittles in their asset column—but not Fish Whistle on the scenic Chester River in Chestertown. As the chef told us, "Fish Whistle is all about the

food," and he walks the talk with an expansive menu that features a variety of Eastern Shore seafood and produce as well as homemade ice cream and to-die-for pies by in-house baker Lisa Powell. The restaurant itself is plain-brown-wrapper simple from the outside, sharing space with a busy boatyard and located across the street from the Historical Society of Kent Island and a pocket-park marked with a bronze sculpture of a Japanese goose. Inside, the wall of windows simulates a mural of water activities; in-season tables on the deck are prime spots to enjoy both the view and the food and service by a cadre of young ladies, among them a charmer named Kristen. Local oysters are a big seller here, with an appetizer sampler the chef prepares in four styles: the classic Rockefeller and casino plus a fried oyster and a gumbo topping, with a wee crab fritter as garnish. He also makes a rave-worthy Eastern Shore version of cioppino and dresses up pasta dishes with bay scallops delivered daily from Ocean City waters or a mix of seafood in a cream sauce. Fish (cod) and chips are a popular item as is the fish taco and Thursday's unlimited oyster bonanza. On a busy night, patrons have been known to slurp 3,000 bivalves, washed down with one of the restaurant's wide selection of beers. Boaters should call ahead for space availability at the city dock next door to the restaurant.

Harbor Shack, 20895 Bayside Ave., Rock Hall, MD 21661; (410) 639-9996; harborshack.net. A self-described "neighborhood hangout" by its owners, Harbor Shack in Rock Hall is popular with local watermen as well as boaters who like the convenience of motoring up to one of the restaurant's shore side slips. The Johnson family has run this y'all-come eatery since 2006, pleasing customers with a mix of Mexican specialties with local seafood and man-pleasing steaks and ribs. Harbor Shack doesn't pretend to be fancy or foodie. Its special appeal is its friendliness, prime location overlooking Rock Hall Harbor, two outdoor dining decks, and a round bar where the margaritas are cold and strong and the beer flows freely. The restaurant's specialty is a jumbo lump crab cake on a ciabatta roll lavished with avocado mayonnaise and layered with bacon, Swiss cheese, lettuce, and (in season) local tomatoes. Good eating . . . as is a fish sandwich featuring a 6-ounce grilled or blackened mahimahi fillet and the fish and chips featuring crispy fried haddock. There is an interesting selection of light fare, including calamari, coconut shrimp with an orange-infused horseradish sauce, and the cook's inventive preparation of yellowfin tuna, described on the menu as "dusted with 14 spices" before being pan-seared rare, sliced, and served on a bed of edible seaweed dressed with hot wasabi. More traditional choices include steamed clams bathed in garlic butter and white wine and mussels in an Alfredo cream sauce. Live music and DJs draw big crowds on weekends, when Harbor Shack rocks. Other worth-mentionables

are that well-behaved leashed dogs are welcome in the outdoor dining areas, fair weather is the best time to go, and don't worry about any dress code—this is Rock Hall, after all.

The Kitchen at Rock Hall, 5757 Main St., Rock Hall, MD 21661; (410) 639-2700; kitchenatrockhall.com. Petite and understated, this little gem was opened in 2011 by Steve and Monica Quigg, successful IT workers in the Washington, DC, area. Little by little, words of praise for the Kitchen at Rock Hall's creative cuisine have spread beyond the boundaries of Rock Hall, and it is being discovered by regional foodies and boaters docking at the many local marinas. Winner of 19 local awards, including Best Crab Cake on the Chesapeake Bay three years in a row from *Chesapeake Bay Magazine*, The Kitchen is an American bistro known for casual fine dining, with lunch and dinner menus featuring seasonal, locally sourced ingredients, including a variety of fish, oysters, house-made pasta, and award-winning crab cakes, as well as a nice selection of meats. On one recent day, seafood dinner choices included diver scallops over a lovely butternut squash risotto, crispy-skinned rockfish resting on a circle of rice surrounded by shrimp and bathed in an intriguing sweet Asian broth, Parmesan-crusted swordfish moistened with a light lemon butter sauce garnished with capers, and a pair of The Kitchen's famous 5-ounce jumbo lump crab cakes. Meat eaters had their choice from among a man-size braised lamb shank, a half a roasted chicken, and either a petite or double cut beef tenderloin. The Kitchen, sitting modestly on a corner in the colorful town of Rock Hall not far from Chestertown, seats 18 inside and 12 on the patio. So reserve early. Note: The Kitchen qualifies as a "best-kept secret"—but feel free to share. Open 11:30 a.m. to 9 p.m. Thurs through Mon. Open for breakfast at 8 a.m. on weekends.

Osprey Point Inn, 20786 Rock Hall Ave., Rock Hall, MD 21661; (410) 639-2194; ospreypoint.com. Casual upscale describes Osprey Point Inn, a charming oasis at the edge of the working waterman's town of Rock Hall. Open since 1993, the Williamsburg-style mini-resort has become a favorite of boaters

for its well-kept marina on scenic Swan's Creek (easily accessible from the Chesapeake Bay) and a 55-seat restaurant featuring a small but well-chosen menu that changes every month. John Evans had just come aboard as chef as we were writing about Osprey Point, but he promises to keep standards high. Monkfish, bass, and trout as well as mussels, oysters, and crab are regular items on the menu, together with lamb, beef, duck, and Eastern Shore quail. Mussels cooked in a winey broth tinged with saffron surround the chef's monkfish entree, garnished with juicy pieces of grapefruit. His crab bisque studded with local corn and sweetened with crab lumps is a palate pleaser, as is the oyster stew. Osprey Point, a short drive from Chestertown, is a destination where you can dine well and sleep well in one of the inn's luxuriously furnished guest rooms or its more rustic Farm House annex. The well-manicured grounds include a pool and charcoal grills for guests; the marina boasts a spanking-clean bath house. Marina slips available for patrons; call dock master at (410) 639-2194. Note: Inn and restaurant closed for month of Jan.

Waterman's Crab House, 21055 Sharp St., Rock Hall, MD 21661; (410) 639-2261; watermanscrabhouse.com. Situated on the shores of the Chesapeake next to a working marina, Waterman's Crab House has evolved over the past 40 years from a local seafood market to a favorite destination for casual crab feasts, seafood dinners featuring fresh local products, and weekend music fests. Today, the two large inside dining rooms and the outdoor dining deck and bar draw crowds in the summer months. They come primarily for the all-you-can-eat crab feasts (including corn and coleslaw), for the cooks' creative take on seafood nachos (overflowing with crab, shrimp, and tiny scallops), for fat crab cakes drizzled with Dijon mustard, for the friendly service, and for the sunset cruises offered through the marina next door that provide a grand finale to the evening.

COLORFUL CHARACTERS
Artist Nancy Hammond's Chesapeake Seafood Dinner "Recipe"

Follow these steps to create the perfect fresh-from-the-bay "meal," a whimsical recipe from an artist whose work is inspired by the Chesapeake Bay region.

1. Take the dog straight from the dock, not directly from beach muck, if possible.

2. Rinse well.

3. Run for the bow before "the shake."

4. Start up the engine and cruise on down the creek to open water.

5. Speed up the motor.

6. As the bow begins to rise, catch the sliding dog, who is trying to grip the fiberglass bottom with his nails, to no avail.

7. Hold the wheel and extend your leg to the side to catch the rump end of the dog sliding by and about to hit the gas tank in the stern.

8. Use fresh bait.

9. Cast line and use wrist as if flipping an omelet.

Queen Anne's County

Bridges Restaurant, 321 Wells Cove Rd., Grasonville, MD 21638; (410) 827-0782; bridgesrestaurant.net. Bridges made its debut in 2000, all dressed up in a custom-designed waterfront building with a formal-looking façade that belied its informal interior. The inside dining room is distinguished by high ceilings, a long bar with big-screen TV, a fireplace, and a pretty view of Kent Narrows. This asset shines in fair weather, when tables on the spacious deck bring diners closer to nature.

Artwork, *Dinner on the Chesapeake*
COURTESY OF NANCY HAMMOND, NANCY HAMMOND EDITIONS

10. When line tightens and dog barks, dinner is almost ready.

11. Reel in large catch with whisk-like motion.

12. Remove hook from mouth of fish.

13. Toss back into the Chesapeake.

14. Head to nearest crab house for dinner.

Executive Chef Nathan Ebersole is proud of his "made from scratch" menu and the fact that most of his suppliers are local. He is also conscious of special needs among guests at the restaurants, apparent in his wonderful rockfish chowder, which is gluten free. His small plates, the designation for petite portions and lower prices, make it interesting and affordable to sample some of his signature dishes. Among the choices are a creamy risotto studded with scallops, crisp mahimahi in taco shells, shrimp and grits, and oyster po' boy sandwiches. Boaters appreciate the convenience of complimentary docking at one of the restaurant's 16 slips. Call ahead to reserve.

Fisherman's Inn and Crab Deck, 3116 Main St., Grasonville MD 21638; (410) 827-8807; fishermansinn.com. "Fisherman's Village" is the name sometimes given to this family-owned seafood paradise just off Route 50 in Grasonville on Kent Island. Sonny Schulz, a third-generation member of the family, is a fisherman himself and particular about what is served at the Fisherman's Inn and the Crab Deck next door as well as what is sold at the family's nearby seafood market. There is no end to the choices on the inn's extensive menu, sure to send shivers up the spines of seafood lovers. The feast can begin with steamer pots filled with crabs or a selection of clams, mussels, crab, and lobster accompanied by drawn butter or steamed lobsters fresh from the market. Or, more elegantly, begin with the kitchen's divine asparagus-crab bisque, a delicious tempura-style soft-shell crab or Ipswich whole-belly clams (not strips). We did not encounter a larger seafood selection or such a variety of preparations in our travels for this book. Chesapeake Bay striped bass (aka rockfish), for instance, is available six ways: potato-crusted with lobster-sherry cream sauce; crowned with crab imperial; Tidewater style, with lump crab, country ham, corn, and cream sauce; and fried, broiled, or blackened. Gluten-free people will like to order from the restaurant's new gluten-free menu. While there is a strong traditional theme to the menus here, the kitchen is not afraid to experiment. Fresh sea scallops lounge on a bed of orzo pilaf enlivened with a green chili beurre blanc; Atlantic swordfish steak sided with lump crabmeat is prepared "Tuscan style" with fresh oregano and lemons; pan-seared yellowtail snapper is teamed with grilled shrimp and creamy stone-ground grits redolent of garlic and cheddar cheese. Have your crabs on the deck overlooking the busy waters of Kent Narrows, enjoy simple fare in the newly renovated bar area, or dine in style at the inn. No visit to the Eastern Shore is complete without a stop at this "seafood central"—where the Shulz family and a friendly staff are skilled in the art of Southern hospitality.

Harris Crab House & Seafood Restaurant, 443 Kent Narrows Way North, Grasonville, MD 21638; (410) 827-9500; www.harriscrab house.com. Harris Crab House & Seafood Restaurant is an Eastern Shore classic, best appreciated during fair weather so you can sit on the second-level deck and watch the sailboats skim over the Kent Narrows and maybe spy a boatload of crabs being delivered by local watermen. Open and flourishing since 1981, Harris is favored by families and others seeking an authentic "crab feast" complete with brown paper-covered tables, picking knives, and wooden mallets. The atmosphere is casual (flip-flops welcome) and the service friendly. The earlier you get there, the better the chances are for ordering the size crabs you want. Priced by the weight of the specimen and the time of year, these are Maryland crabs that are at their fattest in the fall—though sweet no matter what the size. Beer is the best accompaniment to crab for those of legal age, but younger diners will be happy with a Shirley Temple. Crabs may be the main attraction at Harris, but by no means are they the only seafood on the menu. Local oysters are beer-battered and fried up just right and may be ordered with a side of either rockfish or a crab cake. Chef Mike Roberts uses Bay Shore Brand Oysters that are shucked at the Eastern Shore's last surviving oyster processing house in Maryland. Harris has a good selection of steamed seafood—large shrimp (16/20 count per pound), mussels (available in a buttery garlic sauce), and cherrystone clams (served two dozen to a pail). For the extravagant seafood lover, the restaurant has a namesake "basket" that includes shrimp, cherrystones, mussels, and crabs for $42, as well as two ears of local corn when in season. Harris gives you a taste of Maryland seafood and Eastern Shore hospitality—a winning combination. Sweeten it up with the restaurant's signature homemade "Nutty Buddies" and you'll be a happy camper.

The Narrows, 3023 Kent Narrows Way S., Grasonville, MD 21638; (410) 827-8113; thenarrowsrestaurant.com. You would never guess that this very popular waterfront restaurant sits on the foundation of an old oyster packing plant on scenic Kent Narrows, where you can observe fishing boats and other watercraft while enjoying some of the best food on the Eastern Shore. Bo Hardesty built a charming restaurant on this site in 1983, hiring Jerry Dammeyer as manager and staffing it with servers who understood his concept of upscale dining in a tasteful atmosphere warmed with Southern hospitality. Seating along the window of walls on the enclosed porch overlooking the water is prime time, though the layout of the dining room provides most everyone with a nice view. In recent years, Hardesty has delegated some responsibilities to daughter Kelly, but Dammeyer is still going strong and seeing to it that the restaurant's wine list passes muster. The menu notes that Dammeyer and his staff have prepared meals in California for Joseph Phelps and the Murphy family of Murphy-Goode fame. "They loved the food—especially our cream of crab soup and crab cakes," says Dammeyer. "Our crab dishes paired well with their wine." Chef Matt Cohey still sticks to the traditional "r-month" oyster season, when his classic oysters Rockefeller is a big seller. While buying corn, greens, herbs, and tomatoes from local farms and seafood in season from local sources, out-of-region suppliers provide the restaurant with the grouper, flounder, mahimahi, and haddock that appear on the menu. Crab soup comes with a flacon of sherry—and (seafood aside) we highly recommend starting with a cup of The Narrows' version of black bean soup, accompanied by little bowls of rice and chopped onion—if you ask nicely. It is a "secret recipe," developed by a chef named Jimmie at Middleton Tavern in Annapolis when Bo was a partner there. We've never had better.

Rustico Restaurant & Wine Bar, 401 Love Point, Stevensville, MD 21666; (410) 643-9444; rusticorestaurant.com. Stevensville, a quaint village just off the first eastbound exit after crossing the Bay Bridge, is centered with a sweet stop called Rustico Restaurant & Wine Bar. Open since 2007, the tastefully decorated dining rooms and adjacent wine bar are housed in an historic building dating back to the 1800s when it was a general store. Today, Rustico's menu is very much a la minute, serving Italian-accented appetizers and entrees with an emphasis on freshness. While their flatbread pizzas (11 "flavors" including a crisp-crusted crab bruschetta) are a drawing card in the bar area, the selection of appetizers and entrees in the dining areas includes a variety of seafood dishes. Among the favorites is the chef's lovely Seafood Diavolo, rich with lobster, shrimp, mussels, clams, scallops, and calamari in a spicy marinara sauce resting on

PHOTO COURTESY OF RUSTICO RESTAURANT & WINE BAR

a bed of homemade linguini. His *zuppa di pesce*, a traditional fisherman's stew, has shrimp, scallops, clams, and mussels in a zesty marinara sauce tempered with a seafood broth. It is a hearty dish that, when paired with a house salad, warm homemade bread, and a glass of wine chosen from Rustico's well-stocked cellar, adds up to a satisfying main course. The chef does calamari two ways—flash fried and served with pesto aioli or bathed in a spicy tomato sauce. And Rustico's original take on ravioli is delicious: house-made pasta stuffed with lobster pieces, crab, mushrooms, and peas afloat in a creamy rose bath. A special seafood dish one evening was a thick slab of fresh halibut encrusted with Parmesan cheese—the fish impeccably fresh and seasoned. Worth mentioning is Rustico's crab bruschetta, its perfectly cooked risottos made with Arborio rice, and two heavenly desserts—one a classic tiramisu and the other the Orange Creamsicle Cheesecake made by Peace of Cake, a marvelous little bakery just across the street from the restaurant. Rustico has a staff of food-savvy young people who seem to love their profession and a sommelier who knows his craft. It is a little gem in a town that's made for walking. Check out the interesting little shops next door.

Somerset County

Bayside Inn, 4064 Smith Island Rd., Ewell, MD 21824; (410) 425-2771; smithislandcruises.com/food. Cruise boats leave from Somers Cove Marina in Crisfield, arriving 40 minutes later in the little town of Ewell on Smith Island. There to feed them between the hours of 11 a.m. and 4 p.m. are the friendly folks at Bayside Inn, a 100-seat waterfront restaurant serving homemade soups, crab cakes, soft-shelled crab and fried oyster sandwiches, fried shrimp platters, and an Eastern Shore family-style feast that has a little bit of everything on the platter. You've gotta be hungry to polish off two crab cakes, a couple of clam

PHOTO COURTESY OF BAYSIDE INN

fritters, baked ham with gravy, corn pudding, stewed tomatoes, green beans, coleslaw, macaroni and cheese, homemade rolls, and a delicious applesauce custard pie. But a lot of people do, according to Betty Jo Tyler, manager of the restaurant and daughter of Captain Alan Tyler, who until recently was the longtime proprietor of Captain Tyler's Crab House in Crisfield. Betty Jo does a fine job of carrying on the family's legacy as proud Smith Islanders who make visitors feel welcome. Open seasonally.

Blue Crab Cafe, 801 W. Main St., Crisfield, MD 21817; (410) 968-0444; bluecrabcafe.com. Carolyn and John Marquis came to Crisfield in 2008 after raising their five children in Annapolis. She runs the Blue Crab Cafe and he is in charge of the Marquis Manor—their charming bed-and-breakfast a few blocks away. As a Naval Academy graduate (class of 1984) John insisted on a "blue and gold room" in the refurbished historic home that was once owned by the Taws family. Carolyn likens a stay there to "going home to Grandma's house." The restaurant and the nearby inn each face the Chesapeake Bay. Seafood is a specialty at both establishments. Carolyn is the main cook and menu planner, known for her rich crab and shrimp dip, crispy Tangier oyster fritters, Maryland crab soup made with local vegetables in season, a CLT (crab-lettuce-tomato) sandwich, and a happy marriage of a perfectly grilled sirloin steak split down the middle and filled with oysters. She buys her produce and seafood locally and serves only Maryland crabs. She is also the one who orchestrates the special seafood feasts at the Marquis, served on the wraparound screened porch overlooking the Chesapeake Bay. They are part of a package that also includes 2 nights' lodging, 2 gourmet breakfasts (cheese soufflés, eggs Benedict, muffins, a signature Bloody Mary), the use of a kayak, and "crabbing lessons" for kids of all ages. The seafood feast features a dozen hard-shell crabs, 2 pounds steamed jumbo shrimp, 3 dozen clams, oyster fritters and corn on the cob (in season), and a salad. Carolyn makes the tartar and cocktail sauces herself. Locals love the congenial atmosphere of the Blue Crab Cafe, and tourists find its laid-back vibe contagious. The bar is always busy and there's dancing on most weekends. One blogger compared the experience to meeting some of the characters from John Steinbeck's novel *Sweet Thursday*. An outdoor deck seats 20, with indoor tables for 50, and a busy bar pouring your choice of spirits, wine, or a selection of craft beers. This is a fun place—convenient to the ferry that takes you to Tangier Island or Smith Island for another Eastern Shore adventure. Boaters can dock at the Somers Cove Marina, and some even fly into the small Crisfield airport. For information on the Marquis Manor, go to marquismanor.com or call (240) 298-1195.

Chesapeake Crab House & Tiki Bar, 923 Spruce St., Crisfield, MD 21817; (410) 968-1131. A lively tiki bar attracts folks to this casual waterfront restaurant, once the site of Captain Tyler's Crab House. New management has spruced up the premises and extended hours to 7 days a week from 11 a.m. to 9 p.m. Local crabbers and oyster harvesters not only supply the kitchen but also like to eat at the restaurant, where the service is friendly, the beer is cold, and the food is hot. There is a variety of selections on a menu that includes options for carnivores and vegetarians as well as seafood lovers. In addition to Maryland hard-shell crabs and oysters, one of the restaurant's specials is a trio of sliders featuring crabmeat, steamed shrimp, and fish-of-the-day. Combine a tiki bar with a crab deck and when the hard-shells are heavy, you have a recipe for a fine ole' Maryland crab feast with a Caribbean beat. Open seasonally.

Crisfield Crabhouse, 204 S. 10th St., Crisfield, MD 21817; (410) 968-2722; facebook.com/crisfield.crabhouse. After lots of work repairing damage caused by Hurricane Sandy, this old standby has reopened under new management by Billie Jo Tyler. Tropical frozen drinks and oyster shooters are popular items at the waterside tiki bar, and a full menu is available on two levels of dining space that include an outdoor deck sheltered by an awning. The restaurant faces Tangier Sound and is directly behind a low building where crabs swim in tubs and shed their shells to provide the very freshest soft shells you can find most anywhere. Three chefs cook up a storm in the kitchen, using down-home recipes learned from their mothers and grandmothers. One of them is Dewey, the cook who makes the restaurant's signature Seafood Deviled Eggs from

MARITIME MUST-SEES
Crisfield's National Hard Crab Derby

Crisfield, known since the 1800s as "The Crab Capital of the World," takes this honor seriously. Since 1947, this colorful small town on the Chesapeake Bay in Somerset County has hosted an annual Labor Day Weekend bash that's all about Maryland crabs. Contests, games, rides, food and craft vendors, and live entertainment are on an agenda that appeals to kids of all ages and boaters who like the convenience of easy access for big or small watercraft.

Sponsored by the Crisfield Chamber of Commerce and held at the festival grounds of the Somers Cove Marina, the festival kicks off with Thursday's crowning of Miss Crustacean. The weekend continues with Friday's crab cooking contest, Saturday's colorful street parade, and the famous gathering of about 400 crabs that "race" in the National Hard Crab Derby.

On Sunday, a purse worth $30,000 attracts skilled captains to Sunday's Boat Docking Contest, aka The Waterman's NASCAR Event. The annual event, which attracts an estimated 8,000 visitors to Crisfield, ends with a spectacular fireworks display on Sunday night.

a family recipe and on special occasions bakes bread for catered events. The kitchen teams up to make Crabby Fries (fresh-cut potatoes topped with crabmeat), a delicious seafood sauce used as a topping for a rockfish-crab entree, and Skeeter Salad, named after a loyal customer who liked his greens garnished with garlicky shrimp. The restaurant buys most of its seafood locally. Service is down-home friendly and on most weekends there is live music in the tiki bar. Billie Jo and her staff do a good job. Open seasonally.

Drum Point Market, 21162 Center St., Tylerton, MD 21866; (410) 425-2108; drumpointmarket.com. This old-time market has a killer quarter-pound crab cake that could "knock your socks off," a verdict expressed by a friend in Somerset County who knows her seafood. Drum

Note: The Crisfield Chamber of Commerce is currently putting together a 50th anniversary binder book of winning recipes for the event's Crab Cooking Contest. To order, or for more information, call Valerie Howard at (800) 782-3913 or email info@chrisfieldchamber.com.

Point Market's crab cake has won accolades of another sort, this one from the Food Network's *Hook, Line and Dinner* TV show that featured the regional delicacy several years ago. Those luscious cakes, made with Maryland crabmeat, are from a recipe developed by market Owner Duke Marshall and his mother Mary Ada. Over the past 21 years, the recipe has been tweaked to its current "perfection" and is Drum Point Market's best seller. "We ship them all over the world," says Marshall, whose day job is with Nationwide Insurance. If you are there on weekends, it's likely that Marshall and Sally Tyler will be on-site to make the market's famous sandwiches—not just the seafood varieties but an Italian sub that makes you think you're in Philadelphia, maybe. Weekdays, Patty Laird is the woman who makes the sandwiches, which may be enjoyed at outdoor or indoor tables. Check out the market's assortment of novelty items, T-shirts, and souvenirs to add to your collection of oddities. Mary Ada Marshall's crab cakes may be ordered for shipment by the dozen or half-dozen. Open seasonally.

Hide Away Grill, Goose Creek Marina, 25763 Rumbley Rd., Westover, MD 21871; (410) 651-1193; goosecreekmarina.com. Enter through an opening in a weathered wooden fence on Rumbley Road and be prepared to discover a delightful surprise. Hide Away Grill, open since 2007 and owned by Adam Dannenfelser, knows how to make the most of this little gem on Goose Creek Marina in rural Somerset County. In 2014, he added a new tiki bar where the grill gives off tempting aromas of steak and shrimp kebabs, hamburgers and hot dogs. You've discovered an ongoing "beach party," and you're invited to take a place at picnic tables set up on the sand. Hide Away Grill has another waterfront dining area, where crab cakes made from Dannenfelser's "secret recipe" (he's not telling) are the restaurant's most popular item. They compete with a Crabby Mac and Cheese, fish sandwiches, steamed shellfish, and fresh salads made with local produce. This is a "hidden" stopover for boats, bikers, and automobiles—one you will likely recommend to your fun-loving friends. Open seasonally.

Linton's Crab House & Deck, 450 Crisfield Hwy., Crisfield, MD 21817; (410) 968-0127 or (877) 546-8667; lintonseafood.com. You may see the Linton Seafood trucks around the Eastern Shore, making deliveries to other establishments who appreciate its reputation for quality and freshness. And if you find Linton's Crab House & Deck on the side of Route 413 about a mile outside Crisfield, pull over when you see a big blue sign. Step into a seafood market and place your order for the restaurant's famously huge flounder sandwich, cooked to order while you wait, or crabs and shellfish just about any way you like them. While you're waiting, check out the seafood sold here—everything from crabs to alligator meat to frogs' legs. Talk to the folks behind the counter about the fish of the day, decide if you want some takeout for your campsite at nearby Jane's Island State Park, and wander out to the adjacent little "crab house" or the screened-in crab deck, with additional outdoor picnic tables shielded by big umbrellas. Service couldn't be nicer. Linton's serves Smith Island cakes in six different flavors and has "crab lollipops" for kids. It is a good place for families, and either the deck or the crab house is available for rental by groups. Open seasonally.

INSIDER TIPS
Smith Island Cake: Maryland's Official State Dessert

There are as many stories about the origins of the Smith Island cake as there are layers in this towering treat, officially designated by the state legislature in 2008 as the official state dessert of Maryland. Some claim the recipe was brought to the shores of the Chesapeake in the late 1600s by early settlers whose wives baked the cakes for the watermen to take with them when they set off for the fall oyster-harvesting season. Legend has it that the cakes were originally four-layered but grew to 10 as each baker tried to build a higher cake.

What is known for sure is that since the 1800s, generations of Smith Islanders have continued that tradition, sometimes adding candy in between layers and experimenting with different kinds of icing. It was found that fudge frosting kept longer when the watermen were gone for weeks, and it remains the favorite.

Currently, the Smith Island Baking Company (known as "SIBC") is the only bakery on Smith Island. The company began in 2009, when Maryland entrepreneur Brian Murphy teamed with local residents to found a business that brings a sweet dimension to the economy of Maryland's last inhabited island. SIBC currently has nearly 30 employees, and their cakes are offered at Oriole Park at Camden Yards, through Neiman Marcus and Hammacher Schlemmer, and to customers throughout the US and around the world by visiting SmithIslandCake.com.

Murphy keeps the Smith Island Baking Company's recipe a secret, but you will find out how to make your own colorful variation of Smith Island Cake in the recipe section of this book, courtesy of Chef Henry Miller from Two If By Sea Restaurant on Tilghman Island.

Ruke's Seafood Deck, 20840 Caleb Jones Rd., Ewell, MD 21824; (410) 425-2311; rukesgeneralstore.com. Ruke's has been around "forever" (since 1960, to be specific), distinguished by its rustic building with reddish weathered shingles and down-home selection of seafood and sandwiches. There are ramps leading to the entrance, making it wheelchair accessible, with a warm welcome waiting inside. Local cooks are ready to make crab cakes, soft-shell crab sandwiches, rockfish, tilapia, and shrimp as well as cheesesteak subs, burgers, and cold cuts on rolls or bread. The story goes that the original establishment was a grocery store known as "Ma Willies." Ma's daughter Chart found herself on the mainland during hurricane season, learned to make submarine sandwiches, brought the idea back to Ewell, and the local residents called it "Ma Willie's and Chart's Subs." Today, subs take second place in popularity only to Ruke's crab cakes, made with Maryland crabmeat. Folks like to sit on a screened porch, accommodating about 25, or at inside tables seating about 30. A visit here is a step back in time, with the homey clutter of past decades lending charm to a Smith Island landmark worthy of a visit. Open seasonally.

Watermen's Inn, 901 W. Main St., Crisfield, MD 21817; (410) 968-2119; crisfield.com/watermens. It was 1988 when Brian Julian and Kathy Berezoski, both graduates of the prestigious Johnson & Wales culinary school in Rhode Island, returned to Kathy's Eastern Shore roots and opened the Watermen's Inn 2 blocks from the City Dock and the Somers Cove Marina in Crisfield. The two had worked at several other East Coast restaurants along the way and wanted to try going it alone. Julian is the executive chef, and Kathy, who has an additional degree in pastry arts as well as a bachelor's degree in food service management, brings a set of complementary skills to the partnership. Their goal is to provide a gourmet dining experience for their guests, while keeping things appropriately Crisfield-casual and to offer full catering services to the area. It's hard to miss Watermen's Inn, housed in a Day-Glo orange building topped by a hand-painted mural. Just inside is a tempting display of gorgeous pastries, a selection that changes daily and is one of Watermen's strongest drawing cards. There's a cozy taproom where they promise "the perfect martini" as well as a limited selection of wine and beer. While Watermen's is open year-round, its finest times are the months when crabs are plentiful, produce is fresh, and its herb garden is abloom. Some of the chef's special appetizers are blackened shrimp and "cheesy" grits, steamed mussels with pancetta ham and tomatoes, and steamed clams with chorizo sausage and saffron broth. Entree selections at dinner change nightly but if it's crab season, ask about the crab cakes. Other popular choices are the chef's preparation of scallops, shrimp, and crab in a silky cream sauce topped with puff pastry; shrimp in a garlicky butter-wine sauce with sun-dried tomatoes, spinach, olives, and pine nuts over linguini; and a unique rockfish encased in kosher salt for cooking, then released from its "cage" and sauced with a divine crab cream sauce. Watermen's is a good choice for folks seeking a taste of fine dining in a pleasantly casual setting where the two dedicated owners are on-site to see that their guests are well-fed.

Talbot County

Bartlett Pear Inn, 28 Harrison St., Easton, MD 21601; (410) 770-3300; bartlettpearinn.com; @BPearInn. Childhood sweethearts Alice and Jordan Lloyd are the proprietors of the highly regarded Bartlett Pear Inn on the prettiest street in Easton. While the inn's guest rooms are beautifully decorated and the amenities top-drawer, the inn's kitchen is the heart and soul of the operation. Here, Chef Jordan, who has worked under noted chefs Thomas Keller and Michel Richard in California and Manhattan, is inspired by his Eastern Shore roots as well as the sophisticated menus embraced by his mentors. His menu changes with the seasons but always includes several seafood dishes. Jordan has a fondness for rockfish and other breeds of bass, coming up with innovative ways to prepare them. (The recipe for Crispy Skin Bass that he shared for this book is one that he demonstrated when I attended one of his popular cooking classes.) While many of his sources are local, he is also supplied by seafood companies offering a broader range of products that keep his menu varied throughout the year. Bartlett Pear's dining room is small and simply appointed, with long windows suggesting the historic nature of the handsome building. A cozy bar next door is a delightful place where a trained mixologist creates unique libations and small plates from Chef Jordan's kitchen provide samples of his skills. Sometimes there's live music—and always the food and drink will make you sing. PS: Most everything at the restaurant is housemade, including the extraordinary ice cream that Lloyd supplies to the distributors of Maryland's famous Smith Island cakes. Wine is very much a part of the scene at the Bartlett Pear Inn, with pairings suggested on the menu and recommendations offered by a savvy staff. The Lloyds reach out to the community with an ongoing series of food and wine events as well as cooking classes. If you are looking to celebrate, call for reservations.

COLORFUL CHARACTERS
Waterman Al Poore Continues
Family Traditions

Waterman Al Poore, 58, sees the dawn breaking most mornings from the deck of his 38-foot work boat, moored in Broad Creek near his home in the small town of Bozman near St. Michaels on Maryland's Eastern Shore. He needs no clock to awaken him at 3:30 a.m.—his internal alarm does the job. "Most people see the sun go down at day's end, but watching the sun rise is a beautiful reminder that a waterman's day has just begun," says the 6-footer with a booming voice and a physique muscled from hard labor.

"An hour before sun-up through mid-morning is the best time for crabbing," says Poore. He uses a 5,000-foot trotline, tying on bags of bait every 6 to 8 feet. Bait could be razor clams or bull lips, which he buys in 40-pound bags. Most days he is alone on the boat, getting as many as 10 bushels or as few as 3 bushels a day that he sells to special customers and a few lucky restaurants.

Recreational crabbing, once limited to kids using string and chicken necks, has increased over the years as more waterfront homes with docks have sprung up along the shores of the Chesapeake. "Back in the 1970s, the only crabbers were watermen," says Poore. He has seen the price of crabs quadruple, rising to $100 a bushel in recent years. His family's crabs have always been prized for their size and quality. He attributes this to experience in where to find and catch the biggest and best. "It takes knowledge of the time of day, the time of year, and the tides," he says.

Poore harvests oysters with hand tongs, as opposed to the high-tech hydraulic dredging used by commercial boats. Times have changed dramatically for Eastern Shore watermen over the years, with seafood harvesting permitted 12 miles offshore according to a law passed in the late 80s. "It's hard on all of us," says Poore.

Poore's working calendar is separated by seasons, dictated by what's running in the bay or flying in the fields. From early spring until late fall, he is out on the water looking for crabs and oysters. During hunting season, he is in demand as a professional guide for duck hunters. His is a demanding job, one that follows the patterns of his dad, "Big Al," and his forebears going back three generations.

He remembers getting his first boat at the age of 10 and learning to crab with his two younger brothers under the guidance of "Big Al," now retired after 40 years as a waterman and owner of a legendary seafood market across the street from the upscale Inn at Perry Cabin in St. Michaels. Young Al stayed with him as a helper, choosing a life on the water while his two brothers went off to college and moved on to other careers.

"My summer work uniform consists of shorts, a T-shirt, and sandals," he says with a grin. "It takes me about 40 seconds to get dressed." In cold weather, he layers on warm clothes and at all seasons has the standard green rain gear at the ready. "Being a waterman may be tough—but, best of all, the only one I have to answer to is Mother Nature."

Bistro St. Michaels, 403 S. Talbot St., St. Michaels, MD 21663; (410) 749-9111; bistrostmichaels.com. Fans of this charming little restaurant in the heart of St. Michaels are happy to have it back in business after a hiatus of several years. Gone are the French father-son team who made it so popular, but young Rob Pascal and his wife, Caroline, are doing a fine job as the newest proprietors. They were smart to hire David Hayes, a gifted chef whose culinary career began as an intern at the posh Inn at Perry Cabin and escalated as he cooked in the kitchens of other first-rate Eastern Shore restaurants. Hayes has a sure hand with seafood, putting his own spin on local favorites and depending on respected suppliers for quality and freshness. He takes deliveries three times a week for his catch of the day (halibut is a favorite item) as well as for the scallops, crabs, shrimp, mussels, grilled octopus, and Maine lobster that have a seasonal space on the bistro's menu. The chef's artistry is evident in appetizers of a smoked salmon and asparagus terrine, steamed mussels swimming with andouille sausage in a wonderful white wine bath, and a savory bruschetta featuring lobster, fennel, house-made tomato jam, and avocado. Entrees have their own appeal—whether a simple seafood platter starring oysters, shrimp, miniature crab cakes, and fried oysters; a savory seafood risotto cooked in a lemongrass-saffron broth and studded with crab, scallops and mussels; or grilled scallops surrounded with vegetables of the season (maybe grape tomatoes or corn kernels) and sprinkled with crisp pork belly. It's hard to resist the special appeal of the Bistro—whether at dinner or at its popular weekend brunch, where a favorite wake-up call comes as a crab cake Benedict topped with the chef's tomato béarnaise sauce. Yum. PS: Many menu items are gluten free and identified as such with a symbol.

Brasserie Brightwell, 206 Washington St., Easton, MD 21601; (410) 819-3838; brasseriebrightwell.com; @BB_EastonMD. A well-stocked raw bar is one of the attractions at Brasserie Brightwell, an authentic-looking brasserie created in a former gas station in the upscale city of Easton. A wood-fire oven is another. The bistro's tagline is *"Se pedre n'est qu'une autre facon de dire aller explorer."* Translation: Getting lost is just another way to say going exploring. The decor and casual ambience makes you wonder if you took a wrong turn and landed on the Left Bank instead of the Eastern Shore. Ceilings studded with paddle fans soar above a stunning antique bar restored to its original glory and is a fine place to feast on grilled oysters and clams or the day's selection of briny and sweet oysters from Chincoteague, Hoopers Island, the Barren Islands, or Prince

Edward Island. Check out the accessories (a huge clock like those found in French train stations) and the many varieties of imported beer that go well with the raw bar items. The short menu for lunch and dinner features seasonal seafood choices, among them trout and snapper prepared by Chef Brendan in the wood-fire oven. Or go for mussels (classic style, tomato saffron, or red curry) or a creative variation on Maine lobster salad that involves fennel, tarragon, mango, and a Dijon vinaigrette instead of mayo. Brasserie Brightwell is one-of-a-kind and draws patrons from many parts of the Eastern Shore who factor in lunch or dinner as part of their visit to the Talbot mini-mall. Check out the farm-raised produce, homemade baked goods, and gourmet specialties at the Easton Square Market next door— where the stall owners are eager to talk about their wares.

Chesapeake Landing Seafood Restaurant, 23713 St. Michaels Rd., St. Michaels, MD; (410) 745-9600; chesapeakelandingrestaurant .com. Say "Spurry" to local residents, and they associate the family name with seafood. Joe Spurry spent many years as a waterman before opening his own packing plant and (in 1991) the Chesapeake Landing Restaurant, a few miles outside of St. Michaels. Shipments of his Miles River Brand crabs and oysters are still in demand by "big city" restaurateurs, but the family saves some for customers who buy from their well-stocked seafood market or dine in their large dining rooms. One of the few local restaurants open year-round, it draws guests at area overnight establishments as well as the locals. Chesapeake Landing's Friday Night Buffet is famous for its freshness and variety of local oysters (in season). Because Spurry trucks make deliveries along the East Coast, you will find Maine lobsters and mussels

PHOTO COURTESY OF CHESAPEAKE LANDING SEAFOOD RESTAURANT

INSIDER TIPS
Beating the Midwinter Blues
at an Easton B&B

This article originally appeared in Maryland Life. *It is reprinted here with permission from its author, Holly Smith.*

They say elegance and coziness don't go hand-in-hand. But what do they know?

Here at the Bartlett Pear Inn in Easton, I feel positively genteel sitting at the graceful vanity in the dressing area of the airy, powder-blue Concorde Pear suite.

And my husband, Ben, plopped down on the stylish wrought-iron bed and catching a *Daily Show* rerun on the flat-screen? He looks downright comfy.

We've never thought of ourselves as B&B people, but the historic Talbot County inn is making a persuasive case.

"We are going for quality instead of a particular 'feel,'" says enthusiastic proprietor Alice Lloyd, who renovated the 220-year-old structure with husband Jordan.

"We want people to leave the Bartlett Pear with satisfied, happy hearts and souls!"

Having themselves left the Eastern Shore several years ago, innkeeper Alice and chef Jordan found the Bartlett Pear the ideal project to lure them and their two young kids back to their hometown.

"The ability to be involved in our small community is both personally and professionally rewarding," says Alice. And as a bonus, "Now we can make a living in a town where we are comfortable and happy!"

Which is how Ben and I are feeling right about now: comfortable and happy. Tucked into the Bartlett Pear's snug bar area as we wait for our dinner reservation, we sip a not-too-pretentious vintage and look out the window onto South Harrison Street.

It may be a bracing late-winter night out there, but it's toasty and intimate in here. So intimate, in fact, that it takes me a minute to realize my knee keeps bumping up against the guy sitting next to us.

Did I mention the bar is snug?

Finishing our drinks, we cross the foyer to the Bartlett Pear's restaurant, a chic but friendly space where the affable Jordan—a veteran of name-brand establishments along the East Coast, including Citronelle in DC and New York's Per Se—works his magic.

Our nestled-in-an-alcove table overlooks the inn's garden. I notice an artsy pear statue perched out there, but Ben's oblivious to it. Thanks to the arrival of his hangar steak with caramelized shallots and béarnaise sauce, he's oblivious to me, too.

Good food can do that, and Jordan's is some of the best.

Using locally sourced organic ingredients wherever possible, the chef describes his ever-evolving menu as "upscale American." In other words, the offerings may be highfalutin and stunningly plated, but they're also recognizable and soothing.

Not that my roasted-vegetable ratatouille in any way resembles what's often considered a pedestrian dish. Instead, Jordan has managed to elevate a handful of simple veggies into something sublime. (Tomorrow at breakfast, he'll perform similar culinary voodoo on the scrambled eggs.)

Sated and sleepy, Ben and I head up the wide wooden staircase to our second-floor room. Other guests and diners will laugh, eat, and amble to bed or back to their homes over the next couple hours. The clatter—easy to hear as we drift off under a thick duvet—sounds fun and collegial, not intrusive.

And that's when it occurs to me: Maybe this is the attraction of B&Bs. Unlike hotels, they offer the camaraderie and good cheer of connecting with fellow guests while also providing a private cocoon where you can blissfully escape the hubbub.

It's not about the claw-foot tubs, careworn floors, and ubiquitous hearths (although they're nice, too). It's about the big-time thrill of a night away writ small and sweet.

And just like that, the Bartlett Pear Inn turns us into B&B people.

The Bartlett Pear Inn is located at 28 S. Harrison St. in Easton, MD. For more information, visit bartlettpearinn.com.

on the menu as well as Maryland rockfish and some of the freshest native crabmeat available. One of my favorite entrees is their Seafood Norfolk, baked ham crowned with lumps of crab and buttery shrimp. And, oh yes, about that fried chicken . . .

Hunter's Tavern at the Tidewater Inn, 101 E. Dover St., Easton, MD 21601; (410) 822-1300; tidewaterinn.com; @TheTidewater Inn. Tucked into a wing of the historic Tidewater Inn, Hunter's Tavern is open daily for breakfast, lunch, dinner, and lovely weekend brunches. New owners have updated the decor, once reminiscent of a gentleman's club, to give the premises a fresh look. With seasoned Chef Paul Shiley in charge of the kitchen, the menus reflect a refreshing take on what appeals to modern tastes—i.e., more varied appetizers, lighter entrees, a focus on Maryland cuisine (Shiley's Eastern Shore-born), and a sprinkling of vegetarian options. These days, in season, you may find snap turtle soup (that old Maryland favorite that is a rarity today because of the scarcity of the main ingredient) side by side with a sherry-touched and very rich Maryland crab bisque, Chesapeake gumbo featuring local seafoods, crab pizzas, rock and chips (as in rockfish), lobster tail tempura, blackened grouper, a smoked tuna melt or blackened grouper sandwich, and a lobster roll that could pass muster with native New Englanders. Access to the restaurant is through a delightful sidewalk terrace, but I suggest entering through the Tidewater Inn's heavy double doors, leading into the beautiful lobby. It is all very grand and reflects past traditions of Southern-style elegance and hospitality.

Latitude 38 Bistro & Spirits, 26342 Oxford Rd., Oxford, MD 21654; (410) 226-5303; latitude38.org. Wendy Palmer, proprietor of Latitude 38 on the edge of Oxford, goes the extra mile when it comes to hospitality. If you are docked at a local marina or staying at the Robert Morris Inn or a local bed-and-breakfast, she is likely to be the driver picking you up so you can enjoy a meal at her delightful restaurant. When you get there, don't be alarmed at the sight of the exterior (a former gas station) and do be delighted when you go inside to discover two white tablecloth dining rooms (one with a fireplace) and a busy bar area where locals like to gather. "It's true—we are the Oxford version of *Cheers*," says Wendy, who opened Latitude 38 in the early 90s after a successful run as the owner of The Masthead on a quiet Oxford side street. It was a local favorite for its food and friendly service, and so is her current operation. The menu is seasonal, changes every 2 weeks, and gives equal billing to seafood and beef (its prime rib is legendary among local meat mavens). A nice touch is the availability of entrees in either petite or regular portions. Seafood lovers will appreciate appetizers such as the house-cured gravlax, dilled and properly presented with chopped egg, chopped onion, and capers; hefty yet tender prawns, grilled and sided with fresh fruit; and mussels steamed in white wine and served in a buttery sauce studded with slices of andouille sausage and topped with crisp frites. A popular Sunday brunch (11 a.m. to 2 p.m.) item is the chef's Chesapeake omelet featuring oysters and lumps of sweet crabmeat. Everything is cooked to order at this fresh-conscious bistro, where one evening rainbow trout was a treat, flecked with tomato relish

PHOTO COURTESY OF LATITUDE 38

and bedded on wild rice sweetened with cranberries and pearl onions tossed with green beans. And if it's the tomato season, discover how good the fried green variety can be by trying them in mini sandwiches layered with mozzarella cheese and basil leaves. If you are staying in the area or arriving by boat, give Wendy a call.

Mason's Restaurant, 22 E. Harrison St., Easton, MD 21601; (410) 822-2304; masonsgourmet.com. The sheer longevity of this family-run restaurant, located in an historic house in an historic town, speaks volumes. Mason's has a legion of loyal locals who appreciate the tasteful decor (including some entertaining poster art) and the skillful service by staffers

INSIDER TIPS
Maryland Strawberries:
A Season Sweet & Fleeting

Local strawberries are a seasonal favorite—one of the gifts of late spring and early summer. Fragile white blossoms precede the fruit, named because long ago its berries were brought from the fields impaled on straw in order to prevent bruising the harvesting procedure. Even today, strawberries are laboriously hand-picked and sold at roadside stands along country roads or sold to specialty food stores during their short season, which peaks in July.

Maryland's Eastern Shore strawberries are in a class by themselves, with a heady perfume and intensity of flavor that sets them apart from other members of the genus *Fragaria*. More petite than its outsized California cousins found in the supermarket year-round, the Maryland fruit is also juicier and richer in color when ripe.

Cream, either poured or whipped, is this crimson beauty's perfect partner when served simply sliced or perhaps by itself with a light dusting of powdered sugar. In Colonial times, a staple on the tables of the gentry would include a special silver shaker with holes at the top big enough to release the sugar inside.

who are apt to remember your name after a second visit. A fireplace in winter makes the "red room" cozy, banquettes opposite the bar in Mason's popular candy shop are perfect for a relatively quiet lunch or dinner, and a brick-paved courtyard is a delightful seasonal option. Owner Matt Mason likes to patronize local sources for produce and seafood, changing his restaurant's menus to match what's available. I believe his mother was one of the first to introduce the now-famous crab dip—and it's still a popular item. At lunchtime, a seafood quiche is consistently good, the filling generous and the piecrust crisp. Fresh tuna is used in the colorful tuna nicoise salad, and Canadian mussels steamed with wine, garlic, and tomatoes are seasonally available. Catch of the day could be pan-seared fresh rockfish with cheddar grits and grilled asparagus or (lucky you) jumbo scallops paired with creamy lobster risotto and arugula salad kissed with truffle oil. Mason's has built a reputation as a reliable Easton institution—so see for yourself the reasons why—among them the iced tea and the attractive waitstaff.

The Masthead at Pier Street Marina, 140 W. Pier St., Oxford, MD 21654; (410) 226-5171; themastheadatpierstreetmarina.com. Kick back, relax, and enjoy the boats and birds bobbing on the scenic Tred Avon River. That view—and the spectacular sunsets—are big draws for The Masthead, a seasonal restaurant run by Wendy Palmer. Palmer and partners oversaw a major renovation of the property after it was severely damaged by Hurricane Sandy. The new Masthead at Pier Street Marina is cheerful and casual, with beachy colors, a spacious outdoor deck seating 250, an 85-seat dining room and a lively tiki bar. It is a fun place for a traditional Eastern Shore crab feast and trendy beverages. Be aware that the size and availability of Maryland crabs can be iffy and that soft shells appear during a short window in late spring or early summer. Palmer acknowledges this "fact of life" and instructs her staff to share any such information with diners. So ask before you order. But there are other seaworthy options at The Masthead, if you can take your eyes off the view long enough to concentrate on the menu. Check out a delicious lobster grilled cheese (made with mozzarella), blackened tuna tacos sweetened with a grilled pineapple relish, steamed clams served New England style with drawn lemon butter, crispy calamari served with a sweet Thai chili sauce, and a rockfish sandwich. Note: Hurricane Sandy destroyed the piers on the river, but there is docking for 60 at an adjacent marina. Call The Masthead for information on availability. Fancier fare includes The Masthead's top-notch crab cake, crowned with crab imperial and served two to a plate. Mahimahi gets the Rockefeller treatment, garnished with steamed spinach, bacon, and parmesan, and the crab bisque is noteworthy.

Out of the Fire, 22 Goldsborough St., Easton, MD 21601; (410) 770-4777; outofthefire.com. Amy Haines left her high-profile job with a West Coast biotechnology company to follow her food dreams and open a "green" restaurant on the East Coast. She chose Easton, opened a small restaurant and eat-at bar, and quickly gained respect and popularity for her health-appropriate and innovative menu. A huge wood-fire oven makes her pizzas outstanding and gives flavor to the roasted vegetables, fish, and meats. Amy buys and serves sustainable seafood only, depending on two highly rated suppliers for the best that money can buy. Her reference point is the Monterey Bay Seafood Watch, an outfit that provides information on sustainability. Spring is the time for char, a finfish that tastes like a cousin

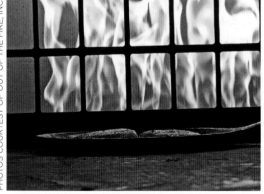

to salmon, roasted on a wooden plank on a bed of herbs with a potpourri of fresh vegetables and garlic. The same technique adds flavor to seasonal produce. Her main supplier of herbs and vegetables is Cottingham Farm, where Owner Cleo Braver (a former attorney) is a pioneer in organic farming at her sprawling gardens and greenhouse on the outskirts of Easton. Come casual and be prepared for fresh tastes in a friendly place, with Amy on-site to see that her high standards are met for the benefit of her patrons—and the environment.

Scossa Restaurant, 8 N. Washington St., Easton, MD 21601; (410) 822-2202; scossarestaurant.com. *Scossa* means "surprise" in Italian—a fitting name for this elegant Northern Italian restaurant in the heart of Easton. Under the skilled oversight of Chef-Owner Giancarlo Tondon, the kitchen turns out some spectacular plates. An example is the signature appetizer named Scossa Tagliere, an artistic mélange of scallops and mushrooms sautéed in butter, fresh asparagus spears, two kinds of ham (Parma and prosciutto), and a discreet shower of Stracchino cheese. Chef Tondon, a native of the Italian city of Trento, began his career at the legendary Harry's Bar just off St. Mark's Square in Venice. Harry's famous Bellinis are (of course) featured at the bar, where customers may pair the restaurant's extensive wine options with small plates that could feature a soothing lobster risotto, smoked salmon with capers, and crispy calamari escorted with a side of spicy arrabbiata sauce. Among the more spectacular seafood entrees in the dining room are Branzini Venziana and wild salmon in a pinot noir sauce. Chef Tondon is a master at sauce-making, using them to enhance but not overwhelm his creations. Scossa is special, made so by the oversight of Chef Tondon, his wife, Talley, and her sister Gini. It is an elegant place inside (with decor by local designer Jami Marida) and out, where one may dine in good weather at wrought-iron tables shielded from the street by attractive white pillars. You can't miss it.

PHOTO COURTESY OF SCOSSA RESTAURANT

COLORFUL CHARACTERS
James Michener: Bard of the Chesapeake

Taking the reader on a journey spanning 3 centuries, James Michener's iconic novel, *Chesapeake*, published in 1978, remains fresh and fascinating to readers interested in the history of this unique region of the US. Michener traces the lives of four families who represent the culture of the Eastern Shore of Maryland and lived in an area spanning the historic towns of Easton, Oxford, and St. Michaels.

Visitors may learn more about the author and the settings for his novel by following this itinerary:

Easton: The Talbot County Free Library at 100 W. Dover St. (several blocks away from the Tidewater Inn) stores Michener's original manuscript in its Maryland Room, where the author carried on much of its research. The library is open Mon 9 a.m. to 9 p.m., Tues and Wed until 6 p.m., Thurs and Fri until 5 p.m., and Sat 9 a.m. to 1 p.m. Summer hours are extended to 9 p.m. on Thurs and 5 p.m. on Sat. This is a beautiful library in an historic building and is a wonderful place for book lovers to browse. The Third Haven Meeting House, 405 S. Washington St., is mentioned in the book as the place the Quaker family Patmore worshipped. It is the oldest religious building in continuous use in the US.

Oxford: It was in the Tavern at the historic Robert Morris Inn that Michener wrote the original outline for *Chesapeake*. He frequently dined there and on more than one occasion proclaimed that the crab cakes at the Inn were "the best on the Eastern Shore." Today, the Inn's kitchen is in the capable hands of Master Chef Mark Salter—so a meal here will give you the chance to judge for yourself if Michener was on target.

After lunch, stroll over to the famous Cutts and Case Shipyard to see Byeberry, the oldest house in Oxford. Together with other historic houses in Oxford, it dates back to 1668. On workdays at the busy boatyard, you can watch craftsmen building elegant wooden yachts, using traditional materials on vessels equipped with state-of-the-art engineering and design.

To continue your Michener tour, hop the Oxford Bellevue Ferry (your car can come too) for a scenic cruise across the Tred Avon River on the oldest continuously running ferry in the country. Head to **St. Michaels,** another town that figures prominently in Michener's novel. Many of the homes are historic, among them the handsome brick house at 200 Green St. known as the Cannonball House, the only structure that was hit when the British bombarded St. Michaels in the War of 1812. Their fire was deflected when clever local residents hung lanterns in the trees, making the British aim high above the town's buildings—thus missing their targets.

St. Michaels is home to the Chesapeake Bay Maritime Museum, an important stop on your route. There are always wooden boats under loving construction in the Boat Building Shed, and old log canoes and other vessels associated with life on the bay are on display. *Rosie Parks* is the name of an authentic skipjack permanently docked at the waterfront Chesapeake Bay Maritime Museum.

From St. Michaels, drive on to Tilghman Island, a community once largely inhabited by watermen and the original home of the skipjacks. Black Walnut Point, at the end of town, has free parking to access the Naval Radar Station and the adjacent wildlife refuge maintained by the Maryland Department of Natural Resources. Open daily from 8 a.m. to 5 p.m., it offers a view across the Choptank River that includes the place where the fictional Devon Island was located in Michener's *Chesapeake*.

Leaving St. Michaels, keep an eye out for Railroad Avenue, where Michener lived at the end of the street while working on his renowned book.

St. Michaels Crab & Steak House, 305 Mulberry St., St. Michaels, MD 21663; (410) 745-3737; stmichaelscrabhouse.com. Eric Rosen is the chef-owner-manager of this likable landmark at the St. Michaels marina. Rosen is a genial and accommodating host, pledging customer satisfaction with a mantra on the menu that says "The meal I promise and serve is my reputation. If you enjoyed it, tell others; if not, tell me." He's been keeping his promises since 1992, when he opened this restaurant just after graduating from restaurant school in Philadelphia. Rosen may have learned the finer points of culinary art while a student, but he prefers to serve what the locals and tourists want: fresh seafood in a salty waterfront setting. On fair days, his two outdoor docks are the scene for crab feasts and beer, as well as oysters, clams, calamari, shrimp, fish, and a Crab House Bloody Mary, served in a glass rimmed with Old Bay. Steamed Maryland crabs are market-priced and sold by the dozen or half dozen, as are steamed or raw oysters and cherrystone clams. In addition to these bottom-line favorites, the restaurant offers an appealing selection of seafood entrees featuring crab cakes, soft-shell crabs, and oysters topped with crab imperial; broiled scallops, salmon, rockfish, and catfish; grilled or blackened tuna steaks; shrimp scampi over linguini; and fried clams, oysters,

and flounder. While the location itself is a winner, it is the well-prepared food and the friendly vibe that makes this place special. The building dates back to the 1830s when it was an oyster shucking shed. Rosen is proud of the diversity of his clientele—"from town folk to entertainers and artists"—and says he and his staff stand ready to oblige customers' special dinner requests—as long as they have the ingredients. Note: The restaurant is open daily, except Wed, and closes from the second Sat in Dec until Apr 1.

208 Talbot, 208 Talbot St., St. Michaels, MD 21663; (410) 745-3838; 208talbot.com; @208TalbotMD. Seafood lovers as well as carnivores will find much to like at 208 Talbot in the delightful town of St. Michaels. Curt Cummings and Executive Chef David Clark are co-proprietors of a restaurant that deserves its sterling reputation. It has a split personality, with a casual tavern as you enter (hang your jackets on a hook and stay awhile) and several small, well-appointed dining rooms that are quieter and more formal. Chef Clark has a penchant for seafood, evident in his creamy version of a New England-style chowder studded with tender clams and smoky bacon bits; fat day-boat sea scallops, seared and served on a cloud of pureed cauliflower rimmed with a ribbon of balsamic; and local oysters tricked out with jalapeño-cilantro lime butter. He treats fresh tuna to a quick sear, thinly slices the rare fish fan-style, and serves it on a bed of crab-fried rice. His version of a crab cake has an Asian twist, while his oyster potpie is Maryland-style comfort food. Another oyster preparation is more sophisticated, adding prosciutto ham and toasted pistachio nuts to the dish and bathing the bivalves in a champagne cream sauce. Mussels are steamed with a saffron shellfish fume, to which the chef adds morsels of house-made sausage, tomatoes, shallots, and lots of garlic. While Chef Clark works his magic in the kitchen, Cummings stays busy keeping patrons happy and the service flowing. It's a winning combination.

Two If By Sea Restaurant, 5776 Tilghman Island Rd., Tilghman, MD 21671; (410) 886-2447; twoifbysearestaurant.com. The website for the quirky Two If By Sea shows a collection of antique cars parked out front of this endearing restaurant on the side of a road just outside the town of St. Michaels. It was enough to bring us to this rural destination on Tilghman Island, where we had the pleasure of meeting Chef-Owner Henry Miller and his partner, Scott Spittler. The photo, they explained, was a bit of serendipity, taken by one of their first patrons on the day they opened in 2008. Truth is, the cafe itself is the definition of serendipity—from its

INSIDER TIPS
Cooking with the Pros

While you won't earn credits, you'll learn some tricks of the trade from this lineup of Eastern Shore chefs who offer cooking classes at their respective restaurants.

The Robert Morris Inn: Central casting would pick Master Chef Mark Salter for a starring role in any TV food show. Salter, a photo-worthy guy who was for many years the executive chef at the upscale Inn at Perry Cabin in St. Michaels, expanded his horizons by becoming a part-owner and full-time chef at the charming and historic Robert Morris Inn in nearby Oxford.

One of his "side jobs" is as a teacher at Salter's popular cooking demonstrations, which begin at 10 a.m. and culminate with a festive luncheon and glass of wine. His menus follow the seasons of the Eastern Shore and are built around three themes: Signature Dishes, Specials, and Seafood Recipes. Thirteen sessions are held throughout the year.

In the spring, for instance, his demos could include spring pea and mint soup with crab; grilled lamb with cauliflower puree, asparagus, new potatoes, and raspberry bread pudding; local oyster on the half shell, oyster chowder, oyster potpie, and oysters Rockefeller; jumbo lump crab and mushroom gratin; and Pavlova with mixed berries and Chantilly cream.

The Robert Morris Inn is located at 314 N. Morris St., Oxford, MD 21654; robertmorrisinn.com. Classes are held every 2 weeks, and reservations should be made in advance by calling (410) 226-5111 or emailing enquiries@robertmorrisinn.com.

The Bartlett Pear Inn: Chef-Owner Jordan Lloyd keeps the mood light at his cooking demos in the small dining room of the Bartlett Pear Inn in Easton. Using a small table equipped with a cook stove and the tools of his trade, Lloyd moves quickly at the cooking station and peppers his "how-to" directions with interesting and amusing anecdotes about the recipes and information about his local suppliers.

I was amazed at his ability to both instruct and entertain at a recent class that started with a sample of "Caipirinha Twister," a play on Brazil's national drink created by the inn's personable mixologist. After this mood-setter, Chef Lloyd began his demo with a Turtle Boy Farms salad with Champagne vinaigrette, crispy-skin rockfish enlivened with a classic sauce Vierge, Maryland Farms chicken ballotine (including techniques on stock and sauce work using the whole chicken), and a sweet finale lesson in how to make the classic apple tart with crème Anglaise.

Lloyd and his wife, Alice, dream up a stream of special events that include wine dinners as well as the cooking lessons that are well-attended by regional residents as well as guests at the inn who often plan their stays to coincide with Chef Lloyd's professional performance as a modest but exceptional chef and teacher. But most of all, his sessions are a lot of fun.

The Bartlett Pear Inn is located at 28 Harrison St., Easton, MD 21601; (410) 770-3300; bartlettpearinn.com. For more information, email info@bartlettpearinn.com or call.

Two If By Sea Restaurant: Chef Henry Miller of the 1950s-style Two If By Sea Restaurant on Tilghman Island is a graduate of the Culinary Institute of America in Hyde Park. He is a talented baker who makes his own varieties of the famous Smith Island cakes and is happy to share his considerable knowledge and love of food at his popular Sunday afternoon cooking classes.

His schedule for 2014 reflects his versatility and his fascination with global cuisines as well as his ability to make cooking fun for all. All classes are held at 4 p.m.

Two If By Sea is located at 5776 Tilghman Island Rd., Tilghman, MD 21671; (410) 866-2447; twoifbysea restaurant.com. Call to register for a Sunday class.

decor to its menu, which changes seasonally and at the whim of the chef. Miller, a graduate of the Culinary Institute of America in Hyde Park, is one of the most passionate and creative cooks around. Baking is his first love, proven by the pies, cakes, and pastries on display in the front of what was once a general store. Cooking up breakfast, lunch, and dinner is an art he performs at a stove at the rear of a long narrow room where the cast of *Mad Men* would feel right at home. It is decorated with retro souvenirs that include stools covered in green leather in front of a dining bar and shelves of memorabilia featuring an amazing collection of cookie jars. Two If By Sea started as a breakfast and lunch destination, and has morphed into the "Best Kept Secret in Talbot County" (*What's Up* magazine) with the addition of weekend dinners and a new beer and wine license. Seafood specialties of the house include Chef Miller's original rockfish soup, scallops with snap peas and pancetta, rockfish with a rich crab-infused butter sauce, softshell crabs piccata, an eggplant and crab napoleon that tastes as good as it looks, and a crisped fish and chips special featuring in-season rockfish. The restaurant's hearty breakfasts are legendary and its luncheons likewise. Vegetables and herbs come from a garden out back, and most everything is made "from scratch." Two If By Sea is one-of-a-kind, just waiting for you to walk in the door and find yourself in a nostalgic time warp. Note: Breakfast (voted "Best on the Eastern Shore" by *What's Up Eastern Shore* magazine) is served daily, lunch daily except Mon, bistro fare Thurs through Sun, and dinner in the 35-seat back room Fri and Sat.

Wicomico County

The Red Roost, 2670 Clara Rd., Whitehaven, MD 21856; (410) 546-5443; theredroost.com; @theredroost. Back in the late 1940s, Eastern Shore native Frank Valentine built a chicken house of cinder block and oak, where Frank Perdue used to get stuck delivering poultry feed. High

tides drowned all the chickens in the 1960s, but in 1971 a subsequent owner converted the chicken house into a general store catering to patrons of his campgrounds. Locals flocked in to sample his local crabs and corn, and in 1974 The Red Roost restaurant opened its doors to the public. Today, there are four dining rooms seating 400. Tourists on buses from Philadelphia, New Jersey, and New York make stops at the rustic crab house to feast on the Red Roost's legendary "All You Can Eat" special featuring mounds of steamed blue crabs, homemade hush puppies, and fried chicken, clams, and shrimp. "Folks usually spend 2 hours

at our tables, picking crabs and socializing," says manager Katie Deckenbeck. Brothers Tom and John Knorr, owners since 1996, are "keeping the old traditions alive," much to the delight of the multigenerational local followers. Though Red Roost is not on the waterfront, an access road leads to its docks on the Pocomoke River, where customers can tie up and take advantage of the restaurant's complimentary pickup service. Note: Red Roost is open Mar 17 through Oct 31.

Restaurant 213, 213 N. Fruitland Blvd., Fruitland, MD 21826; (410) 677-4880; restaurant213.com. Chef-Owner Jim Hughes of Restaurant 213 is a culinary genius who wows patrons with a menu that infuses Chesapeake-inspired dishes with French twists that speak of his early years as a protégé of famed Chef Roger Verge at Le Moulin de Mougins in the hills near Cannes. He has earned fame for superior cuisine since launching his restaurant in 2003, making a coveted guest chef appearance

at the Beard House in Manhattan and receiving the highest rating from *Frommer's Guide*. His version of the ubiquitous crab dip features a silken béchamel sauce, and his preparations of day-boat scallops, black sea bass, oysters, and lobster (from Ocean City) reflect his extraordinary talents. Seasonal fresh produce and herbs come from his 10-foot by 60-foot garden on the premises. Hughes enjoys meeting patrons of his unique restaurant, a charming oasis where food lovers are welcome and the service embodies Eastern Shore hospitality. 213's extensive wine list numbers 50 pages, handsomely illustrated with colorful wine labels and featuring wines from many first-rate vineyards. The *Wine Spectator* recognizes the wine list and the restaurant as among "the best in the nation." Though this little gem is off the beaten track, the detour from Route 50 is well worth it. PS: Remember to preorder the soufflé of the day and ask about the "Breakfast Dessert."

Worcester County

Drummers' Cafe, Atlantic Hotel, 2 N. Main St., Berlin, MD 21811; (410) 641-3589; atlantichotel.com. Tucked demurely into a corner of the historic Hotel Atlantic in the quaint town of Berlin near Ocean City, the Drummers' Cafe is a little jewel. Open at 11 a.m., the cafe seats 80 inside and 30 in a screened porch perfect for people watching—as well as for wonderful lunches prepared by Chef Leo and his staff. I love the variety of appetizers and the option of making a meal by ordering a couple of them, perhaps mixing seafood with meat by ordering jumbo sea scallops seared in brown butter and served on tomato slices on a bed of shoepeg corn and fordhook lima beans lightly bathed in coconut milk followed by twin kabobs of fork-tender filet mignon partnered with a mini salad of baby arugula and picked red onion and grilled bread. Grilled wild-caught salmon paired with field greens in balsamic vinaigrette is another good choice, as are pan-roasted Prince Edward Island mussels sharing the bowl

with homemade sausage and a zesty white wine and herb butter sauce. For Asian flavors, the kitchen crusts ahi tuna with sesame seeds and coriander, sears it quickly, and serves it with a seaweed salad, crispy wontons, wasabi, pickled ginger, and ponzu. And the cafe's popular fish tacos get a Cuban twist, grilled and served in a soft tortilla with Havarti cheese, cabbage, and cilantro-avocado sauce. Starting at 5 p.m., while still preparing appetizers, the kitchen proves its versatility with celestial lobster bisque and entrees that include rockfish, salmon, and oysters as well as a memorable rack of lamb. The atmosphere is elegant, complete with a single sparkling chandelier and Victorian loveseats flanking the fireplace, while the mood is casual and the service smooth. Mark it on your map and enjoy exploring the sweet town of Berlin, where time seems to stand still.

Fager's Island, 60th on the Bay, Ocean City, MD 21842; (410) 524-5500; fagers.com. If there is a single restaurant in Ocean City that defines excellence and consistency, it's Fager's Island on Assawoman Bay hard by the 60th Street Bridge. And if there is a single reason for this success, it

is legendary Owner John Fager. Fager is a hardworking hands-on person, often on the premises and occasionally bussing tables. He is also a world traveler, as evidenced by the numerous works of art scattered throughout the premises, which include a casual downstairs bar-restaurant, an upscale upstairs dining room, an outdoor deck, a "secret garden" with benches and tables, and a dock leading to a romance-inducing gazebo. Head Chef John Laws has been onboard since 1976, initially drawing crowds with super burgers, overstuffed sandwiches, and a raw bar. Over the years, Fager's has evolved, earning accolades for fine dining in a window-walled room reminiscent of a cruise ship's showplace, while retaining its reputation as a prime place for casual fare, live music, and an energetic vibe. Seafood—both shell and fin—stars on the menu of the upscale second-story dining room (although carnivores would vote for Fager's legendary 16-ounce prime rib). Laws sources locally when he can and uses other suppliers for the Chilean sea bass garnished with jumbo

prawns and Thai basmati rice, lobster dishes, and the occasional Dover sole. His oven-roasted tomato bisque is enhanced with Maryland lump crab, and there is a changing selection of house-smoked fish. A final note: Every night the inspiring throb of Tchaikovsky's "1812 Overture" fills the entire premises—"magically" timed to coincide exactly with the setting of the sun. Genius.

MARITIME MUST-SEES
Fager's Island: A Tribute to One
Man's Imagination

This article originally appeared in Shore Living. *It is reprinted here with permission from Mary Lou Baker.*

John Fager, creator of Ocean City's legendary Fager's Island, is supercharged, emanating an energy that could light up a room—or an island. A Baltimorean by birth, he has lived most of his life in Ocean City, where Fager's Island stands as a tribute to his imagination and determination in the face of multiple challenges. He spent summers there as a child, worked there as a teen, and returned after college to begin an amazing career as entrepreneur.

Back in the '70s it was Fager's then-revolutionary idea to build environmentally friendly condos on the bay side. "Hey, this is Ocean City—not Bay City," said the skeptics. But Fager stuck to his vision, even when a recession dried up the funds he was counting on to develop the land he had purchased for development. Ever entrepreneurial, he built a bar on stilts and expanded the concept to include music, music, music.

Opening date was June 16, 1975, a day celebrated with the cannon volleys, chimes, and brass fanfare of Tchaikovsky's "1812 Overture"—played over loudspeakers at 5 p.m. "We still do that today—but now we time it to coincide with the setting of the sun," says Fager, noting that first-timers are startled by the sounds and often emotionally moved to tears at this seemingly miraculous phenomenon.

Fager's Island was an instantaneous slam-dunk with both local residents and summer people—especially when John began serving humungous Baltimore-style deli sandwiches generously stuffed with first-rate meats he roasted himself. Back then, he was a one-man show—making his signature sandwiches, serving drinks in Mason jars, and cleaning up after his customers went home happy.

When his blossoming business called for an expansion, he recruited longtime friend and Culinary Institute of America graduate Mike Meyers to come to his simple kitchen and create a limited number of dinner entrees for his rapidly expanding clientele. Meyers, an accomplished chef who was between jobs, stayed long enough to establish Fager's as a popular dining destination for his French onion soup, prime rib, duck, scallop, and crab entrees. John's culinary contribution was barbecued shrimp wrapped in bacon—something new at the time and still one of the restaurant's signature items.

Always a hands-on kind of guy, John took on the role of waiter. "We had five or six tables back then—and if I had more than four at a time, I was buried," he says.

His previous experience in the hospitality industry was as a teenage bus boy at Phillips Crab House and (in his 20s) as the co-owner of the Purple Moose, a lively bar on Ocean City's boardwalk. He sold it in order to focus on Fager's, which had by this time become wildly popular.

What started as a waterfront watering hole quickly evolved into a multifaceted operation known for its "fun factor," as John added a kaleidoscope of live bands that attracted a dancing crowd. Adding to the operation's "wow factor" were outsize furniture from Baltimore's Antique Row, stained-glass windows, and an authentic tin ceiling. Fager's eclectic decor was in contrast to the planked wooden floors that remain today in the first-level bar area.

Gradually, a series of decks were built around the building, together with a made-for-romance gazebo at the end of a pier jutting into the bay. An upstairs dining room, its arched windows overlooking the water reminiscent of a cruise ship, was added in 1996.

With longtime Executive Chef John Laws dazzling diners with his culinary legerdemain and weekday specials featuring half-price lobsters (from both local and Maine waters) and fabulous prime rib, Fager's became, and remains, a magnet dining destination.

Fager takes pride in his wine cellar, stocked with bottles he has collected since the '80s specifically to pair with his restaurant's foods. "In the early days, our wine cellar was out of proportion to the restaurant—but over the years we created a good balance," he says with characteristic modesty. The prestigious *Wine Spectator* has consistently recognized its quality with its Best of Awards for Excellence and named it the only restaurant in the state of Maryland to exceed industry standards.

Fager's Island is one of the few restaurants with its own Private Label wines. Fager is a savvy buyer of varietals, choosing three Merlots from France, two from Italy, a French Bordeaux, and a California Pinot Noir as worthy of his label.

Listening to Fager recount the evolution of Fager's Island, it becomes clear that his operation qualifies as a bona fide engine of local economic development. Inspired by boutique hotels he patronized while traveling in Mexico and the Caribbean, he designed and built the 85-suite Coconut Mallory in 1988. The property, painted pale yellow and decorated with island-inspired furnishings, was an immediate drawing card for visitors seeking luxury lodging.

Encouraged by this success, Fager purchased the replica of the Thomas Point Lighthouse in 1988 and again expanded the scope of his magical island. He built a bridge over the canal separating the restaurant from the octagonal red-roofed structure, and totally gutted what had been a failing restaurant. With the help of Larry Peabody, a prominent designer of hotels in Haiti and the Cayman Islands, he transformed the eight-sided structure into a unique hotel with 23 octagonal-shaped suites and a reputation for superb service. The Lighthouse Club opened in 1988, within 6 months of Coconut Mallory's debut. Peabody designed the golden-hued rattan furniture for the club's spacious guest rooms (complete with marble Jacuzzis), and Fager had the four-poster beds, armoires, chaises, and couches custom made.

Fager and his longtime assistant, Angela Reynolds, teamed up to decorate the hotel's fabulous Great Room. Here folks are welcome to relax before the fireplace or watch native waterfowl swim past in the water. Arriving guests are greeted with sangria or mimosas upon check-in and throughout their stay are welcome to help themselves to homemade cookies, fancy teas, and Starbucks coffee. The Lighthouse Club is full of surprises, including gas fireplaces in each room, complimentary breakfasts delivered to the room, and wonderful nautical photographs on the walls alongside a dramatic three-story spiral stairway.

Although both hotels proved successful, the recession and financial considerations forced Fager to sell his beloved Coconut Mallory hotel in 1997. Fager took a temporary break from entrepreneurial activities to travel. His itineraries included trips to Thailand, where he embraced the compassionate concepts of Buddha (563–483 BC), the Indian philosopher. Spending time with Fager, you can detect a sense of perhaps hard-won peacefulness within him and a deep-seated kindness at his hard-wired core.

"I was brought up Lutheran, with religion pretty much confined to an hour or so on Sundays," he says. "With Buddhism, there is a constant awareness of a person's relationship to the world and to others—and a consciousness of the importance of compassion." Fager is quick to point out that while his belief in the basic tenets of Buddha is an important influence in his life, he is not a Buddhist. "But I do meditate—though not enough," he adds.

Fager's status as something of a world citizen is confirmed with a tour of the 12-room Edge Hotel he built in 2002 between the Lighthouse and the restaurant. Each of the stunning suites has a different global theme, created with furniture and artifacts that Fager collected in his world travels. There are curtained four-poster beds, antique furnishings, and whimsical accessories Fager brought back from afar, fireplaces and chaise lounges in every room, massive bath suites, in-room

The Grove, 12402 Martins Neck Rd., Bishopville, MD 21813; (410) 252-5055. The Grove Market is a totally unique and out-of-the-way restaurant and smokehouse with some amazing food. Sitting on the side of a country road in Bishopville (just over the 64th Street Bridge), the weathered building hints at the unique atmosphere inside. You're as likely to see trucks as limos parked outside this favorite foodies' destination, where the

Jacuzzis, soaring floor-to-ceiling glass windows, and individual balconies overlooking a swimming pool and the bay beyond.

"Glorious" is too mild a word for this world-class jewel, blushing sight-unseen in Ocean City.

Apart from his full-time job as the mastermind of his tiny empire, Fager is a philanthropic member of the community. He stepped in to rescue the historic Atlantic Hotel in Berlin when previous owners skipped town, thus ensuring the continuance of this valuable Victorian property. He contributed and campaigned for funds to help a local hospital fend off closure. And he donated his time and talents to the restoration of Rackcliffe Plantation House, an historic landmark in Berlin that opened to the public in June.

Fit and youthful at 60-something, Fager works out regularly and keeps in touch with friends far and wide. One of them is Charlie Smith, his now-retired managing partner for 26 years. "In the beginning we had just a handful of helpers—now we issue 200 paychecks to a staff that includes many college graduates and lots of longtime employees," says Smith. "There aren't enough words to describe John Fager—he's an absolutely splendid fellow and I admire everything about him."

Fager, an expert equestrian and avid skier, lives on a farm in Worcester County with his wife, Michelle, and their three sons, who play lacrosse, soccer, and Little League baseball with their dad cheering them on. Life for this extraordinary human being is good—the reward for many years of hard work and the belief that nothing is impossible if you follow your dreams.

menu changes like the weather and the kitchen is open only from early May until the end of Dec. There's always seafood on the menu—crabs, oysters, scallops, mussels, or what's fresh in the finfish category. Chef Dale changes the menu depending on his whim and the season, but different varieties of fish smoked on the premises are usually available (unless they get scarfed up early in the evening). In addition to local seafood, The

Grove's oven-roasted duck is a huge favorite, reports Co-owner Leslie Lunga, whose on-premise garden supplies the restaurant with herbs, some vegetables, and all the flowers. It was back in 1987 that Lunga and Dale started their food adventure as a steamed crab operation and seafood market in a former general store. Since the early '90s, The Grove has evolved into a "best-kept secret" destination with about 22 seats. Do call for reservations in advance of your arrival. The few tables sell out fast.

Harrison's Harbor Watch, 806 S. Atlantic St., Ocean City, MD 21842; (410) 289-5121; harrisonsharborwatch.com. For the quintessential Ocean City experience, Harrison's Harbor Watch at the end of the boardwalk fits the bill. Gulls swoop, surf foams on the jetty, and the Atlantic Ocean crests outside the window-walled 2-story building that has been a local landmark since opening in 1984 on this scenic Ocean City inlet. Though the Harrison family has several other establishments in the area, this is their flagship restaurant and the place to slurp its famous Oyster Shooter, belly up to its bountiful raw bar, and choose from a selection of seafood fresh from local waters. Patrons of the raw bar enjoy a sideshow of staff shucking oysters and opening clams as they fill each individual order. In addition to raw on the half shell, oysters may be had "Baltimore style" (baked with mushrooms and diced ham in a garlicky chardonnay cream sauce) and clams come steamed with drawn butter or dressed up a la casino. At the table, you'll have a hard time choosing from one of the biggest selections of seafood we encountered in our research. Fresh fish from local watermen is delivered daily to Harrison's kitchen from local watermen, as they have been doing for the past 3 decades. Depending on the season and other factors, look for rockfish, tuna, mahimahi, flounder, swordfish, and the occasional native lobster. Have them broiled, blackened, or pan-seared—plain or with complimentary sauces of mango-pineapple salsa, tomato-basil lobster cream, chimichurri (fresh herbs-garlic-olive oil), or, for an additional $11, topped with crab imperial or asparagus and crab. Entrees come with unlimited side dishes of fresh vegetables, wild rice, red potatoes, and coleslaw as well as a basket of Harrison's famous homemade rolls. Harrison's quarter-pound crab cakes are the best-selling item on its menu, but if you have eaten your quota of this Maryland delicacy, there are many other options at this people-friendly destination. Topping off a meal with the kitchen's authentic Key lime pie is another good idea.

THE EASTERN SHORE

Have Some Fun, Hold the Cash

Just how much budget-conscious stuff is there to do in Ocean City? Tons! And the biggest draw is also the most affordable.

"Some destinations charge for beach access, but Ocean City never does," says Donna Abbott, the town's communications manager.

"Kids of all ages love the beach, and it is, without a doubt, the top no-cost activity around."

Beyond the big blue, OC offers such a large assortment of no-cost diversions that, says Abbott, "On almost every night of the summer, there's something free for families to enjoy, including movies and concerts on the beach, family beach Olympics, concerts in the parks, and more."

Also totally free, naturally, are the simpler pursuits that make Ocean City a wonderful summertime—or anytime—destination.

"I love to go to the beach and just put up my umbrella, sit back, and relax with a good book," says Abbott.

"There's something about the sound of the waves, the smell of the salt air, and the feel of the sand between the toes that just totally relaxes me."

For more information on Ocean City, MD, including a current list of promotions and events, visit ococean.com.

Jules Fine Dining, 11805 Coastal Hwy., Ocean City, MD 21841; (410) 524-3396; ocjules.com. Jules Fine Dining restaurant made a quiet debut in a quiet strip mall in a not-so-quiet city in 2003—and has gathered a huge fan club since then. Owner Julius Adam Sanders and Executive Chef Michael La Bombard each have impressive culinary credentials and a passion for excellence that is apparent in their menu, the spare but elegant decor of the restaurant, and the attentive service of a skilled staff. You will probably want to get a little "dressy" (in Ocean City parlance, this means wear shoes) for dinner at Jules. It will be a special occasion, even if it's nobody's birthday or anniversary. Maybe start with oven-roasted tomato soup (especially in-season) and the chef's original Hail Julius

Caesar salad, "broken hearts" of romaine tossed with toasted pine nuts in a creamy house-made dressing and topped with tangy Asiago cheese and grated Parmesan. Or go for a tower of the chef's fried green tomatoes in a macadamia nut shell sandwiched between jumbo lump crab and showered with beurre blanc. Other standouts are a plate of house-brined and smoked rockfish, bacon-wrapped day-boat scallops glazed with an Asian barbecue sauce and bedded on an edamame seaweed salad, oysters Rockefeller, and a seafood sampler of fried calamari, coconut shrimp, and oysters. Entrees, on a menu that changes with the seasons, might include scallops, shrimp,

"Stinky Beach" Is for the Dogs

This article originally appeared in Maryland Life. *It is reprinted here with permission from its author, S.C. Torrington, sctorrington.com*

The Worcester County Department of Recreation and Parks' sign reads "Homer Gudelsky Park," but to locals, it's simply Stinky Beach—one of the few year-round, dog-friendly area beaches.

"Stinky Beach received its nickname from fish waste that would wash up on shore from the nearby fish docks and commercial maritime activities in West Ocean City," says Carol J. Cain, technical coordinator for the Maryland Coastal Bays Program.

But that was a half-century ago.

Visible from the Route 50 bridge, this football-field-size beach provides panoramic views of Sinepuxent Bay and Ocean City. Adjacent Martha's Landing (named for the late philanthropist and widow of Homer Gudelsky, whose family donated the land) features luxurious million-dollar homes, many with private piers.

Visit Stinky Beach and, from sunrise to sunset, your leashed pet can enjoy the sand, small waves, and marshy area with all their glorious scents. Several "doggie bag" dispensers and trashcans are available, with a potential $100 fine as motivation to use them.

So don't leave Stinky Beach stinky.

and lobster in a divine tomato-seafood vodka cream sauce twirled with angel hair pasta or the kitchen's innovative version of jumbo lump crab cakes, these scented with curry and paired with a red pepper remoulade sauce, toasted coconut and cashew salsa, and (for some reason) mashed potatoes. Another popular dish, recommended by an Ocean City friend who is a regular at Jules, is a main course of jumbo shrimp crusted with coconut and almond, kissed with coconut cream sauce, and served with shrimp risotto and vegetables of the day. Sanders takes pride in his establishment's well-chosen wine list and encourages guests to ask about the flights of wine that illustrate its breadth. If you are looking for a gourmet-lover's experience, Jules is for you.

THE WESTERN SHORE

A loosely defined region, Maryland's Western Shore consists primarily of Baltimore City and Baltimore and Anne Arundel Counties. (Be careful not to confuse the Western Shore with "Western Maryland." Otherwise, you'll end up way out in the mountains wondering where all the seafood went.)

Anchoring the region is Baltimore City, an irresistibly quirky, sometimes gritty town that is first and foremost a working port (the nation's second largest, in fact). Residents of "Charm City" boast their own patois, culture, and cheap beer (National Bohemian, aka "Natty Boh"). They also love crabs almost as much as they love their Baltimore Orioles and Ravens. Almost.

With its famed Inner Harbor—a bustling waterfront commercial district filled with shops, restaurants, and more than a few pushy seagulls—plus historic seafaring neighborhoods like Fell's Point, which sits along the Patapsco River, Baltimore is unmistakably anchored to the water. And even though few residents of the city and surrounding county make their living on the waves these days, most appreciate their home's watery roots.

The same can be said for Anne Arundel County, home of the state's capital, Annapolis (which itself is home to the legendary US Naval Academy). Not only does the county border the Chesapeake Bay, but the Magothy, South, and Severn Rivers snake through it, too, giving thousands of residents quick access to the water. Happily, everyone in the county has quick access to phenomenal seafood, from raw oysters at Annapolis' City Dock to crab bruschetta in Deale. Eat up!

Anne Arundel County

Blackwall Hitch, 400 6th St., Annapolis, MD 21403; (410) 263-3454; theblackwallhitch.com; @BlackwallHitch. In case you are wondering, Blackwall Hitch takes its name from a type of sailor's knot named for the Port of Blackwall on London's Thames River. This new addition to the cluster of restaurants in Eastport, a colorful nautical neighborhood on a peninsula within the city limits of Annapolis, made an immediate splash when it opened in May 2014. Its main attractions are a marble-topped oyster bar, a rooftop deck with a view of the Annapolis Harbor, numerous dining

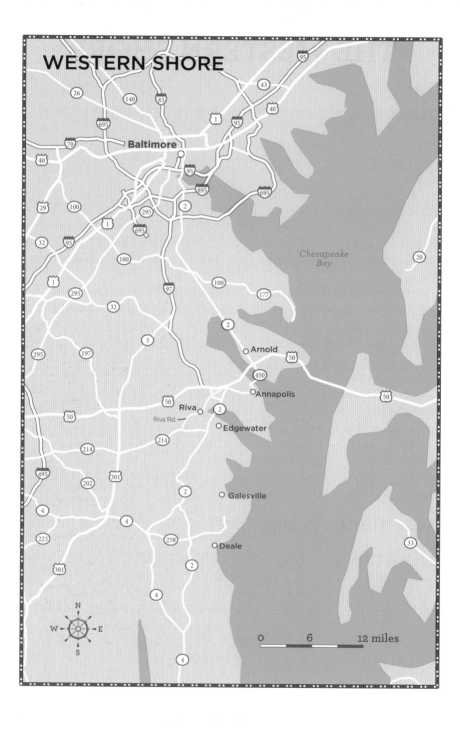

options that include four private dining rooms, an extensive bill of fare, and an eager-to-please young waitstaff. Serious seafood lovers gravitate to the oyster bar in a corner of the restaurant, where a personable bartender mixes pretty cocktails and pours draught beers from a list of 20 unique brands. We're talking Flying Dog Raging Bitch Belgian, Heavy Seas Loose Cannon, Fat Tire Amber, and Angry Orchard Crisp Apple Cider. Feel free to request "tastes" in order to make an informed decision. An overhead blackboard lists the day's oyster specials—5 or 6 varieties from Maryland, Virginia, Canada, Maine, and Massachusetts when we visited. It's fun to have one of each, served on an ice bed in a big round tin, sailor style. The nautical theme is repeated throughout the attractive premises with hanging translucent lamps shaped like casks casting a flattering glow in the 125-seat dining room and the Oyster Bar, which includes a rustic communal dining table. It's a perfect place to share Castle Blackwall, an ice tower displaying oysters and clams on the half shell, chilled Maine lobster tails, and jumbo shrimp ($50). Or to sample the kitchen's crab and shrimp ceviche, sparkling with citrusy flavor in an avocado half, drizzled with avocado cream and sided with a crisp tortilla; or to share the restaurant's signature starter—Blackwall Prawn, a 7-ounce serving of this delicacy enhanced by a garlic-chive butter sauce. We also recommend the fire-roasted Prince Edward Island mussels and a trio of quesadillas overflowing with crab lumps, roasted corn salsa, cheese, and chopped cilantro. We focused on Blackwall's raw bar, but the restaurant's menu has many options—from wood-fired pizza and sandwiches to the braised short ribs that are a specialty here. Plenty of parking behind the restaurant gives Blackwall another edge.

MARITIME MUST-SEES
The Annapolis Maritime Museum
Preserves a Slice of History

Eastport, a peninsula separated from Maryland's capital city of Annapolis, has a quirky personality all its own. It is home for many small marine businesses, a nucleus of good restaurants, and the Annapolis Maritime Museum, a unique educational resource that attracts 10,000 visitors a year from the US and abroad who come to learn about the heritage, culture, and ecology of the Chesapeake Bay.

Housed in the former McNasby's Oyster Packing Company at the mouth of the Chesapeake Bay, the museum's keystone exhibit is called "Oysters on the Half Shell" and features an authentic oyster workboat called *Miss Lonesome*. The boat has been cut into three sections, with Plexiglas bulkheads and decks to illustrate how they were built and used for tonging oysters. The exhibit area's concrete floor and rows of tables piled high with oyster shells give visitors a sense of what a shucking room looked like in the mid-'50s.

Visitors get a close-up of an oyster's anatomy via an interactive exhibit featuring a large-scale fiberglass bivalve in the main exhibit area. Along one wall, another display features authentic processing equipment, complete with a stack of old tin cans carrying the label "Pearl of the Chesapeake Oysters." Two interactive touch screens show videos of harvesting and shucking techniques, and visitors hear recordings of the gospel songs sung by the women who worked as shuckers decades ago.

Boatyard Bar & Grill, 400 4th St., Annapolis, MD 21403; (410) 216-6206; boatyardbarandgrill.com; @BoatyardBandG. Join Annapolis boaters at their favorite hangout, the hail-fellow-well-met meeting place established in 2001 by Dick Franyo. Franyo, a successful stockbroker in his former life, knows how to please folks looking for above-average food

The museum's campus also includes an historic wooden boat exhibit and a rustic dog-friendly waterfront park. From its shores, visitors may launch their canoes and kayaks, fish, and crab on the three transient piers and picnic on a deck overlooking the Chesapeake Bay. The museum is one of four partners in a consortium that shares ownership of the iconic Thomas Point Lighthouse and offers a once-in-a-lifetime 3-hour boat trip and tour of the lighthouse by prior arrangements with the museum.

Inspiring a sense of environmental responsibility for the Bay and instilling an awareness of Maryland's maritime heritage are the goals of the museum, according to museum director Alice Estrada. "It is as a programmatic museum that we really shine," says Estrada. "Our museum interprets its themes more by programs than by exhibits."

Note: While it is a serious endeavor year-round, the museum gets playful every year when it hosts its annual Annapolis Oyster Roast and the "Burning of the Socks" to signal the arrival of spring and the beginning of the boating season. Sailors of all stripes throw their footgear into a roaring fire to the lusty cheers of onlookers, there to attend the Annapolis Oyster Roast, a popular annual fundraiser for the museum. Hundreds of people come every spring for the chance to sing along with the locally famous Jeff Holland and his Oyster Boys, eat their fill of Maryland crab soup and oysters, and sample oyster-based dishes from seafood restaurants.

The Annapolis Maritime Museum, 723 2nd St., Annapolis, MD 21403. Open Thurs through Sun noon to 4 p.m. Call (410) 295-0104 or visit amaritime.org for more information.

(and beer) at reasonable prices in an atmosphere that most evenings is supercharged with energy. A sailboat with a flying jib graces the cover of an extensive menu that begins with a selection of oysters (and oyster shooters), plump and rosy Prince Edward Island mussels in a fragrant garlicky broth studded with slices of onion, steamed clams, and jumbo

Gulf shrimp steamed Baltimore style in Copperhead ale. Boatyard Grill smokes fish on the premises every day and is known for its excellent crab and artichoke dip, fresh calamari southwestern style, and conch fritters paired with a mango chili sauce. The kitchen takes honest pride in its crab cakes ("all killer/no filler") and the "neighborhood's favorite" of fish tacos (either mahimahi or cod loin) served on a platter overflowing with Spanish rice, ranchero beans, and sour cream. A fleet of cooks perform in view of patrons in the main dining room, while a rear dining room is favored by families. This is a no-frills but fun place to taste the true flavor of Annapolis. From house-made whole-wheat pizza to its famous crab cake dinner and the Saturday-only lobster rolls, the "everything is good here" mantra rings true. Note: Boatyard Grill donates a portion of its sales to the Chesapeake Bay Foundation and other Bay conservation causes.

Cantler's Riverside Inn, 458 Forest Beach Rd., Annapolis, MD 21409; (410) 757-1311; cantlers.com; @Cantlers. Located deep in the woods overlooking Mill Creek, Cantler's Riverside Inn is a slice of Americana just outside Annapolis. Opened in 1974 by Jimmy and Linda Cantler, it is an offshoot of the family's 5-generation history of working in the seafood industry. During high oyster season, Cantler's serves 15 to 20 bushels of the bivalves weekly—all supplied by the family's oystering operation. In high crab season (May through Sept) patrons pick an average of 100 bushels a week at long picnic tables covered with brown paper. While Cantler's has long been the place to go for a good old-fashioned Maryland crab feast, in recent years the once-simple menu has become decidedly upscale, if not trendy. You could easily run up the tab by sampling from a bill of fare that now includes jumbo shrimp stuffed with crab imperial, blackened rockfish bites, and your choice of sliders (fried oyster, fried crab cake, tuna, and shrimp at $4.50 each). Soft crabs fresh out of the holding tanks at the rear of the restaurant are a seasonal specialty ("properly" served on white bread with lettuce and tomato), while smoked fish is a daily special. Prime rib is on the menu for meat lovers.

Manager Dan Donnolly, who has been with Cantler's since 1994, recounts a story about being invited to put on a crab feast at the James Beard House in Manhattan. When he arrived to survey the dining room, he was startled to see the tables set with fine china, silverware, linens, and crystal. "We were asked to put on an authentic, down-home Chesapeake Bay–style crab feast," he told the maître d. "This just won't do." The maître d became indignant and stormed out of the room. But soon the misunderstanding was resolved, and out came the brown butcher paper and wooden mallets that Donnolly had brought, and a fine time was had by all as they reveled in the splendidly messy informality of such a Maryland-style crab feast.

Carrol's Creek Cafe, 410 Severn Ave., Annapolis, MD 21403; (410) 263-8102; carrolscreek.com. "One of America's best waterfront restaurants," proclaimed a national food and travel magazine after a visit to Carrol's Creek Cafe in Maryland's capital city. Annapolis residents were not surprised at this news, since this pretty place is where they themselves take visitors and enjoy lunch, dinner, and wonderful brunches on Sunday and special holidays. Jeff Jacobs, son of the original owner, has been at the helm for a number of years, ably assisted by longtime front man Richard McClure. Their hands-on management style shows in the seamless service by a cadre of waiters who are as at ease on the breezy outdoor deck as in the elegantly appointed interior rooms whose expansive windows provide water views from most tables. Carrol's Creek has an expansive list of appetizers that include the house special of large sea scallops encased in shreds of phyllo, deep fried to a crisp and served on a bed of steamed spinach studded with lump crab and prosciutto ham in a shrimp cream sauce. It's a personal favorite, and the recipe is in this book. A well-trained kitchen staff guarantees the consistent excellence of the food here, whether it's one of the town's best crab cakes; sherry-scented cream of crab soup (onetime winner as "Maryland's Best"); creamy crab artichoke dip to spread on the accompanying baguette; plump Prince Edward Island mussels steamed with shallots, garlic, basil, and tomatoes in Chardonnay; or Choptank Sweets oysters crowned with house-made bacon and Vermont cheddar. Main course options include salmon grilled and served on a bed of pureed cauliflower with wilted Chinese cabbage and a delicate saffron cream sauce, and native rockfish, roasted and served on a bed of risotto flecked with sun-dried tomato, baby spinach, and lumps of jumbo crab. And a robust cioppino featuring fresh fish, clams, mussels, scallops, and shrimp in a vibrantly seasoned tomato broth. Carrol's Creek shines especially bright in fair weather, when you can sit under an umbrella table and watch the boats go by on Spa Creek and enjoy the view of the Naval Academy on the other shore. That said, it is a good choice for all seasons—and the bar's happy hour is one of the best around. Note: The shuttle between Annapolis and Eastport will drop you off at Carrol's Creek.

A Cook's Cafe, 911 Commerce Rd., Annapolis, MD 21401; (410) 266-1511; acookscafe.com. From the minute you walk into A Cook's Cafe, obscurely located in an Annapolis office park, you've come to the right place. That is, if you are a true "foodie." Cookbooks and food magazines are stacked on shelves in the small space, which includes a half-dozen tables and stools at a counter beneath a big picture window overlooking the parking lot. Choosing from the ever-changing blackboard, you place your order for the seasonal soup de jour, sandwiches, and desserts and either take out or sit down and browse away. Chef-Owner Craig Sewell opened this very special oasis in a neighborhood of chain restaurants in 2002, offering cooking classes and serving as headquarters for the Annapolis area's CSA program as well as superior foodstuffs. His eggs come from a farm just down the road, vegetables and meats are supplied by local farmers, and seafood is supplied by Two Oceans Seafood, a Marine Council Certified business. His breads and croissants are wonderful. If it all sounds too precious for words, it isn't. Sewell, experienced in both the restaurant and corporate catering worlds, says A Cook's Cafe "was created to keep good food and good cooking down to earth, inviting, and intimate." Most days he is on-site, overseeing the action in the large kitchen in the rear and keeping up with what's going on upfront. Seek it out for light fare weekdays from 11 a.m. to 4 p.m. Or call ahead for a special catered dinner at home.

Harry Browne's Restaurant, 66 State Circle, Annapolis, MD 21401; (410) 262-4332; harrybrownes.com. Harry Browne's has earned a reputation as an Annapolis institution since it opened in 1974, just after Owner Rusty Romo's 21st birthday. More than 3 decades later, the ebullient Romo shows no signs of slowing down, constantly cultivating a restaurant known for its excellent food, friendly service, and casual elegance. His secret to success is himself—usually on-site to greet guests like old friends—which many of them are. Situated on State Circle, opposite the State House, Harry Browne's (named for Romo's uncle, a longtime coach at the USNA) is distinguished by its pleasantly retro decor accented by a huge antique chandelier rescued from a 1920s luxury ocean liner. Browse a menu that begins with a wonderful sherry-tinged cream of crab soup, plump Prince Edward Island mussels bathed in an aromatic white wine sauce, a citrusy ceviche of lobster and scallops, Spanish-style garlic shrimp, crisp calamari jazzed up with spicy chipotle aioli, and mini-crab cakes served with a honey-sesame sauce. There's a new French chef in Harry Browne's kitchen, his skills reflected in a rich (and deliciously retro) Coquille St. Jacques, slow-cooked halibut in a tomato-fennel ragout, and a memorable seafood cassoulet of shrimp, calamari, mussels, and chorizo in a deluxe saffron cream. "Werthmann" grilled salmon, named after longtime patrons of the restaurant, is crowned with a hash of leeks, crab, and ham and moistened with a white wine sauce gently flavored with Madagascar vanilla. It was the Werthmanns' favorite dish, and may become yours. Caesar salad, prepared tableside, is a house specialty. The restaurant's extensive wine list (and private wine list) deserves attention. Ask Rusty or Jason for details. Note: Window tables overlooking State Circle are prime time for people-watching. An upstairs lounge is famous for weekday 4-7 p.m. happy hours and an extensive bar menu nightly featuring the restaurant's famous burger for $5.

Jalapeños, 85 Forest Dr., Annapolis, MD 21401; (410) 266-7580; jalapenosonline.com. We went a bit inland to recommend Jalapeños, a unique Spanish-American establishment located in a strip mall across from the upscale Annapolis Town Center on the outskirts of Annapolis. Owner Gonzalez Rodriquez had a stellar reputation as a restaurateur when he opened Jalapeños in 1999. At the outset, the gregarious Gonzalez was the main draw to a plain-faced place that surprised with classically prepared Spanish food. Over the years, the interior has been totally transformed and the menu has acquired a Mexican accent from Gonzalez's chef-partner Alberto Serrano, whose son Obed is now in the kitchen after a stint in Spain learning that country's cuisine. The marriage of the two ethnic styles is a happy one. Seafood is very much a part of Jalapeños' extensive menu, with Spain winning out as the dominant partner with some, others voting for Mexico, and everyone able to mix and match. First off, I need to mention the excellence of Jalapeños' traditional seafood paellas—either in red sauce or a lighter saffron stock. Either is a great group dish. You may have trouble choosing from the many options, though I recommend the black bean soup, the shrimp in a lobster cava cream sauce, sea scallops finished with a cream sauce spiked with sherry and flavored with basil and house-made fish stock. On the Mexican side of the tapas menu, you'll find mussels bathed in a spicy blend of tequila, white wine, tomato sauce, and red pepper; a ceviche of scallops, shrimp, and calamari in a citrusy sauce flavored with garlic and cilantro; and scallops sautéed with "Mexico Mix" and finished with a touch of Mexican beer. Gonzalez, usually up front greeting guests, will be glad to see you. PS: Jalapeños is noted for its generous "happy hours" in the bar only, when a nice selection of 20 tapas are priced from $5 and drinks (try the red or white sangria) are half price.

Les Folies Brasserie, 2552 Riva Rd., Annapolis, MD 21401; (410) 573-0970; lesfoliesbrasserie.com. The years have flown since French-trained Chef Alain Matrat opened Les Folies on New Year's Day, 1999. It didn't take long for Annapolitans to embrace this authentic bistro, which has only increased in popularity since then. Matrat, when not performing as the restaurant's executive chef, often greets patrons by name. And if he needs coaching, his longtime spouse and head server, Lawrence, is there to remind him. Be forewarned that Les Folies is located on a main artery on the fringe of Annapolis, next to Bowen's Farm Store. It is not until you step into the restaurant, inhale the heady scent of good things cooking, and get seated in the bi-level dining area that you realize you've found a very special place. For openers, Les Folies's raw bar has an astonishing variety of shellfish: Malpeque and Raspberry Point oysters from Canada; Blue Points from Connecticut; Belans and Wianno from Maine; Gigamoto from Washington State; periwinkles and Taylor Bay scallops from Maine; clams and sea urchins from Rhode Island; stone crab claws from Florida; shrimp from Georgia; and Maine lobster. Matrat, who for years worked at a well-known restaurant in the nation's capital, obviously has good connections with seafood suppliers. And what of the seafood dishes that come from his kitchen? Try an appetizer of luscious lump crabmeat flan finished with lobster sauce; buttery escargots baked in their wee shells; mussels baked with herbs, garlic, and butter and finished with cognac or steamed with white wine and shallots; and La Soupe de Poissons, a medley of seafood swimming in a saffron-touched fish broth topped with a dollop of rouille. It's a meal in itself. Les Folies is as appealing at lunch as it is at dinner, with a sheet of daily specials augmenting an already extensive menu that includes a variety of seafood preparations in the inimitable style of Chef Matrat: trout amandine, pan-seared salmon topped with a tasty red pepper puree, Le Gateau de Crab Maison (airy crab cakes crowned with lobster sauce), and a signature seafood bouillabaisse that sings. The restaurant's fish of the day, marinated in herbs and garlic olive oil, is grilled to order and filleted tableside. *C'est magnifique.*

PHOTO COURTESY OF LES FOLIES BRASSERIE

McGarvey's, 8 Market Space, Annapolis, MD 21401; (410) 263-5700; mcgarveys.net. Mike Ashford is the dynamic personality who launched this iconic Annapolis bar restaurant in 1975. A gentleman sailor, he wanted a place where like-minded folks could gather for a beer and a burger—and they did so in droves. Among them were such luminaries as the late Walter Cronkite, Ashford's sailing buddy and a down-to-earth guy who liked the honesty and quality of the place. Ashford gave a moving

10-minute eulogy at Cronkite's funeral, viewed many times on YouTube. Today, McGarvey's sits modestly on the City Dock, still drawing celebs ranging from Cal Ripken to Gary Jobson and politicos of every persuasion as well as locals of all ages. Many come for the raw bar, voted Best in Annapolis by *What's Up Annapolis* magazine for the 9th year in a row and cited as among the top 21 in America by the *Daily Meal*. They come for the freshest oysters and clams on the half shell at the bar, also available steamed and served with drawn butter or dressed up Rockefeller or casino style. They come for dry-packed scallops from New England, broiled and buttered so their flavor speaks for itself. They come for a humungous seafood sampler (oysters, clams, shrimp, and mussels piled high on an enormous plate) and for grilled fish sandwiches featuring an assortment of finfish delivered 6 days a week to the restaurant. And some come for McGarvey's famous burgers, made with humanely raised beef from Piedmont Farm in western Maryland. Along with the raw bar, Mike Ashford's place is known for one of the best burgers around—and for an atmosphere reminiscent of the bar at *Cheers*, where everyone knows your name. Longtime manager (since 1981) Jim Fishback told me that Norm from that long-running show has dropped in on occasion.

Mike's Crab House, 3030 Riva Rd., Riva, MD 21140; (410) 956-2784; mikescrabhouse.com. Since 1958, Mike's Crab House has been a magnet for seafood lovers—especially those of the "picking persuasion" who consider picking crabs and drinking beer to be the ideal seasonal outdoor exercise. The original Mike's was established by the late Mike Piera, whose legacy is continued by his four sons. To their credit, nothing much has changed except for the addition of a popular tiki bar, 20 flat-screen TVs in the main bar, and live music on weekends. If you are a novice in the art of crab picking, go to the restaurant's website for a quick class on the subject. Information there includes the "beautiful swimmer's" anatomy, gender identification, their nicknames, and the types of meat in their bodies: lump, back fin, special, and claw meat. It's well worth the research so amateurs will know what they are ordering. Prices for crabs vary with the season, so be prepared for some variations. Mike's blue crabs come from Maryland, Louisiana, and Texas, but all are prepared Maryland-style—cooked to order with lots of the restaurant's special crab-seasoning blend. Mike's has lots more on its extensive menu than crabs—although it is obvious from the paper-covered tables that they are the star attractions. Their sweet meat is used in crab dip, crab soup (both the tomato-based Maryland-style and the creamy bisque), crab imperial, and as an ingredient for the cook's preparation of rockfish and flounder. Meat eaters are also welcome—the menu includes burgers, steaks, and chicken as well as a good grilled pork chop. A panoramic view of the South River comes with your meal—either from the spacious outdoor deck or the inside dining rooms. Boaters are welcome to dock

CHERISHING THE CHESAPEAKE
The Chesapeake Bay Foundation

As its simple yet powerful "Save the Bay" motto says, the Chesapeake Bay Foundation (CBF) has tasked itself with preserving and reinvigorating the Mid-Atlantic's most vital body of water.

Based in Annapolis, the nonprofit hopes that, by 2015, "The federal government, with state cooperation, will be fully enforcing the Clean Water Act and all other federal statutes applying to the Chesapeake Bay watershed system's environmental health and productivity . . . [and] a precedent-setting program for pollution reduction will have been developed and will be enforced."

It's a lofty goal. Decades of overfishing, pollution, neglect, and general misuse have left the bay a shadow of its former self. If successful, the CBF—through its multipart strategy that includes education, advocacy, litigation, and restoration—may one day restore the enormous estuary to its past glory. In the meantime, the organization continues fighting the good fight in the name of the mighty Chesapeake.

For more information on the Chesapeake Bay Foundation, call (888) 728-3229 or visit cbf.org.

here and stock up on whatever they need at Mike's Country Store, which also offers carry-out from the menu. Service is always friendly and the place becomes "party central" on the weekly Friday Karaoke Nights. Mike's is a fun place to pick crabs. Note: Mike's Crab House North, its sister restaurant (and nearly identical twin), is located in the White Rocks Marina on Rock Creek, not far from Annapolis. Complimentary docking is available for its patrons. Open in season (Apr through Nov) weekdays (except Mon) 3 p.m. to close; weekends 11 a.m. to close. (Closing times vary.)

The Point Crab House and Grill, 700 Mill Creek Rd., Arnold, MD 21012; (410) 544-5448; thepointcrabhouse.com. One of the most attractive crab houses in the region sits on prime real estate next to the Ferry Point Yacht Club and marina just outside Annapolis. Walls of windows insulated with wind-resistant glass permit year-round operation, with 120 seats inside and about 100 outside at picnic tables along the shore. The look is clean and airy—with a great view of the Magothy River and boats in the marina. Opened in 2012, The Point Crab House and Grill has established itself as a family-friendly place to meet friends and neighbors. Crabs, of course, are a specialty, but there's more to the story. Chef-Owner Bobby Jones snagged a Top Chef designation from *What's Up Annapolis* within a year of opening The Point, recognized for his innovative twists on traditional Maryland dishes. He and his wife, Julie, have an extended

family that includes "Mom-Mom" (the delicious Maryland crab soup recipe is hers) and "Nanny," who is credited for her picture-perfect deviled eggs. Worth noting is that Jones uses Maryland jumbo lump in his crab cakes, a designation that ensures the best of the best. "If I can't get Maryland blues, we're all out of luck," says he. Among the culinary amenities at this friendly place are homemade cheddar biscuits and corn fritters, homemade soft pretzels, and crab dip spiked with sherry and served in a bowl of house-made brioche. Prince Edward Island mussels swimming in a garlicky white wine and lemon sauce come with house-made focaccia to sop up the delicious broth. Jones, who grew up on the Bay, has fond memories of festive family crab feasts at his grandparents' home on Kent Island. "We want people to come to The Point to feel like they're hanging out with family," he says. "I start the day with my six prep people by reminding them we are expecting guests at a special party—and it's right here in our restaurant." Note: Slips available for small boats.

Sam's on the Waterfront, 2020 Chesapeake Harbour Dr. East, Annapolis, MD 21403; (410) 263-3600; samsonthewaterfront.com; @samonthewater. Proud Mary's Dock Bar is a popular place for boaters who can pull up to the dock for live entertainment Friday nights and Sunday afternoon and happy hour specials from 3 to 7 p.m. It is a seasonal feature at Sam's on the Waterfront, a lively spot snuggled in the middle of the marina at Chesapeake Harbour, an upscale condo development just outside of Annapolis. You know you're in the right place when you spy a lighthouse modeled after the historic screwpile structures that dotted the bay back in the day. Opened in 1986, the property has changed hands several times but retains its reputation for creative cuisine and a lovely view. At this writing, Jim Wilder is the talented executive chef and has a number of seafood options on the menu. Personally, I am a fan of his lobster roll—a praiseworthy imitation of the New England version right down to the split roll overflowing with sweet meat. Wilder, former chef-owner of two successful Annapolis restaurants who was wooed away to Sam's, also uses the Maine favorite in a mac and cheese creation rich with Vermont cheddar that is a menu staple. He tops Maryland rockfish with a fresh-tasting pesto sauce and combines linguini with Chincoteague clams in a Parmesan-enriched cream sauce redolent of garlic. The menu offers several options for oyster lovers: Florentine style, with spinach, shallots, Pernod, and Parmesan; a fried po' boy featuring a crisp cornmeal coating; and in a seafood sampler combining them with clams and shrimp. Maryland crab shines in a jumbo cake and in the excellent cream of crab soup. One of the more innovative dinner entrees is Scallops Napoleon, seared, sauced with sautéed mushrooms and leeks, and served with a sweet potato pancake and lime garnish. Sam's has two levels of indoor space—so pick your favorite at a restaurant that goes out of its way to please its patrons. PS: If you like chicken livers, you'll love an appetizer called "Dirty Grapes"—an original family recipe.

Severn Inn, 1993 Baltimore Annapolis Blvd., Annapolis, MD 21409; (410) 349-4000; severninn.com; @SevernInn. With its panoramic view of the Naval Academy and the soaring arc of the Academy Bridge over the Severn River, the Severn Inn boasts one of the most beautiful views in the Chesapeake region. Seated on the spacious two-level outdoor deck under blue umbrellas, sipping iced tea or wine from a list of more than 200 selections, is pretty close to heaven. Unlike many waterfront restaurants, where the ratio of view to food is stacked in favor of the former, Severn Inn earns points for innovative lunch and dinner menus as well as pub fare available in the bar adjacent to a pair of window-walled formal dining rooms. Self-described on its bill of fare as "A Modern American Seafood House," the restaurant takes that promise seriously. Its "no filler" jumbo lump crab cake (sandwich at lunch/entree at dinner) lives up to its name. A seafood sandwich of shrimp, crab, and lobster, piled high on a croissant, is a treat—as is the grilled fish-of-the-day BLT on a brioche roll. "Baskets" of tempura-battered scallops, shrimp, and fish are lunchtime favorites, and a grilled ahi tuna taco takes you south of the border. Chef's specials change daily as well as seasonally, and one spring day featured three varieties of oysters ($2.25 each) and pan-seared black drum fish from Delaware paired with littleneck clams and bacon with baby bok choy in a hot sauce. You will find an occasional Spanish accent at the Severn Inn, especially with Chef Lupe's Salvadorian Seafood Stew featuring shrimp, lobster, crab, clams, and mussels in a tomato-cilantro broth and a memorable main course of Verlasso salmon with a tortilla crust and a red mole sauce. Simple is good, especially with your choice of that same salmon, swordfish, or black drum grilled and graced with a buttery white wine sauce. Your fish comes with a choice of the chef's "signature sides" of fried green tomatoes (recommended), grilled asparagus, mashed potatoes, sautéed wild mushrooms, or spinach (creamed, crisped, or sautéed). There's a lot to like about the Severn Inn besides its seafood and view: friendly service, a sumptuous Sunday brunch with endless mimosas, and one of the best burgers around.

MARITIME MUST-SEES
The Chesapeake Bay Bridge Connects Two Worlds

Crossing the Chesapeake Bay over the William Preston Lane Jr. Bridge is an exhilarating experience—scary for some and inspirational for others. In 2013, 25.5 million vehicles made the 4.3-mile journey that connects the metropolitan areas of Baltimore, Annapolis, and Washington, DC, with the bucolic regions of Maryland's Eastern Shore and the shores of the Atlantic Ocean at its tip. At its highest point, the bridge measures 186 feet.

The dual spans along US 50/301 are among the longest and most scenic over-water structures in the world. The original span, opened in July of 1952 and named after the Maryland governor at that time, provides a two-lane roadway for eastbound traffic. A parallel structure opened in June of 1973, providing three lanes for westbound travelers. Tolls are collected on the eastbound bridge only.

Views from the bridge over one of the most beautiful sections of the Chesapeake Bay are breathtaking. Recreational craft, appearing the size of toy boats in a bathtub, bob and buzz on the churning water below. Tankers and container ships the size of a football field may be seen awaiting their

turn to unload cargo in the Port of Baltimore. Despite their size, they hold very few people and tons of consumer products manufactured overseas and sold in the US.

Sandy Point State Park is visible from the westbound lane, its shores populated in-season with surfers, swimmers, and sun-worshippers. During the winter holiday season, the park sparkles with the elaborate display called "Lights on the Bay" sponsored by Anne Arundel Medical Center.

Eastbound, the bridge overlooks a shoreline edged with elaborate waterfront homes and simple cottages as well as a small airport and busy marina accessed via the first exit after crossing the bridge. Every June, hundreds gather on this shore to welcome the brave souls who have swum more than 4 miles from Sandy Point State Park as participants in the Great Chesapeake Bay Swim.

Brian J. Earley is credited as the inspiration for the event when he swam the bay in 1982 in memory of his dad, who had recently died of diabetes complications. Since then, more than 3,000 swimmers have completed the course, which raises funds for the Maryland Chapter of the March of Dimes.

Skipper's Pier Restaurant and Dock Bar, 6158 Drum Point Rd., Deale, MD 20751; (410) 867-7110; skipperspier.com. Changes have come to this prime location on Rockhold Creek in Southern Maryland, easily accessible by boat and a half-hour away by car from Annapolis. Yes, the deck is stacked with picnic tables for outdoor crab feasts, and the dock bar on a perch high above the water has the same panoramic view. The change has come with the new 20-something proprietors—Jessica Rosage, a Johnson and Wales graduate, and her husband, Dave, an alum of Stevens College with an MBA from Loyola University in Baltimore. Jessica's special dessert is a version of the Smith Island cake, made in-house with chocolate mousse separating the nine layers. Jessica's culinary training is put to work in the kitchen, while Dave oversees the total picture. We suggest starting with Jessica's regional version of bruschetta, hers a warm tomato basil salad tossed with lump crab piled on ciabatta bread, drizzled with pesto, and grilled to meld the flavors and melt the cheddar cheese topping. A native Marylander, Jessica takes pride in offering fresh fish every day, sometimes just off the boats of the local watermen who patronize the place. Choices vary from grilled rockfish over fried green tomatoes with a roasted red pepper aioli, salmon with a cilantro-sweet chili glaze, roasted shrimp and scallop scampi redolent with garlic to a broiled seafood potpourri of tilapia, oysters, shrimp, and mini crab cakes. Worth mentioning is the convenience of the restaurant's take-away steamed Maryland blue crabs sold by the dozen—and the hospitable vibe of this typical (but above average) Chesapeake fish and crab house. A children's play area entertains the kids, and well-behaved dogs are welcome in the Dock Bar, where the view is panoramic and so are the sunsets.

Thursday's Steak & Crab House, 4851 Riverside Dr., Galesville, MD 20735; (410) 867-7200; thursdaysrestaurant.com. At the end of a long pier in the tiny town of Galesville, seafood seekers will find a friendly staff waiting for folks looking for the ideal spot for a crab feast. Thursday's sits on stilts over the boat-busy West River, once a port for shipping local seafood and produce up to Baltimore. While there is an indoor dining room, the best place to enjoy the scenery (and the crabs) is at a table on the sheltered deck or under an umbrella near the bar, where well-behaved dogs are welcomed with a bowl of water by pet-friendly local waiters. Thursday's serves Maryland blue crabs on tables covered with brown paper and mallets to make the picking easier. But there are other choices—among them appetizers of an excellent cream of crab (with sherry on the side), back fin crab dip accompanied by a small loaf of bread, steamed clams or mussels; and (a personal fave) potato skins overflowing with a creamy combo of shrimp, crabmeat, and scallops. Thursday's is best enjoyed in daylight hours, enjoying a leisurely lunch then walking down the lane to admire the boats in the scenic marina. Note: Docking for boaters available at restaurant.

INSIDER TIPS
Consider the Crab

Its Latin name, *Callinectes sapidus Rathbun*, may mean "beautiful swimmer that is savory," but the blue crab's moniker could just as aptly translate as "backbone of Chesapeake Bay cuisine." No other undersea creature—not oysters, not clams, not even rockfish (the state's official fish)—enjoys the blue crab's vaunted status as the Free State's most iconic culinary offering (not to mention its most valuable bottom-feeder).

Voted the official state crustacean in 1989, the blue crab—with its instantly recognizable bright blue claws—holds a place of honor on any respectable seafood establishment's menu, starring in everything from hot crab dip (don't forget to order extra toast points for dipping!) and soft-shell crab sandwiches, to the region's gold-standard dish: the crab cake. (Many eateries' street cred rises or falls solely on their cakes' crabmeat-to-breading ratio.)

As with other bay fauna, unfortunately, the last few decades have been rough on blue crabs. Everything from overfishing and polluted runoff to relentless habitat loss have conspired to hobble the Chesapeake's crab population. (The Maryland Department of Natural Resources reports that the winter of 2013–2014 was especially brutal: Extremely cold temperatures killed off an estimated 28 percent of the adult crabs in state waters.)

And while serious efforts to shore up the blue crab population are now under way—thanks, in part, to entities like the Chesapeake Bay Foundation, the Chesapeake Bay Program, and the joint Maryland and Virginia Bi-State Blue Crab Advisory Committee—there's a long way to go until the "beautiful swimmers" are restored to their former numbers.

In the meantime, Marylanders and visitors to the region will continue devouring the crustaceans, but they'll hopefully do so with the understanding that crabs need to be saved as much as savored.

Blue Crabs at a Glance:

- Blue crabs can grow up to 9 inches across. Male crabs (called "jimmies") must be at least 5 inches across to be legally harvested in Maryland. (There are no size limits on harvesting mature females, known as "sooks.")

- Crabs are harvested as either hard shell, peelers (just prior to molting), or soft shell (immediately after molting).

- Blue crabs are Maryland's most valuable commercial seafood commodity.

- Males have an inverted "T" shape on their abdomen (or "apron"). Mature females have a rounded abdomen with an inverted-bell shape on it.

- Blue crabs feed on clams, oysters, mussels, smaller crustaceans, dead fish, plants, and even other crabs.

- Most crabs live no more than 3 years.

- More than one-third of the US's annual blue crab harvest comes from the Chesapeake Bay.

Wild Country Seafood, 124 Bay Shore Dr., Annapolis, MD 21401; (410) 267-6711; wildcountryseafood.com. Most Annapolis residents don't know about this little gem, tucked away in an alley near the Annapolis Maritime Museum in the Eastport section of Annapolis. Owner Pat Mahoney Jr., who was raised on the water around Eastport, and his dad, Pat Mahoney Sr., are the last commercial fishermen on a peninsula that was once populated with watermen and long-gone oyster packing houses. But the Mahoneys keep the traditions of those days alive and working. The father-son team opened their "seafood shack" in 2009, sharing their morning catch with appreciative patrons daily and year-round (except for Mon). Sitting at the market's five outdoor picnic tables or in the park at the Annapolis Maritime Museum, seafood lovers may feast on crabs, oysters, rockfish, grouper, and perch that the Mahoneys have pulled from the

PHOTO COURTESY OF WILD COUNTRY SEAFOOD

Chesapeake Bay and its tributaries that morning. You can watch while a whole fish is expertly filleted, deep fried, and nestled into a roll for one of the best fish sandwiches around. Or satisfy your craving for oysters with plump and juicy specimens still briny from their bath. The Mahoneys have a 4-acre oyster bed where they practice the art of aquaculture to bolster their supply. Crabs may begin to come in during late May, but they grow fatter as summer wanes and are at their meatiest in September. As watermen, the Mahoneys know just when and where to look for the best of the bay. Their old-style market is sparkling clean, with the day's selection of seafood displayed on ice in a glass case. Outdoor tables are sheltered with umbrellas overlaid with straw, and miniature work boats made by the younger Mahoney hold condiments for your meal. Wild Country was one of the most exciting discoveries made for this book. You will love talking to the Mahoneys about their family's proud history on the Eastport Peninsula. Note: Wild Country is open weekdays (except Mon) from 3 to 7 p.m., Fri through Sat 11 a.m. to 7 p.m., and Sun 11 a.m. to 5 p.m. Weather permitting, the Mahoneys and their crew spend mornings aboard their work boats, *The Baby Boy* and *Wild Country*—busy catching your dinner.

MARITIME MUST-SEES
Can't-Miss Attractions on the Western Shore

Annapolis City Dock: Smack-dab in the heart of Maryland's capital, the Annapolis City Dock is exactly what you'd expect from an upscale waterfront community. Its assortment of boutiques and specialty shops means no end to the retail-therapy options, while its collection of great seafood spots, excellent views of the Chesapeake Bay, and impressive vessels sailing in and out of port mean a day spent at the City Dock is a day spent immersed in Maryland's maritime culture. *City Dock, on Main Street in downtown Annapolis, MD; visitannapolis.org.*

Eastport: Take a short walk over the Spa Creek Bridge from the Annapolis City Dock, and you'll be in the laid-back community of Eastport. Jokingly referring to itself as the Maritime Republic of Eastport, the place is "an enlightened democracy based in the Eastport neighborhood of Annapolis, Maryland, [which] has become a force in the community since its founding on Super Bowl Sunday 1998." Playful and charming, Eastport is a terrific place to eat, explore, or just dip your toes in the waters of the Chesapeake Bay. *Visit themre.org.*

Fell's Point: Located a mile from Baltimore's Inner Harbor, Fell's Point is a cobblestoned waterfront neighborhood with a rich maritime past. Once known for its thriving shipyards and its role as an arrival point for thousands of immigrants, Fell's Point today is a walkable, charming area where visitors will have no trouble finding things to do (not to mention fantastic seafood to eat). Its architecture is diverse, its people unique, and its charm boundless. No trip to the region would be complete without a stop here. *fellspointmainstreet.org.*

Ft. McHenry National Monument and Historic Shrine: Overlooking Baltimore Harbor, the 18th-century Ft. McHenry defended Charm City against the British during the War of 1812. Upon witnessing a pivotal battle there, in fact, Francis Scott Key was inspired to pen "The Star-Spangled Banner." More than just the birthplace of the US' national anthem, however, Ft. McHenry is a vivid example of how integrally tied to the water Baltimore truly is. *Ft. McHenry National Monument and Historic Shrine, 2400 E. Fort Ave., Baltimore, MD 21230; (410) 962-4290; visit nps.gov/fomc.*

The Inner Harbor: Once the country's leading shipbuilding site, Baltimore's Inner Harbor is, today, Charm City's quintessential waterfront destination. Filled with shops, seafood restaurants, boats, and other draws (including the Maryland Science Center and the National Aquarium), the Inner Harbor is an always bustling, always fun place to be. And while there are plenty of touristy things to see and do here, the harbor's underlying authenticity keeps it from lapsing into kitsch. *The Inner Harbor is located on the waterfront in downtown Baltimore. Visit Baltimore.org.*

National Aquarium: A spectacular facility, the enormous National Aquarium boasts thousands of undersea critters, re-created habitats, educational exhibits, the ever-popular "Dolphin Discovery," and much, much more. Located in Baltimore's Inner Harbor, it's a favorite among locals and tourists alike, and that means big crowds most weekends. Ticket lines can be long, so consider purchasing yours online ahead of time. *The National Aquarium, 501 E. Pratt St., Baltimore, MD 21202; (410) 576-3800; aqua.org.*

US Naval Academy: Although technically an undergraduate college dedicated to educating future members of the US Navy and Marines, the US Naval Academy is much more than just a school: It's a piece of living history. Founded in 1845, the academy features monuments, a walkable, tree-lined campus (known as "the Yard"), and an historic chapel. It is also the final resting place of Revolutionary War hero—and father of the modern Navy—John Paul Jones. Overlooking the confluence of the Severn River and Chesapeake Bay, the Naval Academy welcomes more than a million tourists each year, all of them eager to stroll its famed grounds. *The US Naval Academy, 121 Blake Rd., Annapolis, MD 21402; usna.edu.*

Yellowfin Steak and Fish House, 2840 Solomons Island Rd., Edgewater, MD 21037; (410) 573-1333; yellowfinrestaurant.com. Annapolis architect Catherine Purple Cherry has created an eye-stopping exterior and interior for this popular restaurant on a Chesapeake Bay inlet near Annapolis. Seafood of every stripe—from sushi to salmon—is the star of the show at Yellowfin, which opened to rave reviews a decade ago and earned the loyalty of locals over the years. A well-trained cadre of servers takes good care of patrons, whether helping to choose from an extensive list of cocktails, wines, and beers or explaining the restaurant's "Fish List," a selection of finned swimmers that changes weekly. One week, the "Fish List" starred grilled Alaskan halibut, Norwegian salmon crowned with Maryland crab imperial, grouper topped with crab and hollandaise, heart-healthy grilled sockeye salmon or blackened yellowfin tuna, and flash-fried cod and chips. Yellowfin is innovative in many ways, including its recent introduction of a "Nibbles, Small Plates and Sharing" menu that features two dozen mostly-seafood choices at bargain prices. Yellowfin is also famous for its lobster mac 'n cheese or lobster risotto, each crowned with a 5-ounce lobster tail; seafood tacos filled with grilled salmon or haddock; a festive seafood paella featuring lobster, shrimp, mussels, scallops, clams, and calamari; and a fabulous sushi selection. The waterfronts restaurant, owned by local entrepreneur Harvey Blonder (also owns Buddy's Crabs and Ribs in downtown Annapolis—a casual tourist destination overlooking the City Dock that is good for families or large groups), is known for its dramatic sunsets over the South River as well as the freshness of its seafood and the personalized attention of its staff. Guests who arrive by boat are given complimentary docking privileges.

Baltimore City/County

The Black Olive, 810 S. Bond St., Baltimore, MD 21231; (410) 276-7141; theblackolive.com; @bmoreblackolive. Look for the hand-carved sign suspended above a wooden door on a quiet street in Baltimore's Fell's Point neighborhood—and know you have arrived at the Black Olive, a special destination for seafood lovers. Owners Stelios and Pauline Spiladis have transformed a former general store into a true Greek tavern, its three rooms and back deck offering a choice of dining experiences—from formal to rustic. Pauline is the passionate and knowledgeable executive chef, while Stelios is the gregarious host who greets guests and keeps the Greek music playing on the sound system. The restaurant's specialty is whole fish, grilled in the kitchen and expertly filleted at your table. The daily selection, displayed on a bed of ice in the center of the restaurant, might include such rarities as Dover sole, St. Peter fish, Mediterranean sea bass, whole sardines, bronzini, dorade, and red snapper as well as wild-caught salmon, tuna, and Maryland rockfish. It is an original concept, and one that distinguishes The Black Olive from all others. Everything at this restaurant is original, it seems, starting with Pauline's own recipe for a delicious black olive bread and ending with her baklava ice cream or a crimson strawberry sorbet lightly flavored with ouzo. Mediterranean influences are reflected on her extensive menu, which features 15 small plates, vibrant salads dressed with a fine Greek olive oil, and seafood entrees of charcoal-grilled sea scallops, jumbo shrimp, and sushi-quality tuna. Seafood kabobs featuring the fish of the day are wonderful—especially the lobster version. One thing you should sample is Pauline's divine bread pudding made with her olive bread, leeks, portobello mushrooms, artichokes, and feta and manouri cheeses. Another is her crab cake, creamy with a touch of homemade mayonnaise and gently flavored with fresh herbs. Oh, and another is a bottle from The Black Olive's boutique wine list. Ask Stelios for a recommendation. (Note: The Black Olive is a stand-alone restaurant, not to be confused with the restaurant at the Black Olive Inn, which is run by the Spiladis' son Dimitri.)

Bo Brooks Restaurant & Catering, 2780 Lighthouse Point, Baltimore, MD 21224; (410) 558-0202; bobrooks.com; @BoBrooksRest. Bo Brooks has been a familiar name to native Baltimoreans since 1964, when the original restaurant was opened in East Baltimore by a guy with the same name. Bo has not been in the picture for many years, but the restaurant is still known as "the place" for picking Maryland crabs on tables covered with brown paper. Now owned by the Herman Hannon family, who opened the "new" Bo Brooks in 2000 at a prime location on the Baltimore Harbor, it is distinguished as much for its water views as for its seafood. Crabs remain the main attraction, although there are many other appealing options on its extensive menu. At the time of

PHOTO COURTESY OF BO BROOKS

this writing, Cordon Bleu-trained Mary Ann Connell is the restaurant's chef de cuisine—although her talents are underutilized in a kitchen that specializes in seafood. For openers, there are three varieties of oysters on the menu: the sweet and slightly salty Chesapeake; the saltier specimens from Battle Creek; and the sweetest Blue Point from Long Island. Taste-test two of each for about $11. Deep-fried hard-shell crabs are the edible vessels for the restaurant's jumbo crab cake, a holdover from the original Bo Brooks that is still popular with old-timers. One of the newer offerings is Chesapeake Toast, a rich treat featuring jumbo lump crab cakes crowned with creamy crab imperial and served on Parisienne toast. A cheesy crab pretzel is a best-seller at Bo Brooks' popular weekday happy hours, when drinks are half-price from 2 to 6 p.m. For a taste of Baltimore—old and new—Bo Brooks is a good choice. If you are going for hard crabs, I suggest you call ahead to check on availability. But even if they're running low, the view and Connell's cooking is worth a trip.

Charleston, 1000 Lancaster St., Baltimore, MD 21202; (410) 332-7373; charlestonrestaurant.com. Since opening their prize-winning restaurant, Charleston, in 1997, restaurateurs Tony Foreman and Chef Cindy Wolf have been wowing guests with gracious surroundings and phenomenal cooking. With its French-influenced take on Low Country cuisine, the Harbor East establishment boasts a lineup of savories like no other in Charm City (or anywhere else, for that matter). The seasonal menu changes often, but it's always prix fixe and includes 3 to 6 courses, with or without wine pairings. (Opt for "with"; the intelligently curated, 800-plus-label wine list guarantees the perfect pour awaits.) Although meaty fare—in the form of, among other things, veal sweetbreads and grilled beef tenderloin—is expertly presented, it's the underwater offerings that most delight seafood lovers. Think shrimp Creole with saffron basmati rice, spiced andouille sausage, and Creole sauce; pan-roasted wild Alaskan halibut with artichokes, roasted cipollini onions, and arugula oil; bigeye tuna tartare

with lime, cucumber, chives, and crispy potatoes; and grilled Norwegian salmon with local pea-tendril cream, English peas, crispy shallots, and Upland cress. (You should definitely think "cornmeal-fried oysters" and "crab cakes," too, since the everyday favorites are writ extraordinary in Wolf's masterful hands.) Don't let the cheese trolley pass by without sampling a nibble or two, and save room for dessert. Whatever sweets Charleston prepares are sure to be amazing.

Faidley Seafood at Lexington Market, 203 N. Paca St., Baltimore, MD 21201; (410) 727-4898; faidleyscrabcakes.com. When *Gentleman's Quarterly* gave its 1992 Golden Dish Award to the crab cake at Faidley Seafood in Baltimore's famous Lexington Market, it started a landslide of accolades over the years. The most recent praise came from *Smithsonian Magazine*, naming it as one of the "20 Most Iconic Food Destinations Across America" and proving that this tasty iconic Maryland seafood specialty has staying power. Faidley goes back to 1886, when John Faidley opened his seafood stall at Lexington Market, passing it down through generations that now include longtime owners Nancy and Bill Devine, their daughter Dayme Hawn, and her son Will. The secret to the success of Faidley's famous crab cake is simple, according to Nancy: "Not much filler and a lot of Maryland crabmeat." She uses broken saltine crackers for the filler as well as an egg and her special sauce as a binder. Three grades of crab determine the size and flavor of her cakes: claw, sweeter but darker meat, for the small; back fin for the medium; lump for the 6½-ounce large.

With just two lumps per crab, it takes 24 crabs to make a pound, says Nancy, who prefers the crunchier exterior of her deep-fried cakes, which are also available broiled. Faidley has served up to 1,000 people in a single day from a menu that also offers fried soft-shell crabs served Baltimore-style between layers of white bread with lettuce and tomato. Fried or broiled hake, catfish, haddock, flounder, and rockfish are popular sandwich material for the lunch crowd, and are stocked in Faidley's seafood market section. Lexington Market is a busy place, so be

prepared for a lot of action as well as what the media has called "the best crab cakes in the world." Note: Faidley is open Mon through Sat 9:30 a.m. to 5:30 p.m. They deliver their crab cakes to customers worldwide. To order, call (410) 727-4898 between 10 a.m. and 5 p.m. Mon through Sat.

COLORFUL CHARACTERS
John Shields, Culinary Ambassador
of the Chesapeake

Chef, author, and TV personality, John Shields is the owner of Gertrude's Restaurant at the Baltimore Museum of Art and the star of the popular PPS series *Coastal Cooking with John Shields*, based on the title of his latest book. That TV show follows him to locations across the continent—from Maine to New Orleans to Charleston to Whidbey Island in the Pacific Northwest—where he interviews folks who grow, raise, and cook the foods of their regions.

But Shields is most at home in his native Baltimore or traveling throughout Maryland gathering material for two new books—one celebrating the 25th anniversary of his original *Chesapeake Bay Cookbook* and the other titled *The New Chesapeake Bay Kitchen*, focusing on Chesapeake Bay cuisine in the 21st century.

Often called "The Culinary Ambassador of the Chesapeake Bay," on most days Shields may be found at Gertrude's, where he sat down with me one Sunday morning. Shields is one of the most upbeat people I know, with a gentle charisma and a sincere passion for what he does. He reminisced about his childhood and the great affection he had for his grandmother Gertrude and his mother, who was widowed when Shields was 7. "That was where I got my work ethic, by watching them and learning the meaning of self-discipline and responsibility," he said.

As a kid, Shields loved playing the piano and as a teenager, dreamt of becoming a "rock star." But instead, he went to college, majored in business, and got his first job at a local financial institution. He still played in the band as a creative outlet—and one day impulsively stowed his beloved piano in the back of his truck and took off for Provincetown on Cape Cod. Though he hoped to land a gig in a band up there, he found himself cooking in a local hotel.

Shields discovered he liked the restaurant business, and while on vacation in California took a job in a restaurant next door to Alice Waters' now-legendary Chez Panisse. He identified with the culture of "California cuisine" that Waters pioneered, and had no trouble finding work at several well-known restaurants in the area and fitting in with what was called "The Berkeley Gourmet Ghetto." "We all shopped for the freshest of everything at the Monterey Market," he says.

He cooked under Chef Jonathan Waxman at the prestigious French A la Carte, and when Waxman left for a job in Los Angeles, Shields was asked to take over. He "hit the floor running" and discovered an affinity for French cooking. "I had to create a new menu every day—and write it in French," he recalls. He remembers when former *New York Times* critic Frank Prial gave him a good review and a reviewer for a French newspaper did likewise.

Those youthful experiences reflect different chapters in Shields' story. Another began when he returned to Baltimore 25 years ago, introducing himself—and his first cookbook—at the first Baltimore Book Fair. Baltimoreans embraced him as the maestro of the newly upscale restaurant at the Baltimore Museum of Art, putting Gertrude's on the map of go-to places for lunch, teatime, dinner, private parties, and receptions. You are likely to spy Shields at Sunday brunch when the sounds of jazz in the background add to the ambience. And, while Shields has little time to play his own piano anymore, there is no doubt that he has earned a reputation as a "rock star" of the 21st-century food world.

Gertrude's Restaurant, Baltimore Museum of Art, 10 Art Museum Dr., Baltimore, MD 21218; (410) 889-3399; gertrudesbaltimore.com; @GertrudesBalt. Chances are good that Owner John Shields will be working at his delightful restaurant on the ground floor of the Baltimore Museum of Art. And busy as he may be, chances are good he'll take a minute to say hello—unless he's cooking in the kitchen. Open since 1988 and named after his beloved grandmother, Gertrude's is one place you won't want to miss if you are hoping for a taste of the Chesapeake. A self-described "Bawlmer boy," Shields puts together menus that speak to the season. He uses Maryland blue crabs as they are available, oysters from Chincoteague, rockfish from the Chesapeake Bay, scallops from the Atlantic Ocean, and can convert you to the sweet taste of local catfish with an original "Southern fried" version sided with cheese grits. True to Gertrude's bay-inspired theme, crab is the star of Gertrude's show. Crab soups—your choice of the traditional tomato-based or the sherried cream of crab—are laden with lump meat. Crab cakes are prepared three ways: from his grandmother's original recipe; a spicy version hot with serrano chilies, ginger, and garlic that are called "crabettes"; and a vegan "I Can't Believe It's Not Crab" that could fool a waterman. But there are lots of other tasty morsels to tempt the seafood lover: Gertie's Seafood Gumbo, thick with scallops, shrimp, crab, mussels, and andouille sausage; a wonderful

entree called Salmon Alla Bella, the wild-caught fish crusted with herbed Parmesan, napped with a light butter sauce, and served with wild rice pilaf and asparagus; rockfish stuffed with crab imperial and sauced with pecan butter. Vegetarians can find good choices on the menu, like the Middle Eastern platter laden with carrot salad, tabbouleh, stuffed grape leaves, and house-made hummus. Gluten-free burgers shine. And Pastry Chef Doug Wetzel is a genius at creating sweet treats—from lemon meringue pie to crème brûlée in three flavors (vanilla, coffee, pistachio) to an amazing butterscotch bread pudding. Gertrude's serves lunch and light afternoon fare on weekdays, brunch on weekends, and dinner daily. Closed Mon. Seasonally, the 110-seat restaurant serves diners on its outdoor terrace.

John Steven Ltd. Five Points Tavern, 1800 Thames St., Baltimore, MD 21231; (410) 327-5561; johnstevenstavern.com; @JohnStevens Ltd. It was back in the 1980s that this neighborhood pub got some good press from a *Baltimore Sun* food columnist for the addition of a delicious oyster stew to its mostly liquid bill of fare. It was a time when Baltimore's Fell's Point neighborhood was basking in its good news-bad news reputation as an area with more bars per block than anywhere in the country. In the years since then, Fell's Point has been gently gentrified, retaining its colorful ethnic personality while adding news luster to an historic waterfront deep-water point that was once a center of commerce for coffee and tobacco. Senator Barbara Mikulski still lives there as do many others who value the older homes and the newer restaurants and quirky shops. John Steven has kept up with the times, morphing from a waterman's bar to a seafood-oriented restaurant where Chef Tom Friend (recently of Kali's Court) is showing his skills. With an outdoor patio, a rear garden, and an attractive indoor dining room adjacent to the original bar, it has become a popular meeting place with friendly bartenders and an easy vibe. Belly up to that bar for a craft beer or a "Dark and Stormy," a strong sailor's favorite made with Gosling dark rum. Then check the menu to decide between Friend's four preparations of Prince Edward Island mussels (in white wine, coconut curry, marinara, or Fra Diavalo sauces); a rich crab dip topped with melted cheddar and served with celery and a baguette; jumbo scallops, broiled and moistened with lemon and white wine; steamed shrimp with Old Bay seasoning; or fresh Chesapeake Bay oysters—fried or on the half shell. Broiled rockfish, sesame-crusted tuna, and a daily catch are other items on the menu, which includes Maryland crab cakes as well as farm-raised tilapia. There is a lot else to like about this slice of Baltimore's

Fell's Point, located in a building that was built in 1730 by none other than John Fell himself. "Preserving the past, one pint at a time" is John Steven's motto—and you may want to help with that goal.

Ryleigh's Oyster, 36 E. Cross St., Baltimore, MD 21230; (410) 539-2093; ryleighs.com; @RyleighsOyster. While it works its culinary magic on lots of undersea delicacies, Ryleigh's truly shines when spotlighting—what else?—oysters. Whether at its location in historic Federal Hill or its newer digs in Baltimore County's Hunt Valley, Ryleigh's takes the humble bivalve and elevates it to a work of art. For slurpers, that means your half shells will be remarkably fresh and exquisitely briny; for just-can't-stomach-it-raw seafood lovers, it means (cooked) oysters presented in clever, creative ways you've probably never tasted before. Think char-grilled oysters with garlic-herb butter, tomatoes, and Parmesan cheese; fried oyster tacos with pico de gallo and pineapple salsa (move over, fish tacos!); panko-encrusted oysters with tomato aioli, romaine lettuce, onion, and hardboiled egg; and creamy oyster stew redolent with thyme, garlic, celery, and onions. But what if, for some inexplicable reason, you're just not in the mood for oysters? Tuck into Ryleigh's shrimp, chicken, dirty rice, and andouille sausage jambalaya; its Maryland Shore-style crab cakes with corn salad and sweet-potato fries; or even its seafood-free (egad!) but rich and delicious vegetarian *cavatappi* pasta with roasted red peppers, sautéed spinach, shallots, garlic olive oil, and feta cheese instead. You won't even miss the oysters. (Okay, you will. Better order a dozen on the side, just to be safe.)

PHOTO COURTESY OF RYLEIGH'S OYSTER

INSIDER TIPS
Old Bay Seasoning: A Magical Maryland Mix

Old Bay Seasoning is the not-so-secret flavoring in Maryland crab cakes—and just about anything else that needs a spicy kick. Natives sprinkle the mix on all kinds of seafood, as well as french fries, crab soups, potato chips, vegetables—you name it.

Most households have the distinctive yellow can on their shelves, and many restaurants include a shaker of Old Bay next to their salt and pepper containers. It's a wonder no entrepreneur has come up with an Old Bay aftershave or cologne.

Named after the *Old Bay Line*, a passenger boat that sailed between Baltimore, Maryland and Norfolk, Virginia, in the early 19th century, it was developed in 1939 by German immigrant Gustave Brunn. McCormick & Company bought the company in 1990 and continues to make and market a magical mix that includes paprika, dry mustard, bay leaf, black pepper, celery salt, mace, cloves, allspice, nutmeg, cardamom, and ginger.

When the NFL's Baltimore Ravens won the Super Bowl in 2013, McCormick & Company issued a limited edition can of Old Bay Seasoning honoring six players from the team: Joe Flacco, Torrey Smith, Terrell Suggs, Ray Rice, Haloti Ngata, and Lardarius Web. They sold out fast and are now considered by sports fans to be collectors' items.

Sascha's 527 Cafe, 527 N. Charles St., Baltimore, MD 21201; (410) 539-8880; saschas.com. Sascha Wolhandler has long reigned as one of Baltimore's most colorful personalities—chef, caterer to the movie stars who film in the city, radio show personality, and owner of Sascha's 527 Cafe near Mt. Vernon Square. A glorious town house, at one time a beauty salon patronized by the Duchess of Windsor, is the scene for an everything-fresh cafeteria-style lunch destination and by night a candlelit upscale restaurant where a turn-of-the-20th-century chandelier sparkles under 16-foot ceilings supported by marbleized columns. It is in the evening that Catherine Bind, a 15-year veteran of Sascha's kitchen, creates an appealing and ever-changing selection of fresh foods in a style inspired by Alice Waters. Bind describes her style as "creative American, with global touches from Asia to France, and Moroccan in between." She offers "taste plates" as an alternative to a single entree and reserves a special section on the menu for "From the Water" specialties. Baby crab cakes come as sliders on homemade brioche rolls with a caper-studded remoulade and may be ordered in three different quantities—as an appetizer or one-note main course. Seafood is one of Sascha's specialties, maybe calamari with Chinese lime sauce; a pretty salmon roulade made with wild-caught salmon, lemon gnocchi, fennel, and prosciutto; Prince Edward Island mussels bathed in lemon butter and hot chilies, served with hot garlic bread and frites; red snapper tacos like you've never tasted—hot with roasted poblano and cooled with lime crème fraiche; or Bend's delicious version of shrimp and grits—gluten-free and available in small or large portions. She even does a pad thai with shrimp and mussels in a red curry sauce with rice noodles, cucumber, mango, cilantro, and fried peanuts. Meat eaters will appreciate Sascha's special (and well-priced) grilled filet moistened with a red wine glaze and served with a hot-and-sweet chutney of blueberries and jalapeño peppers with fingerling potatoes, baby carrots, and bacon—all gluten free. Sascha's bartender makes the legendary "perfect martini" and the bistro's boutique-vineyard wine list is chosen to marry well with the food. On weekends, there's usually some live music going on, making a visit here like attending a party at a friend's house. That friend would be Sascha—and her dashing partner Steve, who takes good care of her (and her guests).

Thames Street Oyster House, 1728 Thames St., Baltimore, MD 21231; (443) 449-7726; thamesstreetoysterhouse.com; @ TSOH2011. If you detect a New England accent at this very popular Baltimore restaurant, it's because Owner Candace Beattie studied at the prestigious Berklee School of Music and lived in Boston for a decade before returning to her native Baltimore and opening the Thames Street Oyster House in 2011. In a city lacking in serious seafood restaurants it was an immediate success, earning accolades from *Baltimore Magazine* (Best New Restaurant in 2012, one of Top Ten Restaurants and Best Outdoor Dining in 2013) and bringing in a steady stream of patrons looking for quality in food, service, and ambience. Its location in gentrified Fell's Point was another plus. Beattie, who had worked in numerous restaurants herself, knew the importance of "the chef" and hired veteran Chef Eric Houseknecht, a graduate of Johnson and Wales in Rhode Island, to lead

her kitchen. She also knew the importance of oysters on the trendy food horizon, and set up a spectacular wine bar that every day stocks 10 different varieties of oysters from both coasts and beyond, as well as an appealing list of other bar-appropriate choices. Then she added on four kinds of oyster shooters (Natty Boh, Smirnoff, Antiqua Blanco, and Old Granddad) for good measure. And Houseknecht's menu makes seafood lovers smile. Stand-outs are the marvelous New England-style lobster rolls, whole-belly clam rolls, grilled mahimahi sandwiches, wonderful Block Island scallops, baked hake loin from Maine waters, New Bedford grill-marked swordfish with a Madeira sauce; flounder with a surprise sherry-touched fricassee of escargots, lobster, and potato and pearl onions; a superior bouillabaisse of mixed seafood (shrimp, mussels, fish, baby clams, etc) swimming in a tomato broth with strands of house-made pappardelle pasta and crowned with an authentic rouille. The Thames Street Oyster House stands well above the crowd, with an upstairs dining room overlooking the water, a beautiful terrace, a lively bar, excellent seafood, and an owner who knows how to please her patrons.

INSIDER TIPS
Chartering a Sail around Annapolis

This piece originally appeared on the Annapolis Visitors Center's food blog. It is reprinted here with permission of author Mary Lou Baker.

PHOTO COURTESY OF JENNIFER KAYE

Up the creek without a paddle? Wish you had your own yacht to sail around the waters surrounding Annapolis and get a closer look at the gorgeous boats anchored on its moorings?

No problem.

Annapolis is the homeport for two highly regarded boat charter companies—at your service as long as you let them know you're coming. Both Yacht Charters by Watermark and Woodwind Charters can get you and your guests out on the water in style. Sailing season in Annapolis is Apr 10 through Oct 26 so call ahead to set up a cruise that suits your needs.

Watermark, founded in 1972, has a fleet of 13 yachts that range in size from the luxurious 95-foot yacht *Catherine Marie* to the cozy 24-foot motorized *Miss Anne*. In addition to Watermark's popularity as a unique venue for corporate meetings or wedding receptions (with accommodations for up to 220), it also caters to folks who want to see the "real Annapolis" and understand why it is nicknamed "The Sailing Capital of the World."

Watermark's best choice for small groups is *Miss Anne*, where by prior arrangements food can add another dimension to your cruise. Options include a 2-hour romantic sunset trip, complete with hors d'oeuvres and wine; a dessert cruise, when the *Miss Anne* will pick up your party at waterfront restaurants in Eastport and treat you to a selection of sweet treats to enjoy while cruising on Spa Creek for a few magical hours as the lights come on at the US Naval Academy and the beautiful homes along the shores.

How about a "Boat and Breakfast" adventure? With advance notice, the 75-foot sailing yacht *Woodwind* invites you aboard for its weekend bed-and-breakfast package for as many as four couples. Guests arrive early to stow their gear in one of the schooner's comfortable cabins before setting out for a 2-hour sunset sail on the Chesapeake Bay. They disembark for 8:30-9 p.m. dinner reservations at one of Eastport's top-tier restaurants (not included in the fee). Restaurant options include Carrol's Creek Cafe, the Chart House, O'Leary's Seafood, Lewnes or Ruth's Chris (for steaks), and Boatyard Grill and Blackwall Hitch.

After dinner, passengers return to the *Woodwind* at its designated dockside mooring for a good night's sleep. Next morning, their gourmet breakfast includes crab quiche with asparagus, a delicious apple cake, and the yacht's signature dish of yogurt, berries, and granola topped with Vermont maple syrup. The per-cabin fee is $299 for two, including taxes.

Both Woodwind and Watermark call upon Annapolis caterers Eric Daniels of Palate Pleasers and Ken Upton of Ken's Creative Cuisine to provide the food served onboard their specialty food cruises—whether it's breakfast, brunch, picnics, lunch, or dinner. Brunch cruises are scheduled for Mother's Day and Father's Day. Dinner for special private charters could include crab cakes, tenderloin, salmon, lamb chops, shrimp skewers, and local vegetables. Fees vary according to the occasions and menu.

Visit yachtchartersonthebay.com or schoonerwoodwind.com for more info.

Tio Pepe Restaurant, 10 E. Franklin St., Baltimore, MD 21202; (410) 539-4675; tiopepebaltimore.com. Tio Pepe is one of my all-time favorite places to go for sangria and seafood. Tio's signature sip, a fruity concoction poured from the restaurant's colorful pitchers into stemmed cut-glass goblets, and a greeting from Francesco (the courtly maître-d') is enough to put you in a festive frame of mind. And I love the whitewashed stone walls, the lighting from candlestick chandeliers, and the attentions of waiters dressed in colors that designate their type of service. A longtime star of Baltimore City's dining-out scene, Tio Pepe remains the epitome of "the perfect restaurant," carrying on the legacy of formal service in elegant-but-not-stuffy surroundings and food that sings in a Spanish accent. Chef Emiliano Sanz has been orchestrating the menu since 1972, and his voice is still powerful. "Specialties of the Chef," a daily insert into the regular menu, lists six or seven fresh fish as well as scallops and shrimp preparations. At one recent lunch, Chef Sanz's daily specials were six: silver salmon broiled with béarnaise or poached with Hollandaise; rockfish with crabmeat or jumbo scallops—each glazed with the kitchen's celestial champagne sauce; soft-shell crabs in an amandine or lemon butter sauce; swordfish Riojana, with tomatoes, onions, mushrooms, and multicolored peppers; grouper simply sauced with lemon butter; and tilapia amandine. Entrees are escorted by small dishes of rice and carefully cooked seasonal vegetables—maybe bright green string beans or asparagus. My favorite are the scallops in champagne sauce, so delectable they are candidates for that "last meal" Julia used to talk about. There's lots to love at Tio's—a memorable *sopa de pescado y marisco*, a traditional Mediterranean soup-of-the-sea that combines the flavors of clams, mussels, shrimp, and chunks of fish in a lovely broth; a sherry-tinged black bean soup accompanied by little dishes of rice and chopped onion; the chef's famous Dover sole sautéed with bananas and napped with hollandaise. If you are tired of the pursuit of the newest and trendiest, get your family and friends together and feast on Tio's sumptuous Paella Valenciana while working on a pitcher of sangria.

SOUTHERN MARYLAND

Although Southern Maryland is made up of three counties—Charles, Calvert, and St. Mary's—only Calvert and St. Mary's dip their toes directly in the Chesapeake Bay. But the abundance of rivers and creeks ribboning the region means all three counties offer outstanding seafood options, not to mention natural beauty and rich history. (Just how far back does that history date? Well, the shoreline of Calvert Cliffs State Park is considered one of the best places *in the world* to find prehistoric shark teeth. Which means, ironically, that a region known for its seafood was originally settled by seafood.)

Once home to a large population of Piscataway Indians, as well as to the first English Roman-Catholic settlement (St. Mary's City) in the New World, another of Southern Maryland's historic claims to fame is that it witnessed the flight of Lincoln assassin John Wilkes Booth, who stopped at the Charles County home of Dr. Samuel Mudd—now the Dr. Samuel A. Mudd House Museum—in 1865 to receive medical treatment during what he'd hoped would be a successful flight to freedom. As all good students know, it wasn't.

Throughout (and well beyond) the Civil War era, tobacco was king of the region's economy. Tens of thousands of acres of farmland were dedicated to growing the cash crop; steamboats and other vessels would ship tons of the cured leaves up and down the bay, often hauling passengers, mail, and other cargo, too. Although steamers no longer chug through the waters, and tobacco has been dethroned by less controversial crops, Southern Maryland—designated a Certified Heritage Area—hasn't lost its historic feel and unspoiled, mostly rural makeup.

Today, towns like Chesapeake Beach and North Beach—once the summertime stomping grounds of wealthy early-20th-century city dwellers—have all the charm (and the same beautiful sandy beaches) they once did. Leonardtown is as quaint and walkable as ever, and surrounded-by-water Solomons still welcomes visitors who are as likely to pull up by boat as by car. But regardless of how guests get to Southern Maryland, the smart ones know not to leave before tucking into a few steamed blue crabs, fresh oysters, hand-shaped crab cakes (easy on the breading!), or other good-enough-for-Neptune nibbles.

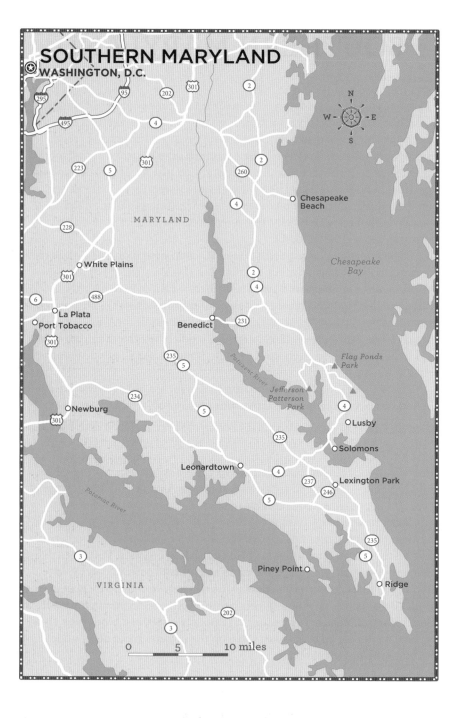

SOUTHERN MARYLAND

WASHINGTON, D.C.

MARYLAND

Chesapeake
Beach

Chesapeake
Bay

White Plains

La Plata
Port Tobacco

Benedict

Patuxent River

Flag Ponds
Park

*Jefferson
Patterson
Park*

Newburg

Leonardtown

Lusby

Solomons

Lexington Park

Potomac River

Piney Point

Ridge

VIRGINIA

N
W   E
S

0   5   10 miles

Calvert County

Abner's Crab House, 3748 Harbor Rd., Chesapeake Beach, MD 20732; (410) 257-3689; abnerscrabhouse.net. Bobby Abner has loved crabbing—and crabs—since he was a kid. In 1966 he turned that passion into an authentic crab shack that's as down-to-earth and friendly today as it was back then. Still family-owned and operated, Abner's Crab House doesn't just serve up great seafood; it serves up a great time, too. (Witness its tongue-in-cheek motto: "The place where it's OK to have CRABS!") That means you don't have to sweat it when you and the kids get your hands dirty digging into a pile of seafood. And that dribble of tartar sauce on your bottom lip? No one will judge. Since it can be tough deciding what to order—fried oysters with a side of slaw? Stuffed flounder and potato salad? A crab ball sandwich and hush puppies?—your best bet may be to go big: Order one of Abner's famed "steampots." Like the name suggests, it's a scrumptious mess o' the ocean's finest offerings: crab, steamed shrimp, mussels, and clams served in a big pot, with a side of garlic butter. And if you'd like to see firsthand where some of that seafood came from, book a day of charter fishing on Abner's *TamShell* or *TamShell II*. What could be cooler than encountering your dinner in its natural habitat?

Anglers Seafood Bar & Grill, 275 Lore Rd., Solomons, MD 20688; (410) 326-2772; anglers-seafood.com. With a name like Anglers, you can guess what gets star billing on the menu. Yep: fish and other seafood. Early risers can head to Anglers (by car or boat) as early as 5 a.m. for a stick-to-your-ribs breakfast of steak and eggs, fluffy pancakes, creamed chipped beef on toast, or a three-egg omelet. But if what you're really after is seafood, plan your visit for lunch or dinner. That's when the eatery, with its lovely waterfront view of Mill Creek, rolls out the treasures of the sea. Think fried rockfish bites with a spicy dipping sauce; a fried soft crab sandwich served with lettuce and tomato on a potato roll; an ahi tuna wrap with cucumber-wasabi sauce on the side; or a battered haddock sub on a toasted French roll. Heartier appetites should make a beeline for the entree section of the menu. That's where you'll find such crowd-pleasers as stuffed rockfish crab imperial, steak & cake—aka a 6-ounce New York strip steak served with a crab cake; and hand-breaded butterflied fried shrimp. For dessert (you saved room, right?), dig into a slice of lemon berry cream cake. It's a sweet way to cap off an evening of dining on—and from—the water.

CHERISHING THE CHESAPEAKE
Public-Private Partnership Helps Oysters Make a Comeback

"As I ate the oysters with their strong taste of the sea and their faint metallic taste that the cold white wine washed away, leaving the sea taste and the succulent texture . . . I lost the empty feeling and began to be happy and make plans."
—Ernest Hemingway, *A Moveable Feast*

Magical powers have long been associated with the ugly-shelled oyster, whose beautiful interior is considered by some to be an aphrodisiac and by others a simple source of culinary delight. While at one time the protein-rich bivalve was considered food for the poor because of their widespread availability along the entire East Coast, today's sophisticated tastes have created a steady demand for oysters—especially those from the Chesapeake Bay, with their signature sweet and slightly salty taste.

Thanks to a series of state-sponsored programs, Maryland's supply of oysters has been restored to healthy levels after an alarming dip in the Chesapeake Bay's native oyster population that began in 1994 when the harvest dropped to an alarming 1 percent of historic levels. Officials attributed the decline in part to the depletion of the oysters' natural habitat, which over the past three decades had catapulted downward to 80 percent—from 200,000 acres to 38,000 acres. Oyster harvesting declined from 1.5 million bushels a year to an average of 142,000 in recent years.

It was Maryland Governor Martin O'Malley who made oyster restoration a priority of his administration. According to the state's Department of Natural Resources, the state and its partners increased Maryland's network of oyster sanctuaries from 9 to 24 percent, planted 1.25 billion native spat in the year 2013, and maintained 76 percent of the Bay's remaining prime oyster habitats. The Oyster Advisory Commission—a group of scientists, watermen, anglers, businessmen, economists, and environmental activists—was established in 2009 and is credited with the strong comeback of Maryland's oyster population and the effectiveness of public-private partnerships.

One of the key partners in the state's restoration efforts has been the Oyster Recovery Partnership (ORP), a nonprofit established more than 20 years ago to focus on protecting the environment and preserving Maryland's cultural heritage. Its oyster restoration program is led by the expert scientists at the University of Maryland Center for Environmental Science in Cambridge. One of the leading scientists working on the project is Elizabeth W. Watkins, Ph.D., an Annapolis native raised on the Severn River who early on developed a fascination with the Chesapeake Bay—and a fondness for oysters that has grown into a personal mission.

"In addition to being delicious, oysters have an important role in the ecology of the Chesapeake Bay," says Dr. Watkins, an associate professor at the University of Maryland Center for Environmental Science. She is proud of the work the ORP is doing, especially its Shell Recycling Alliance Program, which has enlisted many Maryland restaurants to save empty oyster shells so they can be returned to the water. Dr. Watkins says that more than 1,200 tons have been recycled since 2009. "Baby oysters must attach themselves to something hard—and what could be better than a 'mother' shell?"

Back Creek Bistro, 14415 Dowell Rd., Solomons, MD 20688; (410) 326-9900; backcreekbistro.com. Housed in a building that was once home to the power plant for the US Amphibious Training Base during WWII, the Back Creek Bistro more than fulfills its mission "to provide, in an upscale yet relaxing atmosphere, reasonably priced top-of-the-line food, excellent service, and delicious cocktails and wine." Located at the Calvert Marina, the waterfront eatery boasts an extensive menu sure to please everyone at the table. Although landlubbers may opt for one of the bistro's many meat dishes, seafood lovers will head straight to the under-sea offerings. These include champagne scallops (sautéed scallops with orange zest, cilantro, red onions, and champagne sauce), fried Maryland oysters, blue crab gnocchi in a white vodka-cream sauce, shrimp Alfredo, lobster bisque, and (no surprise here) jumbo lump crab cakes. Savor your spread while watching the spectacular sunset over Back Creek, and stick around for the live music. A rotating roster of top-quality musicians means an evening at the Back Creek Bistro will sound almost as good as it tastes. (If you're heading to the bistro by boat, feel free to tie up at one of the big floating docks out front. There's no charge.)

Bistro Belle Maison at the Blue Heron Inn, 14614 Solomons Island Rd., Solomons, MD 20688; (410) 326-2707; blueheronbandb.com. Located inside the lovely Blue Heron Inn B&B, Bistro Belle Maison is Chef (and innkeeper) Amanda Rutledge Comer's homage to "simple, perfect food, warm, comfortable service, and attention to detail." What that means for lucky diners is meals centered on the finest ingredients rather than the latest fads; it means a smart, savvy chef who knows better than to gild the lily on something that's already exquisite. With a menu that changes weekly, you never know exactly what'll be on offer at Bistro Belle Maison, but you can bet it'll be in season, locally sourced whenever possible, and fabulous. The lineup might include ahi tuna carpaccio or seared scallops one week, and stuffed shrimp with artichoke and saffron risotto or yellow lentils with bacon, tomato, prawns, and Parmesan toast the next. Mussels Provençale, trout amandine, soft-shell crab with sweet-pea pancakes, and rockfish with summer succotash also take turns starring on the menu, as do local cheeses, meats, and produce. Check the website to see which stellar dishes will be available during your visit. Or, better yet, just show up and let Bistro Belle Maison wow you. (You don't need to stay at the inn to eat at the bistro, but you really should. Wouldn't a night away feel great right about now?)

The Dry Dock Restaurant, 245 C St., Solomons, MD 20688; (410) 326-4817; zahnisers.com/restaurant-2. Anchored at Zahniser's Yachting Center, the Dry Dock Restaurant doesn't just enjoy a spectacular view of the harbor. It also enjoys a reputation for serving as much fresh, sustainably caught seafood as possible, along with some of the area's finest locally grown produce. What that means for guests at the award-winning Solomons mainstay—whether they pull up in a car or drift in by boat—is that meals here are sure to be memorable. From the appetizers—lobster mac n' cheese, crab cake sliders, fried oysters, and amaretto glazed shrimp, to name a few—to the ever-changing entree lineup, it's impossible to leave hungry. And speaking of those entrees, although they're different week to week (illustrating the Dry Dock's commitment to using seasonal ingredients), they always feature something from the sea. That might mean Pescatore Rigatoni (pasta with shrimp, scallops, and mussels in a creamy marinara sauce) one night, and lemon grilled salmon with sun-dried tomato risotto, Mediterranean pesto salad, and crumbled feta the next. Or it might mean a different—though equally fantastic—dish entirely. Such is the fun of cooking seasonally!

Rod 'N' Reel Restaurant at the Chesapeake Beach Resort and Spa, 4165 Mears Ave., Chesapeake Beach, MD 20732; (866) 312-5596; chesapeakebeachresortspa.com. Delighting guests' discriminating palates since 1946, the Rod 'N' Reel Restaurant at the Chesapeake Beach Resort and Spa is as much of a regional landmark as the quaint town it resides in. Owned and operated for 3 generations by the same family, the place serves its signature seafood dishes 364 days a year—shuttering only on Christmas Day. Must-try draws include the Portobello Neptune—a meaty mushroom topped with sun-dried tomatoes, mozzarella, shrimp, and Maryland crab—and the fresh local stuffed rockfish, brimming with crab imperial and plated alongside a rich rice pilaf. Sunday finds peckish locals and visitors alike queuing up for the Rod 'N' Reel's legendary breakfast buffet—think eggs Benedict, bay fries, sausage gravy, creamed chipped beef, and warm doughnuts—but it's the Thursday-night seafood buffet that truly makes undersea connoisseurs' knees go weak. Picture fresh mussels, clams, steamed shrimp, the catch of the day, crab legs, hush puppies, chowder, and other goodies spread out before you. Now imagine an empty plate in one hand, a pair of tongs in the other, and nothing standing between you and the phenomenal oceanic spread. Who's ready to eat?

Stoney's Kingfishers, 14442 Solomons Island Rd. South, Solomons Island, MD 20688; (410) 394-0236; stoneysseafoodhouse.com. Managing to feel both elegant and casual, Stoney's Kingfishers mixes nature-themed artwork, handcrafted wood carvings of native fauna, and a large Chesapeake Bay-themed mural in a setting that woos highfalutin guests as easily as it makes kid-toting parents feel right at home. The outdoor deck and upstairs bar are terrific spots for watching the rippling Patuxent River inlet, but all eyes will turn toward the table when the food arrives. And what excellent food it is. Smart diners know to kick things off with an order of crab balls—three golf-ball-size spheres of deep-fried crabby goodness, served with a side of tartar sauce—and then stick to the sea for the rest of the meal, too. Whether it's a salmon BLT (grilled salmon, applewood bacon, and fresh lettuce and tomato on Texas toast), an oyster po' boy served with sriracha mayo on a baguette, or Neptune's Platter (the whole megillah, featuring scallops, shrimp, a crab cake, fresh fish, seasonal fresh veggies, and a baked potato), Stoney's seafood fare feeds its guests well, leaving them satisfied and happily stuffed. (Stoney's has two other locations nearby—Broomes Island and Solomons Pier—offering similarly succulent options.)

Traders Seafood, Steak & Ale, 8132 Bayside Rd., Chesapeake Beach, MD 20732; (301) 855-0766; traders-eagle.com. Housed in the same building where the famed Seabreeze once reigned supreme, the family-owned Traders Seafood, Steak & Ale continues its predecessor's reputation for excellent food in an authentic nautical setting. Although it offers lots of not-so-fancy draws—including live music on the waterside outdoor deck, summer luaus, Keno, Racetrax, electronic bingo, and scratch-off lottery tickets—Traders' food is top-notch all the way. That means the flounder stuffed with crab imperial will be light on filler and heavy on succulence; the seafood Alfredo's jumbo lump crabmeat, scallops, and shrimp will star—rather than be treated as an afterthought—in the proceedings; and the barbecue bacon-wrapped shrimp won't leave you asking, "Um, there's shrimp in here, right?" Go rogue and order the "Angels on Horseback"—scallops wrapped in bacon and then glazed with soy sauce—or stick to what you know and ride the crab cake train all the way to dessert. Stop by anytime on "Thirsty Thursdays" and enjoy 2-buck domestic beers and $3.50 glasses of wine or rail drinks with your meal, and make a point of coming out for the weeknight happy hour. Where else can you get a platter of fantabulous crab nachos for just $4.99?

Vera's Beach Club, 1200 White Sand Rd., Lusby, MD 20657; (410) 586-1182; verasbeachclub.com. When is a restaurant more than just a restaurant? When it's also a hotel, marina, private-event venue, concert stage, and all-around great place to hang out and have fun. And that's exactly what Vera's Beach Club is: a legendary Southern Maryland destination where the raucous, playful surroundings are as beloved as the food (and the late Vera herself). That means no matter what you're here for, you're going to have a blast—and you're likely to leave stuffed. Dig your toes into the sand at the beachfront bar while digging your fingers into an order of Old Bay-dusted fries; broiled Hot Island oysters with ham and garlic-butter sauce; or a few sesame-crusted ahi tuna wontons. From there, kick things up a notch by plunging head-first into the entrees. The fried shrimp dinner with a side of Vera's special sauce will leave you all Neptuney and Zen-like, while the hot garlic Alaskan king crab legs may just have you licking the plate clean (don't be embarrassed; you're among friends). Flag down the waiter for another cold one before calling it a night. Or better yet, don't call it a night at all. You surely have room for just one more order of Old Bay peel-and-eat shrimp, right? Of course you do!

MARITIME MUST-SEES
Can't-Miss Attractions in Southern Maryland

Bayside History Museum: With a stated mission to "provide all citizens with an understanding of the role the Chesapeake Bay environment had in shaping the cultures of the bayside communities," the quaint Bayside History Museum tells its stories through exhibits like "Amusement Park at Chesapeake Beach," "Camp Roosevelt," and "A Day at the Beach." Photos, artifacts, and reproductions round out the offerings, and an on-site gift shop means visitors have a chance to nab the perfect take-home souvenir. *The Bayside History Museum, 4025 4th St., North Beach, MD 20714; (410) 610-5970; bayside historymuseum.org.*

Calvert Marine Museum/Drum Point Lighthouse: Situated at the mouth of the Patuxent River in Solomons, the Calvert Marine Museum is a one-stop shop for experiencing a snapshot of the Chesapeake Bay, the men and women who made (and make) their livings on it, and the vessels sailing its waters. Highlights include go-ahead-and-touch fossil displays; an up-close-and-personal encounter with live skates and rays (these can be touched, too; be sure to ask a staffer for assistance); an outdoor marsh walk; and, possibly coolest of all, the on-site, fully restored Drum Point Lighthouse, a screwpile, cottage-style lighthouse—one of only three of its kind left on the bay. The fascinating structure is a destination in its own right. *The Calvert Marine Museum, 14200 Solomons Island Rd., Solomons, MD 20688; (410) 326-2042; calvertmarinemuseum.com.*

Chesapeake Beach Railway Museum: It was in the late 19th century that entrepreneur Otto Mears and associates envisioned and then designed the resort town of Chesapeake Beach. Complete with hotels, bathhouses, gaming—at casinos and a racetrack—and a boardwalk, the place offered plenty to do for the summer guests arriving via passenger steamer from Baltimore. (Non-gambling or swimming vacationers surely appreciated the boardwalk, carousel, and band shell, while thrill-seekers would've headed straight for the roller coaster.) While its glory days as an amusement-park getaway for moneyed city slickers may be long gone, the Chesapeake Beach Railway Museum—housed in the original Chesapeake Beach Railway station—preserves the area's rich history through exhibits honoring the people (and locomotives) that helped make the town what it is today. *The Chesapeake Beach Railway Museum, 4155 Mears Ave., Chesapeake Beach, MD 20732; (410) 257-3892; cbrm.org.*

Cove Point Lighthouse: Owned and overseen by the Calvert Marine Museum, the Cove Point Lighthouse illuminates the Chesapeake Bay yet today. (Because it's still a functioning lighthouse, the US Coast Guard is responsible for its official operation.) Located on 7 acres of land overlooking one of the bay's narrowest points (gaze out across the water and you'll see Dorchester County), the lighthouse's gorgeous keeper's quarters can be rented for overnights or longer stays. Day-trippers can't tour the quarters, but they're invited to explore the grounds and peek inside the lighthouse's towering chamber. *The Cove Point Lighthouse, 3500 Lighthouse Blvd., Lusby, MD 20657; (410) 326-2042; calvertmarinemuseum.com.*

Dr. Mudd House Museum: Was Samuel A. Mudd—the country physician who treated the broken leg of fleeing Lincoln assassin John Wilkes Booth—a traitor, or was he simply an unwitting accomplice caught up in events not of his making? The matter may never be settled, but visitors to Mudd's farm—now a museum—can at least get a feel for the Civil War–era setting where the doctor's controversial actions took place. *The Dr. Mudd House Museum, 3725 Dr. Samuel Mudd Rd., Waldorf, MD 20601; (301) 274-9358; drmudd.org.*

Greenwell State Park: Encompassing 596 gorgeous acres along the Patuxent River, Greenwell State Park boasts 10 miles of hiking, biking, and equestrian trails; a 50-foot fishing pier; a boat launch; and an historic circa-1880 manor house. Almost universally ADA-compliant, the park prides itself on being accessible to visitors of all abilities. That means being in a wheelchair or on crutches is no barrier to enjoying nearly all the park's facilities. *Greenwell State Park, 25420 Rosedale Manor Ln., Hollywood, MD 20636; (301) 872-5688; dnr2.maryland.gov.*

Jefferson Patterson Park and Museum: Home of the Maryland Archaeological Conservation Laboratory—which houses more than 8 million artifacts—the Jefferson Patterson Park and Museum is a unique destination you don't want to miss. Spread across 560 acres along the Patuxent River, the park includes the usual suspects—from a visitor's center and hiking trails to gorgeous waterfront views—to the highly unusual ones: namely, 70-plus identified archaeological sites documenting 9,000 years of human civilization, an impressive number of interactive exhibits, and a re-created Indian village. Each summer, the public is invited to participate in on-site archaeological digs. So bring some sunscreen, water, and a sense of adventure—who knows what you'll unearth! *The Jefferson Patterson Park and Museum, 10515 Mackall Rd., St. Leonard, MD 20685; (410) 586-8501; jefpat.org.*

Kings Landing Park: Looking much like it did during the days of Captain John Smith (who mapped the Chesapeake Bay and its tributaries in the early 1600s), Kings Landing Park offers an outdoorsy, riverfront getaway with a dose of learning thrown in for good measure. Courtesy of the Chesapeake

Bay Gateways Network, exhibits throughout the park inform visitors about the regional importance of the Patuxent River, the flora, and the fauna. With hiking trails, an equestrian ring, and plenty of access to the water for canoers, kayakers, and anglers, Kings Landing has a little something for everyone. *Kings Landing Park, 3255 Kings Landing Rd., Huntingtown, MD 20639; (410) 535-2661; co.cal.md.us.*

Mallows Bay: As eerie as it is enthralling, Mallows Bay, part of the Lower Potomac Water Trail, is a true maritime graveyard. The site of more than 230 intentionally sunken-because-they-were-obsolete ships (including 80-plus wooden steamships from the WWI era), the area is reachable only by boat. (Stay off the adjacent shore; it's private property.) The bay, whose wrecks have now been catalogued by naval historians, was a favorite hide-out of bootleggers during Prohibition.

PHOTO COURTESY OF TOM ROLAND

Today, a small park and boat ramp near Mallows Bay make it easier for intrepid kayakers and canoers to set out on a unique adventure amid seafaring relics. In 2010, the Charles County government opened a small paddle-in-only park (complete with a small beach) near Mallows Bay; plans are in the works to expand the park and make it more accessible. *Mallows Bay is located on the Potomac River in Nanjemoy, MD. For more information, visit charlescountymd.gov.*

Piney Point Lighthouse, Museum, and Historic Park: Sitting 14 miles upriver from the Chesapeake Bay, the Piney Point Lighthouse has, since 1836, illuminated the waters of the Potomac. The circular, 35-foot tower and its adjacent keeper's quarters were once a prized spot for entertaining, having hosted the likes of Teddy Roosevelt, Franklin Pierce, James Monroe, Daniel Webster, John C. Calhoun, and Kate Smith.

Today, the lighthouse is open for tours, rewarding visitors willing to climb the staircase with stunning waterfront views. The Piney Point Lighthouse Museum offers a compelling snapshot of the place's history, while the surrounding park makes for an excellent day of hiking, picnicking, kayaking, or just reveling in the surroundings. *Piney Point Lighthouse, Museum, and Historic Park, 44720 Lighthouse Rd., Piney Point, MD 20674; (301) 994-1471; co.saint-marys.md.us. Hours vary by season.*

Piscataway Indian Museum: Dedicated to preserving the history of Southern Maryland's indigenous peoples, the Piscataway Indian Museum provides a comprehensive overview of cultures far predating the arrival of European settlers. The museum's exhibits "offer a look into the history and culture of the Piscataway and other native people of the US. Each exhibit contains historical and contemporary artifacts from the Eastern Woodlands, Plains, Northwest, and Southwest, while demonstrating how location influenced tribal structure, art, and lodging." One must-see draw (among many) is the full-scale replica longhouse, the traditional Piscataway home in the era of Captain John Smith. *The Piscataway Indian Museum, 16816 Country Lane, Waldorf, MD 20601; (240) 640-7213; piscataway indians.com. The museum is closed in winter.*

Point Lookout State Park and Lighthouse: Sprawled across a peninsula formed by the Potomac River and the Chesapeake Bay, Point Lookout State Park—with its adjacent Point Lookout Lighthouse—is the ideal setting for a day (or weekend) of swimming, sunning, hiking, fishing, boating, and camping. Even more compelling, though, is the park's past as the site of the Civil War's largest prison camp (which once held over 52,000 Confederate soldiers). An on-site museum recounts the area's dubious history; old-timers and ghost hunters will tell you the whole place is haunted by the restless souls of wandering, deceased Rebels. *Point Lookout State Park and Lighthouse, 11175 Point Lookout Rd., Scotland, MD 20687; (301) 872-5688; dnr2.maryland.gov.*

Point No Point Lighthouse: Standing 2 miles out in the Chesapeake Bay from Maryland's Western Shore and 6 miles north of Point Lookout and the mouth of the Potomac River, the Point No Point Lighthouse isn't exactly easy to get to (you'll need a boat, obviously). But seeing it up close is incredibly cool. Completed in 1905, the caisson-style lighthouse includes a two-story brick keeper's quarters, a narrow gallery around the dwelling, an eight-sided lamp, and not much else. (Take more than three steps out the front door, and you'd be in the water.) Serving as a boundary marker for the US Navy's Aerial Firing Range and target area, the now-automated lighthouse—which flashes every 6 seconds—was once put on the auction block, only to be spared when its strategic importance was realized. *Visit lighthousefriends.com.*

Smallwood State Park: Named after William Smallwood, a Charles County native and the highest-ranking Marylander to serve in the Revolutionary War, the 628-acre Smallwood State Park boasts picnic and camping areas, hiking trails, a recycled-tire playground, William Smallwood's restored home (open seasonally), and plenty of waterfront fun. Multiple boat launches mean it's easy to find just the right spot to drop in your canoe or kayak, while the on-site Sweden Point Marina—located on Mattawoman Creek, a tributary of the Potomac River—is ideal for larger vessels and features 50 boat slips and access to some of the region's best fishing. *Smallwood State Park, 2750 Sweden Point Rd., Marbury, MD 20658; dnr2.maryland.gov.*

St. Clements Island Museum and State Park: On March 25, 1634, the first English settlers, sailing aboard the *Ark* and the *Dove*, landed at St. Clements Island. See where it all started during a tour of the 40-acre St. Clements Island Park. Situated in the Potomac River and accessible only by boat, the island's most compelling features include a memorial cross dedicated to those first Marylanders, along with a re-created Blackistone Lighthouse. Boat tours are available via the *Water Taxi II* on weekends during the park's open season. Call ahead for departure times. On the mainland, the St. Clements Island Museum tells the story of the settlers' lives in England through exhibits, watercraft, and the "Little Red Schoolhouse," a replica 19th-century one-room school. *The St. Clements Island Museum and State Park, 38370 Point Breeze Rd., Colton's Point, MD 20626; (301) 769-2222; co.saint-marys.md.us. Hours vary by season.*

Charles County

Captain Billy's Crab House, 11495 Popes Creek Rd., Newburg, MD 20664; (301) 932-4323; captbillys.com. Billy Robertson may have only been 9 years old when he sold his first crabs on Popes Creek, but the kid clearly knew what he was doing. Today, Captain Billy's Crab House, established in 1947, continues what he started by serving up some of Southern Maryland's best seafood in surroundings that say, "Yeah, of course T-shirts and flip-flops are okay!" Whether you motor in by car or drift in by boat, you'll want to bring your appetite. Captain Billy's doesn't ignore its landlubber guests—dishes like mesquite-grilled chicken salad with fresh greens, cheddar and Monterey jack cheeses, and bacon; juicy, drippy cheeseburgers; and chicken tenders with honey-mustard sauce will keep them sated—but it's seafood aficionados who truly enjoy the red-carpet treatment. What does that mean? Among many other things, it means fresh-from-the-water fried rockfish fillets, hand-breaded, deep-fried oysters with slaw and onion rings, blackened scallops with a house salad and fries, light-on-the-breading crab cakes, and baskets of Gulf shrimp with tartar and cocktail sauces for dipping. To toast the perfect meal, order a couple of cold Buds, or head to the more playful side of the drink menu and opt for a rum-soaked Captain Billy's Zombie, a turquoise Blue Hawaiian, a gin-and-fruit-juice "Blue Crab," or a Backfin (the recipe's a secret, so don't ask). For a post-feast recharge, ask for a cup of coffee with dessert; for a boozier recharge, make it Irish. Note: Captain Billy's is open seasonally.

Captain John's Crab House, 16215 Cobb Island Rd., Newburg, MD 20664; (301) 259-2315; cjcrab.com. As much a Southern Maryland landmark as it is a restaurant, Captain John's has been feeding locals and visitors to tiny Newburg since 1963. Overlooking a protected harbor—which is a nice thing to have if you're arriving by boat—the place is exceptional, even though it's far from fancy. That means it's fine to get your fingers greasy when you're tucking into a plateful of crab toast (garlic cheese bread topped with back-fin crabmeat) or an order of fried oysters. It's also fine to order an enormous seafood spread—such as the Island Platter, featuring your choice of crab cakes, deviled crab, fried oysters, fried fish, fried shrimp, and fried clams (want fries with that?)—and somehow polish off the entire thing without giving a single bite to your tablemates. On the other hand, if you're only feeling a little bit peckish, you may want to go with one of Captain John's lighter offerings. A simple, succulent broiled tilapia or flounder fillet with a side of veggies or a salad might be all you need to scratch your seafood-loving itch. (At least for today; come back soon for a deep-fried bacchanal.) Whatever you order, end your visit to Captain John's with a stroll along its short dock. There's just something about being on the water, isn't there?

Casey Jones, 417 E. Charles St., La Plata, MD 20646; (301) 392-5116; casey-jones.com; @caseyjonespub. Feeding La Plata residents and guests to the area for more than 3 decades, Casey Jones is a Southern Maryland institution. Although it bills itself as simply "a place where friends get together to have a great time and enjoy yummy food and tasty beverages," that modest description belies the top-quality dishes served at its tables. From fresh tuna flown in from Hawaii, to garden-fresh salads and hand-tossed pizza, Casey Jones sets a high standard for all its offerings. And nowhere is that more apparent than in the seafood section of the menu. Whether you're in the mood for grilled wild Tasmanian sockeye salmon with lemon arugula risotto and asparagus in a tarragon vinaigrette, Parmesan-crusted scallops with pasta and a vegetable-marinara sauce, orange roughy with Brussels sprouts, or a shrimp salad croissant with lettuce and tomato, you'll find something succulent here. A rotating roster of beers on tap, plus a selection of wines chosen to pair perfectly with its entrees, makes Casey Jones an ideal choice for a special occasion. And the over-the-top dessert menu—featuring wild berry bread pudding with vanilla ice cream, a cranberry cheesecake sundae, strawberry shortcake baked Alaska, and Happy "Un-Birthday" Cake—turns every day into an occasion!

Gilligan's Pier, 11535 Popes Creek Rd., Newburg, MD 20664; (301) 259-4514; gilliganspier.com; @GilligansPier. Looking for a restaurant with its own beach, water-taxi service, and (believe it or not) private island? Head to Gilligan's Pier, "home of the Tropical Beach Party." Along with its stunning view of the Potomac River, Gilligan's Pier offers some pretty stunning options in the entertainment department (not that the palm-tree-adorned tiki bar isn't entertaining enough). Play volleyball, horseshoes, or cornhole before—or after—eating, or just sip your glass of "swamp water" or "pier punch" while waiting for your food to arrive. And what excellent food it is. Playful vibe aside, Gilligan's is serious about its menu—and about supporting local watermen and farmers whenever possible. Everything is made fresh daily, which means the seafood linguini hasn't been sitting in the fridge for a week, the crawfish haven't been hanging out under a heat lamp all day, and the rockfish didn't arrive on a flatbed from points unknown. Family-friendly during the day, Gilligan's turns into a party at night. Think live bands and other draws, flowing drinks, and a raucous good time. Now imagine it happening as the sun sets across the water while you and your friends sway to the music and tuck into a pile of steamed blue crabs. Is there a better way to spend an evening?

Port Tobacco Restaurant, 7536 Shirley Blvd., Port Tobacco, MD 20677; (301) 392-0007; porttobaccorestaurant.com; @PortTobacco Rest. Live music, a waterfront view, and bushels of fresh steamed crabs? What's not to love about the Port Tobacco Restaurant? Nothing, say diners in the know! Kick your meal off with a straight-from-the-sea appetizer:

MARITIME MUST-SEES
The Southern Maryland Blue Crabs

You know you're in serious seafood country when the local baseball team is named after a crustacean. And that's just what you'll find in Waldorf, where the Southern Maryland Blue Crabs have been packing the park for nearly a decade.

A member of the Atlantic League of Professional Baseball Clubs, the Blue Crabs (part owned by Major League Baseball hall-of-famer and former Baltimore Oriole Brooks Robinson) have become a Charles County institution, providing families and other sports lovers with an opportunity to enjoy some big-time fun in an affordable, small-town atmosphere.

Special promotions are often the name of the game at the team's Regency Furniture Stadium, where draws include fireworks, Beer & Wings Thursdays, and, no surprise here, a monthly crab feast. What else would you expect from a team whose mascot is Pinch the Crab and whose league rivals include the Camden Riversharks and the Bridgeport Bluefish?
Learn more about the Southern Maryland Blue Crabs at somdbluecrabs.com.

How about an order of crab and spinach dip with caramelized onions and pita bread; sea scallops wrapped in applewood-smoked bacon and served with honey barbecue sauce; a soft pretzel topped with crab, cheddar-jack cheese, and Old Bay; or some fried mahi nuggets with Thai chili dipping sauce? Sound wonderful? Well, it only gets better from there! For the main event, go for a fish taco with mango salsa and "boom boom" sauce; the 8-ounce Ports fillet, served with garlic mashed potatoes and veggies; an oyster po' boy smothered in Creole remoulade; or a dozen Maryland blue crabs steamed to perfection. If you happen to stop by during Friday happy hour, enjoy dollar beers at the bar. Every night, you'll enjoy the playful cocktails (from the "Malibu Bucket" to the "Vegas Bomb"), flip-flops-are-fine dress code, and laid-back vibe. Who could possibly be stressed out in a setting this relaxed?

The Prime Street Grille, 4680 Crain Hwy., White Plains, MD 20695; (301) 392-0510; theprimestreetgrille.com. True, The Prime Street Grille is famous for its steak, but it's what it does with the "surf" part of surf and turf that makes it a must-try eatery for serious seafood lovers. So leave the 22-ounce rib eye to your shellfish-averse dining companions (why did you bring them, anyway?), and head straight for the undersea offerings. For a truly local taste, opt for the Chesapeake Bay rockfish served with tomato and shallot beurre blanc, the jumbo lump crab cakes with remoulade, or the oyster po' boy (available only at lunch). Better yet, throw calories to the wind and go all in on an order of lobster and crab macaroni and cheese. Rich with chunks of seafood and creamy gruyère, the decadent dish easily requires three extra spin classes, but it'll be worth it. The same goes for the sweeter side of the menu. A slice of vanilla cheesecake, red velvet cake, or chocolate fudge cake—perhaps accompanied by an after-dinner glass of Remy Martin VSOP or Hennessey VS—to wind down the proceedings doesn't just make sense, it's practically mandatory. You're doing those three extra spin classes next week, remember?

The Rivers Edge Restaurant, 7320 Benedict Ave., Benedict, MD 20612; (301) 274-2828; riversedgebenedict.com. Nestled along the shoreline of the beautiful Patuxent River, the Rivers Edge Restaurant welcomes diners year-round to its casual, family-friendly eatery. Boaters can pull up for dockside carryout service, but why not drop anchor and have a seat on the patio or waterfront deck instead? Start off with a cocktail or cold beer, and then dive into the Rivers Edge's many seafood offerings.

If you're not all that famished, head to the appetizer section of the menu. That's where you'll find just-the-right-size-to-share options like crispy shrimp wontons, crab fries (french fries topped with crab dip, cheese, and by-request bacon), vegetable crab soup, and mussels cooked with wine, butter, and garlic sauce and served with garlic bread. Or loosen your jeans a notch and order up a blackened, broiled, or fried rockfish fillet stuffed with crab imperial; a steamer platter of lobster tail, mussels, shrimp, and snow crab legs; teriyaki-glazed tilapia; broiled scallops; a shrimp po' boy wrap with lettuce, tomato, and bayou sauce; or a basketful of popcorn shrimp with fries and slaw on the side. The catch of the day changes frequently, so you'll just have to stop by to see which of Poseidon's treasures happens to be in the spotlight at a particular time. Whatever the fish may be, it'll be even better with a side of hush puppies!

St. Mary's County

Blue Wind Gourmet, 22803 Gunston Dr., Lexington Park, MD 20653; (301) 904-1454; bluewindgourmet.com. Most restaurants don't have mission statements, but Blue Wind Gourmet isn't like most restaurants. Committed to "Producing high-quality products and exceed customer expectations . . . using earth-friendly packaging made from sugarcane and other natural materials which are biodegradable and compostable . . . having the smallest carbon footprint possible on the land and watershed . . . and buying local whenever possible," Blue Wind Gourmet lives its creed. Step into proprietor Rob Plant's hybrid restaurant/spirits shop/brewpub/carryout and you'll discover an impressive array of wines, whiskey, scotch, and beer, plus a menu that's heavy on fresh, organic ingredients and light on pretense. Kick things off by eating your veggies—courtesy of a simple green salad or (even better) an antipasto plate complete with roasted tomatoes, roasted red peppers, fresh mozzarella, fresh basil, and toasted ciabatta and focaccia, all glistening with roasted garlic olive oil—before diving into something from the sea. Chilled shrimp cocktail, pan-seared rare tuna marinated in sesame soy sauce, a Cajun shrimp wrap with green tomatoes and remoulade, catfish with pepper jack cheese and avocado, and crab cakes are just some of the undersea offerings at Blue Wind Gourmet. (Just remember: This place takes its "fresh, local, sustainable" mantra seriously; if ethically procured seafood isn't available at a particular time, it won't appear on that day's menu.) Diners on the move can grab a boxed lunch to go; gluten-free eaters can choose from their own separate menu; and just about everyone can savor the daily wine and whiskey tastings. Seafood, spirits, and sustainability: What's not to love?

Cafe des Artistes, 41655 Fenwick St., Leonardtown, MD 20650; (301) 997-0500; cafedesartistes.ws. Authentic French cuisine in the heart of Chesapeake Bay country? *Oui!* Since 1999, Chef Loïc Jaffres has been feeding—and wowing—diners in downtown Leonardtown with his well-thought-out, accessible menu. A member of the prestigious Academie Culinaire de France, the Moroccan-born chef presides over a four-star establishment that's remarkably friendly and unstuffy. (So leave your black-tie finery and pince-nez at home, unless you're dying to wear it.) Although many of Cafe des Artistes' dishes star beef, lamb, or pork, Chef Loïc puts a masterful Gallic spin on several seafood offerings, too. Start with an appetizer of *Les Moules Bistro* (mussels served escargot-style, with garlic butter and Provençale sauce), *Les Crevettes Scampi* (shrimp scampi), or *La Coquille de Crabe* (creamy crab dip), and then move on to the main event. Whether you opt for *La Poitrine de Poulet au Crabe* (cafe chicken 'n crab) or the more exotic *Le Thon Sauté* (pepper-encrusted pan-seared tuna with green peppercorn sauce), you'll be delighted. Pair your meal with a chilled glass of Pouilly-Fuisse or Hippolyte-Reverdy Sancerre, and you'll feel like you've been transported to a brasserie on the Seine. Better yet, choose

a local pour from Slack Winery or Port of Leonardtown Winery, both of which get the star treatment on the wine list. One sip, and you won't be transported anywhere—instead, you'll be pleasantly reminded that you're already exactly where you want to be.

Courtney's, 48290 Wynne Rd., Ridge, MD 20680; (301) 872-4403; courtneysseafoodrestaurant.com. Way, way off the beaten path and something of a dive (in the best sense of that term), Courtney's is the place to go when you want good, straightforward seafood without a lot of hand-holding. (Translation: Don't expect the staff to come racing and fawn over you; they'll get there when they get there.) Owner Tom Courtney mans the front of the house, while his wife, Julie, works her magic in the kitchen (sometimes using fish caught that morning by her husband). The dining room is no-frills, no fuss; the seafood is outstanding. If it's lunchtime, try a basket of oysters (when they're in season) or shrimp and fries, a bowl of spicy vegetable crab soup, or a good ol' tuna fish sandwich. Later in the day, go bigger: Opt for the local fish stuffed with crab and covered in cheesy cream sauce; the soft crab dinner; or a platter of broiled sea scallops. Entrees include a trip to the salad bar (or, as the menu warns, one trip to the salad bar), soup, and homemade rolls, and everything goes great with a bottle of Rolling Rock, Bud, or Yuengling. There's wine on the menu, too. Just don't go looking for a sommelier.

The Front Porch, 22770 Washington St., Leonardtown, MD 20650; (301) 997-1009; thefrontporchsomd.com. A comfortable community gathering spot as much as a restaurant, the genteel—though never stuffy—Front Porch is as committed to its customers as it is to the environment. Located inside the historic Sterling House in downtown Leonardtown, the eco-friendly eatery feels like a throwback (in a great way) to an unhurried, less frantic age when people had time to savor the food on their plates and the company around the table. Although its focus is on Southern coastal cuisine, the Front Porch offers guests a wide variety of menu options, many focused squarely on the sea. What does that mean for patrons? Rockfish "bites"—panko-breaded, wild-caught Atlantic rockfish served with house-made remoulade; succulent crab cakes rich with lump meat, Old Bay, herbs, and scallion aioli, all served on grilled brioche; beer-battered rockfish sandwiches with lettuce, tomatoes, and onions, all served on toasted ciabatta; a daily fresh fish offering; chilled, pan-seared tuna rolled in black and white sesame seeds and served with wasabi soy sauce and pickled ginger; and

MARITIME MUST-SEES
Maryland Water Trails

MARYLAND
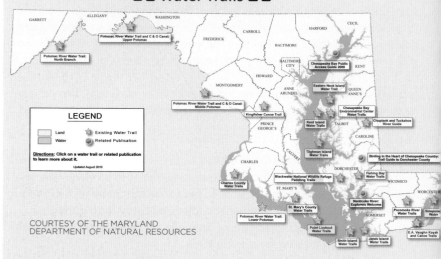 Water Trails

LEGEND

- **Land**
- **Water**
- ★ Existing Water Trail
- **Related Publication**

Directions: Click on a water trail or related publication to learn more about it.

Updated August 2010

COURTESY OF THE MARYLAND
DEPARTMENT OF NATURAL RESOURCES

Not only does the Free State take its seafood seriously, but it also takes the water its seafood *comes from* seriously. In fact, there's an entire program—the Maryland Water Trails Program—dedicated to celebrating the state's navigable waterways and encouraging folks to explore them.

Administered through the Maryland Department of Natural Resources (DNR), the Water Trails Program helps local governments map and promote existing waterways (600 miles' worth, so far); create and distribute user-friendly information about those waterways; and promote boating and paddling safety.

For a route to be considered an official waterway, it must:

- Follow a clearly identified route along a waterway; that route must be recognized by DNR Boating Services.

- Contain public-access points; those points must be open to the general public.

- Have an existing guide or map already drawn.

- Include some kind of interpretive component that emphasizes boating safety and/or regulations; promotes the stewardship of natural resources; and educates users about a particular setting's historical, environmental, or cultural significance.

Popular water trails in the Chesapeake Bay region include the:

- Blackwater National Wildlife Refuge Paddling Trails (Eastern Shore)

- Charles County Water Trails (Southern Maryland)

- Janes Island Water Trails (Eastern Shore)

- Lower Potomac River Water Trail (Southern Maryland)

- Lower Susquehanna River Water Trail (Upper Bay)

- Point Lookout Water Trails (Southern Maryland)

- Sinepuxent Bay Water Trail (Eastern Shore)

- St. Mary's County Water Trails (Southern Maryland)

- Tilghman Island Water Trails (Eastern Shore)

For more information on the Maryland Water Trails Program, visit dnr.state.md.us/boating/mdwatertrails.

a fantastic crab-pesto grilled flatbread sandwich with homemade basil pesto, fresh mozzarella cheese, roasted red peppers, and baby spinach. A well-cultivated wine list makes it easy to pair your meal with an impeccable pour, while the clever cocktail menu makes it nearly impossible to stop at just one drink.

The Ruddy Duck Seafood & Ale House, 16800 Piney Point Rd., Piney Point, MD 20674; (301) 994-9944; ruddyduckbrewery.com. Like all great mottoes, The Ruddy Duck's is straightforward and easy to understand: to "create a fun and exciting atmosphere; serve authentic made-from-scratch food; provide gracious and hospitable service; [and] deliver it all at a great value." Successful on all accounts, it's no reason the restaurant—with locations in Piney Point and Dowell—is such a popular hangout among locals and visitors alike. Illustrating its support for local farmers and watermen, The Ruddy Duck's menu is heavy on fresh, seasonal produce and sustainably caught seafood. That means you can feel good about tucking into an award-winning crab cake sandwich, knowing its star ingredient didn't pull into the Chesapeake region flash-frozen on a flatbed truck. (Go ahead and add lettuce and tomato; they likely didn't travel far, either.) Spice up dinnertime by ordering the shrimp rancheros—grilled jumbo shrimp smothered with ranchero sauce, cheddar cheese, and salsa verde—or jazz things up Louisiana-style with a plateful of Cajun catfish topped with pico de gallo and served with a side of rice pilaf. Whatever you opt for, be sure to wash it down with a house-brewed India Pale Ale, Oktoberfest-style lager, or other signature beer. Suds and seafood: a match made in heaven!

Scheible's Crabpot Restaurant, 48342 Wynne Rd., Ridge, MD 20680; (301) 872-0025; scheibles.com. Scheible's may be part restaurant, part motor lodge, and part marina, but it's fully authentic. Wowing diners for 60-plus years with its fresh seafood and fantastic location along Smith Creek, it's the kind of place that quickly turns into your *favorite* place. You can count on seafood stalwarts aplenty on the menu—including crab cakes, jumbo scallops, beer-battered Gulf shrimp, and grilled fish of the day—along with the sides (coleslaw, french fries, applesauce, house salad, etc.) that you'd expect. What you may not expect is that Scheible's will happily help you book a charter boat with a local captain so that you can try catching your favorite fish yourself. (And if you're staring at a crack-of-dawn departure time, you'll appreciate the fact that Scheible's is a motel, too.) Of course, if you're more into eating food than trolling for it, best just to sit back and let the folks at Scheible's feed you. They're awfully good at it.

Spinnakers Restaurant & Mermaid Bar, 16244 Miller Wharf Rd., Ridge, MD 20680; (301) 872-5020; spinnakerswaterfrontdining .com. Sure, guests at Spinnakers Restaurant & Mermaid Bar can enjoy free Wi-Fi and the big game du jour on the flat-screen TV, but with views of Smith Creek outside and stellar seafood offerings on the plate, why would they want to? Serving breakfast, lunch, and dinner—with a unique menu for each meal—Spinnakers gives diners plenty of delicious options to choose from. At midday, that might mean a deep-fried soft-shell crab sandwich with lettuce, tomato, and tartar sauce; a broiled fish sandwich on a toasted roll; or a basket of clam strips with a side of fries. Come suppertime, Spinnakers kicks the offerings up a notch, wooing hungry patrons with appetizers like rockfish nuggets or fried calamari, plus an array of entrees, including beer-battered jumbo scallops, crab-topped chicken Chesapeake, seafood Alfredo, and the blackened fish of the day. Serious eaters should swing by for the Thursday Night Seafood Special—crab legs, shrimp, and crab balls, plus a choice of two sides—or for Friday's all-you-can-eat steamed shrimp. Whenever you visit, chances are proprietor Kay Carter will be on hand to make sure everything's cooked just to your liking. Odds are, it will be. Note: Guests arriving by boat may dock for free in a transient slip (call ahead for availability).

The Tides Restaurant, 46580 Expedition Dr., Lexington Park, MD 20653; (301) 862-5303; thetidesrestaurant.net. "As a gourmet restaurant in the heart of St. Mary's County, we strive to provide our guests with creative, freshly prepared food utilizing seasonal ingredients produced around Southern Maryland, as well as the best ingredients from all over the world." What does that mean for diners tucking into lunch or dinner at this popular Lexington Park eatery? It means whatever graces their plates will be light-years away from the overprocessed, purposely overseasoned excuse for seafood found on many big chains' menus. (Even a serious dousing of Old Bay—delicious though it may be—can't save subpar fish.) So expect the haddock sandwich with tomato pesto and feta cheese on focaccia to be flaky and rich; the rare ahi tuna, crusted in cracked black pepper, seared briefly in sesame oil with soy sauce, wasabi, and pickled ginger to taste authentically of the sea; and the decadent crab dip with garlic-oil-brushed pita points to be as good for your soul as it is bad for your thighs. And because The Tides takes seriously its commitment to buying seasonally as well as locally, its menu changes often. So even

The Sea Change

The Cove Point Lighthouse keeper's quarters in Lusby may have recently opened to overnight guests, but its metamorphosis took nearly a decade.

"The site was turned over to the museum in 2000. Shortly after that, we began the planning process for its use," explains Vanessa Gill, development director at the nearby Calvert Marine Museum, which oversees the duplex-like quarters.

"Renovations to the sea wall, the lighthouse tower, and finally to the roof of the keeper's house occurred over several years."

Restoring the circa-1828 Calvert County home, which is listed on the National Register of Historic Places, required a dramatic overhaul.

"Since it had been last renovated in the 1980s, there were few to none of its original features in place," says Gill.

"Taking it down to the studs allowed us to upgrade the electric, plumbing, heating, and insulation, and to bring back as much of its original charm as possible."

To capture that charm, the floors were refinished, modern-day closets were removed, and historically correct windows were reinstalled.

Although Gill decorated much of the interior—which is airy and welcoming—herself, she's quick to point out that a project of this magnitude required a dedicated team working very, very hard.

though it always offers *something* exquisite on the menu, it refuses to offer *everything* all the time. Good restaurants know Mother Nature's genius can't be rushed; the finest, freshest ingredients are always worth the wait.

"The key people involved were Doug Alves, the museum's director; Richard Dodds, the museum's curator of maritime history, who oversaw the whole project and even did much of the work; and carpenter Tom Benson," she says.

"And local artist Ann Crain helped design the kitchens, select all the finishes, and purchase all the furnishings."

Donations from numerous businesses, including Tricon Construction, Owens Corning, Woodburn Cabinets, and Building Specialties, helped make it all possible, and the wizardry of local woodworkers like Jim Wilson—who used wood salvaged from the dismantled Cedar Point Lighthouse to craft the kitchen tables—made it magic.

Proceeds from rental of the quarters—which can accommodate up to 16 guests when the duplex's interior doors are opened to create one large space—will support the Calvert Marine Museum and go toward an endowment to cover the long-term care of the Cove Point Lighthouse property.

"It took us almost 10 years to raise enough support to do these renovations," says Gill.

"We don't want the next generation of caretakers to have to work as hard as we did to care for this beautiful site."

The Cove Point Lighthouse keeper's home, located at 3500 Lighthouse Blvd. in Lusby, is available for rental year-round. Proceeds benefit the Calvert Marine Museum. For more information, call (410) 474-5370 or visit calvertmarinemuseum.com.

SEAFOOD & SEA-FUN: ANNUAL FESTIVALS & ACTIVITIES

January

"Bald Pocomoke!" Eagle Watch, Eastern Shore; (410) 632-2566; dnr.state.md.us. Seafood isn't the only thing that makes the Chesapeake Bay so special. Its impressive population of bald eagles and bald cypress is right up there, too. So head to the Milburn Landing area of Pocomoke River State Park, where a park naturalist will guide you on your discovery of some of the bay's mightiest birds and most prolific trees. Snow Hill, MD.

February

Crawfish Boil & Muskrat Stew Fest, Eastern Shore; tinyurl.com/l773tn8. This annual festival in downtown Cambridge features live Cajun music, traditional Louisiana and Eastern Shore foods (including crawfish, muskrat, and oysters), hot-sauce tastings, seasonal libations, and more. The festival is scheduled for the day after the annual World Muskrat Skinning Championships, held as part of the National Outdoor Show. Cannery Way Park, Cambridge, MD.

March

Annapolis Oyster Roast & Sock Burning, Western Shore; (410) 295-0104; amaritime.org. Say "Goodbye, winter! Hello, spring!" in this annual celebration of no-more-socks weather. Listen to a recitation of "Ode to Equinox," enjoy live music and great food, and then peel off your argyles and toss 'em in the flames! The Annapolis Maritime Museum, Annapolis, MD.

A Taste of Solomons, Southern Maryland; solomonsmaryland .com. Bring your appetite to this 1-day food festival showcasing the many wonderful places to eat in lovely waterfront Solomons. Proceeds benefit the Solomons Business Association's annual July 4th Fireworks Display. At participating restaurants. Solomons, MD.

April

Taste of the Town, Eastern Shore; tasteofchestertown.com. Spend an afternoon sampling signature dishes from Chestertown and Kent County's finest restaurants and caterers. Featured goodies include everything from upscale cuisine to down-home classics like Maryland crab soup. Downtown Chestertown, MD.

Ward World Championship Wildfowl Carving Competition and Art Festival, Eastern Shore; ococean.com. An international event where carvers, collectors, and visitors descend on Ocean City for a weekend featuring everything from decorative works of art to functional hunting decoys. Roughly 1,200 different wildfowl carvings representing more than 150 species will be on display at the most prestigious competition of its kind in the world. Roland E. Powell Convention Center, Ocean City, MD.

May

Caroline Paddlefest, Eastern Shore; carolinechamber.org. Enjoy a 7.7-mile paddle down the Choptank River followed by a family-friendly festival at the Choptank River Yacht Club. Paddlers will depart Greensboro for a downriver drift to Denton. Greensboro and Denton, MD.

Dennis Point Marina Spring Fishin' Buddies Derby, Southern Maryland; CharlesCountyParks.com. Catch the excitement during this adult-child fishing tourney, which awards prizes for the biggest (and most) fish caught, along with special honors for snagging trout or catfish. Gilbert Run Park, Charlotte Hall, MD.

Fishing Derby, Eastern Shore; tourcaroline.com. This free, family-friendly event encourages the littlest anglers to come out for a day of fun and fishing. Prizes will be awarded, and all participants get a free T-shirt and lunch. BYO pole and tackle; bait is provided. Greensboro Carnival Grounds, Greensboro, MD.

Havre de Grace Decoy & Wildlife Art Festival, Upper Bay; decoy museum.com. Decoy Carvers, wildlife artists, hunting and fishing suppliers, and outdoor guide services will be displaying and selling their works. Visitors will also enjoy dog demonstrations, carving competitions, and more. Havre de Grace Decoy Museum, Havre de Grace, MD.

Marines Helping Marines Fishing Tournament, Upper Bay; woundedmarinefishing.com. A fishing competition, barbecue, raffle, and all-around great party, the annual Marines Helping Marines Fishing Tournament provides support for injured Marine Corps personnel. Anchor Marina, North East, MD.

Maritime Republic of Eastport's .05K, Western Shore; themre.org. "The Maritime Republic of Eastport, an enlightened democracy based in the Eastport neighborhood of Annapolis, has become a force in the community since its founding on Super Bowl Sunday 1998." Its annual "Not So Ultimate Competition of Strength, Endurance, and Determination" .05K bridge run (complete with a hydration station at the halfway point) begins promptly at the crack o' noon.

Potomac River Waterfowl Show, Southern Maryland; cfsomd.org/ waterfowlshow.html. Award-winning artists showcase their masterpieces—from wildlife art to hand-carved wooden decoys—at this popular annual event. St. Mary's County Fairgrounds, Leonardtown, MD.

Rising Sun Youth Fishing Derby, Upper Bay; (410) 658-5353. Open to anglers 12 and under, this annual fishing extravaganza is sponsored by the Rising Sun Chamber of Commerce. Community Pond, Rising Sun, MD.

Rockfish Tournament, Southern Maryland; dennispointmarina .net. Open to both amateurs and pros, this 2-day tournament offers paid entrants free transient dockage and gratis food during the awards ceremony. Dennis Point Marina & Campground, Drayden, MD.

Solomons Maritime Festival, Southern Maryland; calvertmarine museum.com. Featuring the Antique Boat and Marine Engine Show, traditional foods, free 30-minute cruises, crab-picking and oyster-shucking lessons, live gospel and old-time music, and more, this family-friendly festival is a can't-miss annual event! Calvert Marine Museum, Solomons, MD.

Taste of Indian Head, Southern Maryland; charlescountymd.gov. Enjoy arts, crafts, pony rides, face painting, vendors, and more, all while savoring the finest foods Indian Head has to offer. Village Green, Indian Head, MD.

Wednesday Night Sailboat Races, Western Shore; annapolisyc .com. Head dockside for these popular midweek races (which run through August) where 150-plus boats sail around several marks in the Chesapeake Bay before heading back to Spa Creek for a finish in front of the Annapolis Yacht Club. Annapolis, MD.

June

Honfest, Western Shore; baltimore.org/honfest. Don't miss this silly celebration of all things Charm City! Think beehive hairdos, live music, great food, and funky, only-in-Maryland wares for sale. See you in downtown Baltimore, hon!

Oxford Cardboard Boat Races, Eastern Shore; oxfordcbr.org. Build a sea-worthy cardboard craft, cross your fingers, and hope your vessel stays afloat along the shallow shores of the Tred Avon River. And if it doesn't? No worries. The monies raised still support a great cause—Special Olympics Maryland! Oxford, MD.

Patuxent River Wade-In, Southern Maryland; jefpat.org. Join state and local dignitaries as they wade into the river at Jefferson Patterson Park and Museum in St. Leonard during this annual event that tests the water's clarity. It's all part of an effort to bring attention to Maryland's waterways and the importance of keeping them pristine. Enjoy environmental demonstrations, exhibits, and activities, too.

Rock Hall Rockfish Tournament, Eastern Shore; marylandwater men.com. Hook the Big One during this 3-day pro-am competition in Rock Hall, and you'll end up $10,000 richer. That'll buy a lot of bait!

Rockfish Tournament, Upper Bay; portdepositcc.org. Drop your line and try to snag Maryland's official state fish in Marina Park, Port Deposit. Anglers of all ages welcome; lots of cash prizes up for grabs!

St. Mary's County Crab Festival, Southern Maryland; stmarys crabfestival.com. It's an all-day celebration of St. Mary's County's crab culture and cooking. That means lots of steamed crabs, crab cakes, crab soup, and other undersea delicacies for sale. Enjoy the on-site car and bike show, regional crafters, live music, and children's activities, too! Leonardtown Lions Club, Leonardtown, MD.

Youth Fishing Day, Eastern Shore; fws.gov/blackwater. Come out for a kid-friendly day of catch-and-release fishing on Hog Range Pond. Little anglers who pre-register will receive a T-shirt, lunch, and other freebies. BYO equipment, if possible. Blackwater National Wildlife Refuge, Cambridge, MD.

July

The Big Fish Classic, Eastern Shore; bigfishclassic.com. Entrants in this overnight, offshore tournament vie to catch the heaviest Atlantic Ocean fish they can reel in. Will it be marlin, tuna, swordfish, shark, or something else? Talbot Street Pier, Ocean City, MD.

Cambridge Classic Powerboat Regatta, Eastern Shore; cpbra .com. Experience thrills and spills at this American Powerboat Association-sanctioned inboard-hydroplane and flat-bottom boats race! Visit with the racing teams, admire the vessels, and enjoy great food and drinks, too. Great Marsh Park, Cambridge, MD.

OtterMania!, Southern Maryland; calvertmarinemuseum.com. Lovable otters Bubbles and Squeak are the star attraction at this family-friendly day celebrating all things furry, watery, and adorable. Make otter-themed crafts, learn how to play like the critters do, and listen to Native American myths about "brother otter." The Calvert Marine Museum, Solomons, MD.

Pirate Fest Weekend & Pirate Encampment, Upper Bay; thelock housemuseum.org. Discover where Maryland's first act of piracy occurred! Visit an authentic pirate encampment, complete with skirmishes, music, period clothing, demonstrations, and more. The Susquehanna Museum at the Lock House, Havre de Grace, MD.

Taste of Cambridge Crab Cook-Off and Festival, Eastern Shore; CambridgeMainStreet.com. Enjoy a free street festival featuring live music, kids' activities, a professional crab-picking competition, souvenirs, gallery openings, late shopping, and, of course, a crab cook-off! It's the town's biggest event of the year! Historic Downtown Cambridge, MD.

August

Havre de Grace Seafood Festival, Upper Bay; hdgseafoodfestival .org. With tons of arts and crafts for sale, food vendors, live entertainment, a silent auction, classic car show, and too many undersea delicacies to name, this free event is a can't-miss for seafood lovers and fun lovers alike! Downtown Havre de Grace, MD.

Pirates and Wenches Fantasy Weekend, Eastern Shore; rockhall pirates.com. Arrrrrrr! It's time for a family-friendly weekend of sea shanty sing-alongs, treasure hunts, a beach party, a dinghy flotilla and race, costume contests, live entertainment, and general silly mayhem. Both buccaneers and landlubbers are welcome, and eye patches and peg legs are highly encouraged! Main Street, Rock Hall, MD.

Rotary Club of Annapolis Crab Feast, Western Shore; (800) 327-1982; annapolisrotary.org. Dig in at the world's largest crab feast—it's for a great cause! The yearly all-you-can-eat-and-drink extravaganza includes big male crabs, sweet corn on the cob, Maryland vegetable crab soup, and more. There's a bake sale and cake raffle, too, and all proceeds from the event benefit local organizations and nonprofits. What's not to love? Navy-Marine Corps Memorial Stadium, Annapolis, MD.

Seafood Feast-I-Val, Eastern Shore; seafoodfeastival.com. You may want to loosen your belt before tucking into the spread at Cambridge's annual Seafood Feast-I-Val. With all-you-can-eat steamed crabs, Maryland crab soup, fried fish, fried clams, and sweet potato fries being served up, your self-control doesn't stand a chance. Live music, a car show, and historic town tours add to the party atmosphere, and the setting—along the Choptank River—couldn't be prettier. Sailwinds Park, Cambridge, MD.

White Marlin Open, Eastern Shore; whitemarlinopen.com. Ocean City's most famous fishing tournament lures skilled anglers hoping to reel in a prize-winning white marlin, blue marlin, or tuna. With serious prize money on the line, no one wants to let the Big One get away! Ocean City, MD.

September

Hard Crab Derby, Eastern Shore; nationalhardcrabderby.com. Crisfield isn't known as the "Crab Capital of the World" for nothing! So come out for this incredible ode to all things fishy and delicious held each Labor Day Weekend at Somers Cove Marina. From the legendary hard-crab derby—which is just what it sounds like: a ridiculously silly, ridiculously wonderful "race" that pits the clawed competitors against one another in a contest of speed and will (okay, it's really just random scuttering)—to live music, rides, crab-picking and cooking contests, a pageant, and loads of fabulous food, the event has something for everyone. Don't miss it!

Maritime Museum Crab Feast, Upper Bay; hdgmaritimemuseum .org. Say, "Not so fast, fall!" during this family-friendly event featuring all-you-can-eat Maryland seafood and all-you-can-drink beer. Who cares if Labor Day has already come and gone? Held at the Elks Lodge, Havre de Grace, and proceeds benefit the Havre de Grace Maritime Museum.

Maryland Seafood Festival, Western Shore; mdseafoodfestival .com. "Savor the Bay" during this popular weekend festival in Sandy Point State Park, Annapolis, full of food, live entertainment, demonstrations, a crab soup cook-off, and more! And be sure to bring your appetite—some of the region's best eateries will be serving up their signature dishes.

Wine on the Beach, Eastern Shore; winefest.com. Some of the East Coast's finest wineries offer up their best pours during this popular event in Ocean City featuring live music, Chesapeake region seafood, micro-brewed beers, high-quality arts and crafts, and more.

October

Bull & Oyster Roast, Upper Bay; hdgchamber.com. Sponsored by the Havre de Grace Chamber of Commerce and held at the Havre de Grace Community Center in Havre de Grace, this come-hungry-and-leave-full event features (like the name suggests) roasted bull and oysters, plus door prizes, a silent auction, music, ice cream, and more!

Cambridge Tall Ship Schooner Rendezvous, Eastern Shore; cambridgeschoonerrendezvous.com. Tall ships from across the country gather along the Choptank River in downtown Cambridge during this unique nautical festival. Take a dockside tour of a schooner, sail the waters, dig into delicious Chesapeake region seafood and other treats, and enjoy maritime music. Be sure to take a self-guided tour of the nearby Choptank River Lighthouse, too! Long Wharf Park, Cambridge, MD.

Chesapeake Wildfowl Expo, Eastern Shore; wardmuseum.org. It's a bird! It's a plane! No, it's a bird—lots of them, in fact! Honoring the Chesapeake region's winged fauna (and the geniuses who render it in wood), the festival features thousands of museum-quality decoys, plus folk art, hunting and waterfowling paraphernalia, some serious competitions, and more. The Ward Museum of Wildfowl Art, Salisbury, MD.

Crabtoberfest, Eastern Shore; crabtoberfest.com. Think of everything you love about Oktoberfest—the oompah bands, free-flowing beer, German cuisine, and dirndl-wearing festivalgoers—and imagine how much better the event would be with steamed crabs thrown into the mix. That's Crabtoberfest! Downtown Cambridge, MD.

Fall Festival at the Susquehanna Museum, Upper Bay; thelock housemuseum.org. Celebrate the end of the Lock House's open season during this fall party featuring games, face painting, pumpkin painting, apple cider, and story time. And don't miss the "pirates" on hand to tell the story of the Lock House's nautical past! The Susquehanna Museum at the Lock House, Havre de Grace, MD.

Harbor Day at the Docks, Eastern Shore; ocharborday.com. Celebrate Ocean City's unique nautical heritage during this weekend festival. Highlights include historic exhibits, cooking and fish-cleaning demonstrations, succulent seafood, and more. Sunset Avenue, West Ocean City, MD.

Hot Sauce & Oyster Festival, Eastern Shore; crabigras.com. Dig into piles of freshly shucked oysters—and don't forget to sample some of the more than 100 hot sauces on hand, too! The fun also includes live music, vendors, beer, and more. Downtown Cambridge, MD.

***Sultana* Downrigging Weekend/Tall Ship & Wooden Boat Festival,** Eastern Shore; sultanaprojects.org. Watch vessels from around the Chesapeake Bay as they sail into Chestertown to celebrate the end of the schooner *Sultana*'s sailing season. Offering a little something for everyone, the weekend boasts a Family Day, art exhibits and classes, live museum, lectures, parties, a 5K and half-marathon, and (naturally) lots of good maritime food and fun.

The Taste of Kent Narrows, Eastern Shore; tasteofkentnarrows .org. Savor goodies from some of the area's finest restaurants and crab houses, enjoy the waterfront view, and soak up that relaxed Chesapeake Bay vibe during this afternoon devoted to good fun and good eats. Chesapeake Heritage & Visitor Center, Chester, MD.

November

Maritime Republic of Eastport's Tug O' War, Western Shore; themre.org. Come out for a day of good fun during this so-called Slaughter across the Water, where teams from Annapolis and Eastport are pitted against one another during an all-for-charity tugging match that spans Spa Creek. Win or lose, everyone will enjoy the live entertainment, food, and overall goofiness of the day. Second Street, Eastport, MD.

Waterfowl Festival, Eastern Shore; waterfowlfestival.org. Called "the ultimate weekend for the sophisticated sportsman or art lover," Easton's free Waterfowl Festival brings fabulous wildlife paintings, photos, carvings, sculptures, and other works of art together under one roof. Draws also include fly-fishing demonstrations, a sporting clays tournaments, kids' activities, a concert, and more. Various locations, downtown Easton, MD.

December

Eastport Yacht Club Lights Parade, Western Shore; (410) 263-0415; eastportyc.org. Annapolis Harbor comes "a-light" during this popular wintertime event. Vessels adorned with hundreds of glowing, twinkling lights and holiday decorations bring a dose of maritime magic to the season! Annapolis Harbor, Annapolis, MD.

RECIPES

PHOTO LICENSED BY SHUTTERSTOCK.COM

Carolyn's Crab-Shrimp Dip

Recipe courtesy of Blue Crab Cafe, Crisfield, MD

SERVES 2-4

3 heaping tablespoons backfin crabmeat
4 large shrimp, peeled and chopped
½ cup whipped cream cheese
½ cup freshly grated Parmesan cheese
½ cup pimento-cheese spread
3 shakes Worcestershire sauce
3 shakes Old Bay Seasoning
5–6 shakes Montreal Steak Seasoning
Toasted pita-bread triangles, for serving

Mix all ingredients together in a microwave-safe bowl. Microwave for 3 minutes.

Carefully remove bowl from the microwave and scrape dip into a microwave-safe glass casserole dish. Microwave for 2 more minutes, or until bubbly and heated through. Serve with toasted pita-bread triangles.

Chesapeake Sweet & Sour Crab Balls

First Place Winner, National Hard Crab Derby, Crisfield, MD
Recipe created by Mary Bradshaw of Crisfield, MD

SERVES 4-6

For the crab balls:
2 eggs
1 tablespoons mayonnaise
2 teaspoons mustard
6–8 saltine crackers, crushed
½ teaspoon Old Bay Seasoning
Salt and pepper, to taste
1 pound jumbo lump Maryland crabmeat

For the dish:
1 garlic clove, chopped
1 tablespoon olive oil
2 carrots, thinly sliced
1 green pepper, cut into small chunks
⅓ cup brown sugar
¼ cup ketchup
1 teaspoon soy sauce
¼ cup vinegar
½ cup water
1 can pineapple tidbits, drained and syrup reserved
3 tablespoons cornstarch
2 cups cooked rice

To make crab balls: Mix all ingredients except crab. Add crabmeat, mix, and shape into golf-ball-size rounds. Fry in an oiled skillet until golden brown and set aside.

To prepare dish: In a skillet, brown garlic in olive oil and remove garlic from pan. Add carrots and green pepper to pan, stir-fry until soft, and set aside.

In a saucepan, mix together brown sugar, ketchup, soy sauce, vinegar, ¼ cup water, and reserved pineapple syrup. Bring to a boil and thicken with cornstarch and ¼ water (combined to form a paste), stirring to a smooth consistency.

Add carrots, peppers, pineapple, and crab balls to sauce and serve over rice.

Crab Pesto Flatbread

Recipe courtesy of Jeff Lewis, The Front Porch, Leonardtown, MD

SERVES 1

For the basil-pesto sauce:
4 cups fresh basil leaves
5 cloves garlic
½ cup grated Parmesan
  cheese
½ cup pecans
¾ cup olive oil
Salt and pepper, to taste

For the flatbread:
1 (8-inch) freshly baked
  flatbread
1½ ounces basil-pesto sauce
¼ cup roasted red peppers
2 ounces fresh lump blue
  crabmeat
2 slices fresh Mozzarella
  cheese (sliced thin)
¼ cup fresh chopped
  spinach

PHOTOS COURTESY OF THE FRONT PORCH

To make the pesto: Place all ingredients, but just half the oil, in a food processor. Blend slowly until smooth while drizzling in the remaining oil. Set aside.

To make the flatbread: Preheat convection oven (or conventional oven) to 425°F.

Spread pesto sauce evenly over a piece of flatbread. Add roasted red peppers and crabmeat, and top with mozzarella cheese.

If using a convection oven, bake flatbread for 7 minutes. (A conventional oven may take up to twice as long.)

Remove flatbread from oven and sprinkle with fresh spinach.

To serve: Fold flatbread in half and then cut in half. Enjoy!

Crab Tart

Recipe courtesy of The Narrows, Grasonville, MD

MAKES 6

For the tart topping:
1 cup shredded provolone cheese
1 cup finely chopped spinach
½ cup grated feta cheese
¼ cup diced tomato, strained
1 tablespoon chopped fresh basil
½ teaspoon minced garlic
Crushed red pepper, to taste

Additional items needed:
1 (6-count) pack lavash flatbread
1 (6-ounce) container mascarpone cheese
1 pound fresh Maryland jumbo lump crab, picked over

Preheat oven to 375°F. Place a 12-inch pizza stone in the center of the oven and allow it to come to temperature.

In a large mixing bowl, combine all of the tart topping ingredients, lightly toss, and refrigerate.

Lay out desired amount of flatbreads on a clean, flat surface. Using a rubber spatula, evenly spread a thin layer of mascarpone cheese over the entire flatbread. Top the flatbread with a thin, even layer of the tart-topping mixture, and then add the desired amount of jumbo lump crabmeat.

Place 1 tart at a time on the preheated pizza stone and bake for 8–10 minutes or until done.

Drunken Dancing Prawns

Recipe courtesy of Blue Point Provision Company, Cambridge, MD

SERVES 2

1 tablespoon canola oil
16–20 prawns
1 ounce sake
2 cloves garlic, crushed
1 tablespoon rough-chopped
  cilantro
2 ounces shredded red onion
2 ounces julienned carrot
1 green onion, cut on bias into
  1-inch pieces
1 ounce cognac
¼ cup Thai sweet chili sauce
¼ cup canned coconut milk,
  stirred well
6 ounces steamed jasmine rice
Toasted sesame seeds

Heat oil in heavy skillet over high heat.

While the oil is heating, marinate the prawns in the sake with half the garlic and cilantro.

Sear the prawns briefly in the hot oil.

Add the red onions, carrots, green onions, and remaining garlic, and simmer to soften the vegetables.

Add the cognac, stirring to deglaze the pan.

Add the chili sauce and coconut milk. Adjust to taste, adding more chili sauce for a spicier flavor and more coconut milk for a milder taste.

Place a generous scoop of steamed rice in the center of an Asian bowl and pour the prawns and sauce over the top.

To serve, sprinkle with sesame seeds and the remaining cilantro.

Grilled Chesapeake Bay Oysters

Recipe courtesy of Chef Patrick Morrow, Ryleigh's Oyster, Federal Hill and Hunt Valley, MD

MAKES 12

¾ pound unsalted butter (preferably from
  South Mountain Creamery)
1 tablespoon minced garlic
1 tablespoon chopped fresh oregano
1 tablespoon chopped fresh thyme
1 tablespoon chopped fresh basil
1 tablespoon chopped fresh chives
¼ cup diced tomatoes
12 Maryland oysters (skinny dippers or wilds preferred)
¼ cup cheese blend*
Salt and pepper, to taste

*For the cheese blend: Combine equal parts shredded Hendricks Tomme, Hendricks Swiss, Hawks Hill Garlic Chives, and Pecorino cheeses. Use ¼ cup in the recipe; save the remainder for another use.

To prepare the dish: Place butter in a small saucepan over medium heat. When melted, add garlic, fresh herbs, and diced tomato. Stir and set aside.

Light grill to a medium flame. Shuck oysters and place them on the half shell on the hot grill. Top with butter-herb blend, allowing butter to spill over the edges of the shell (be cautious of the high flames caused by this).

Sprinkle each oyster with a pinch of the cheese blend and salt and pepper, to taste; top with additional melted butter so that the flames melt the cheese.

Once the cheese is melted, the oysters are ready. Enjoy immediately.

Lump Crab & Shrimp Ceviche

Recipe courtesy of Blackwall Hitch, Annapolis, MD

SERVES 10

For the ceviche:

¼ pound jumbo lump crabmeat
¼ pound lump crabmeat
6 large shrimp
½ red pepper, diced small
½ yellow pepper, diced small
1 jalapeño pepper, diced small
1 small red onion, diced small
2 tablespoons chopped fresh cilantro
⅓ cup oil
¼ tablespoon cumin
3 limes
1 orange
Salt and pepper, to taste
5 avocados

PHOTO COURTESY OF BLACKWALL HITCH

For the avocado cream:
1 avocado, halved and scooped out
1 cup sour cream
4 teaspoons lime juice

Cilantro leaves, for garnish
Tortilla chips, for serving

Mix crabmeat in a large bowl. Steam shrimp and shock in an ice bath. Drain, dice, and add to the crab.

Add peppers, onions, and cilantro to the mix. Stir well.

Toss with oil and cumin.

Heat limes and orange for 90 seconds in the microwave. Cut in half and squeeze into mix after removing seeds (or squeeze through a strainer).

Add salt and pepper, to taste.

Cut avocados in half and remove seeds. Set aside.

Prepare the avocado cream by mashing 1 avocado with the sour cream and lime juice. Mix well.

To serve: Fill center of avocado halves with the seafood mixture and garnish with cilantro leaves and avocado cream. Serve with tortilla chips.

Scallops in Phyllo

Recipe courtesy of Jeff Jacobs, Carrol's Creek Cafe, Annapolis, MD

SERVES 4

For the shrimp sauce:
2 quarts shrimp shells
½ cup diced celery
½ cup diced onions
12 ounces heavy cream
1 tablespoon tomato paste
1 tablespoon shrimp base
  (optional)

For the scallops:
8 each U-10 dry-packed scallops
½ cup flour

2 eggs
¾ cup milk
Kataifi (shredded phyllo; Apollo
  brand preferred), available
  at Greek or Middle Eastern
  grocery stores
Oil for frying
1 tablespoon olive oil
2 ounces diced prosciutto ham
4 ounces jumbo lump crab
2 cups baby spinach
8 ounces shrimp sauce

To make the shrimp sauce: Place all of the ingredients in a saucepan. Bring to a boil and then immediately turn down heat to low and simmer for 20 minutes. Strain out the solids and keep the sauce hot until needed.

To make the scallops: Preheat oven to 200°F.

Dust scallops in flour, shaking off the excess. Dip each scallop in an egg wash made by combining the eggs and milk, shaking off the excess.

Spread out about ½ cup kataifi on a plate or baking sheet, and press it into a flat layer. Place a scallop in the middle and roll up the dough to encase the scallop. Repeat the process until all the scallops are coated.

Place about ½ inch oil in a frying pan and heat to 350°F. Place 2 scallop packages at a time in the hot oil. Cook on one side until golden brown and then turn and cook the other side until golden. Drain on paper towels and set aside in a low oven until all the scallops are cooked. (You can also use a deep fryer to cook the scallops.)

PHOTO COURTESY OF CARROL'S CREEK CAFE

In a clean skillet, heat 1 tablespoon of olive oil on medium high, add the prosciutto and crabmeat, and sauté until hot. Next add spinach and sauté until wilted.

To serve: Spoon 2 ounces of shrimp sauce onto a small plate, layer with a quarter of the spinach mixture, and top with 2 scallops. Repeat the procedure on three more plates and serve while warm.

Scallops with Coconut Milk Succotash
Recipe courtesy of Chef Leo D'Aleo, Drummers' Cafe, Berlin, MD

SERVES 2 AS AN APPETIZER

   4 tablespoons unsalted butter
   1 cup white corn
   1 cup lima beans
   1 can coconut milk, stirred well
   2 tablespoons vegetable oil
   6 big dry-packed scallops, removed of chewy side muscle
   Kosher salt or seafood seasoning
   2 sprigs fresh thyme
   6 tomato slices
   3 ounces mild-flavored micro greens or baby lettuces

For the succotash: In a small saucepan, melt 2 tablespoons butter, add the corn and lima beans, and gently sauté for a minute or two. Add the desired amount of coconut milk (you don't want the succotash too soupy) and simmer until the vegetables are done to your liking. Set aside and keep warm.

For the scallops: Heat a nonstick pan on medium-high, add oil, and then carefully add the scallops.

Season the scallops with kosher salt, add the remaining unsalted butter and thyme, and cook until the scallops are caramelized and golden brown—about 3 minutes. Sauté for another few minutes until cooked through. (Note: scallops are quite nice when a little rare. As with any seafood, overcooking is not the way to go.)

To serve: Mound the succotash onto two plates and lay 3 tomato slices on top of each mound. Place one scallop on each tomato slice and garnish the plates with micro greens dressed in a light vinaigrette, if desired.

Seafood Skins

Recipe courtesy of Chef David Hyson, Thursday's Steak & Crab House, Galesville, MD

SERVES 8-10

  10 baking potatoes, washed
  4 ounces butter
  1 pound small scallops (80–120 count)
  1 pound salad shrimp
  3 ounces dry white wine
  1 tablespoon lemon juice
  1 pound claw crabmeat
  2 tablespoons Old Bay Seasoning
  Oil for greasing pan or deep frying
  3 cups shredded cheddar cheese

To prep the potatoes: Preheat oven to 400°F.

Bake potatoes for 60 minutes or until well done. Refrigerate potatoes for several hours.

Slice the cooked, cooled potatoes lengthwise in half, and then into quarters.

To prepare the dish: Preheat oven to 350°F.

Layer butter, scallops, and shrimp in the bottom of a saucepan. Add the wine and lemon juice and begin to sauté over medium heat. When the scallops are almost done, add the crabmeat and Old Bay Seasoning. Sauté for several more minutes until heated through and scallops are just firm. Set aside.

Place the potato skins on a greased sheet pan and bake for 5–7 minutes. (You can also deep-fry the potato skins in 350°F oil for 4–5 minutes.) Remove skins from oven and turn up the temperature to 400°F.

On the same sheet pan, arrange the baked potato skins close together and top with the seafood mixture. Cover the skins with cheddar cheese and bake at 400°F until the seafood mixture is warmed through and the cheese is thoroughly melted and starts to brown on the edges.

To serve: Use a spatula to remove the skins from the pan to a platter. Serve with sour cream. (These make delicious hors d'oeuvres for summer parties!)

Stuffed Crab Avocado

Recipe courtesy of The Tides Restaurant, Lexington Park, MD

SERVES 2

1 avocado, ripe
3 ounces lump crabmeat
1½ ounces seeded and chopped
  cucumber
1 ounce minced red onion
2 teaspoons olive oil
2 teaspoons Baja seasoning
  (ingredients follow)
4 ounces field greens

Store-bought blood orange
  balsamic reduction

For the Baja seasoning:
1 part black pepper
2 parts coriander
1 part cilantro
1 part cumin
1 part dark chili powder

Blend the Baja seasoning ingredients together.

Halve the avocado, remove the pit, and use a spoon to scoop out the flesh, being careful to leave a thin layer of avocado remaining (to hold the shell together).

In a bowl, mix the avocado, crabmeat, cucumber, and red onion together. Drizzle with olive oil and add Baja seasoning. Toss until evenly distributed and then scoop filling back into avocado shells.

Divide the field greens between two plates and top each with half the stuffed avocado. Drizzle each plate with the blood orange balsamic reduction and serve.

PHOTO COURTESY OF THE TIDES RESTAURANT

Chipotle Lime Crab Salad

Recipe courtesy of Chef Bob Steele, Backfin Blues Bar and Grill, Port Deposit, MD

SERVES 4

For the crab salad:
1 pound jumbo lump crabmeat, picked over
1 chipotle pepper in adobo sauce
2 tablespoons diced red onion
2 sliced green onions
½ cup mayonnaise
Zest of 1 lime

For the avocado puree:
1 ripe avocado
Juice of 1 lime
¼ cup mayonnaise
1 tablespoon finely diced red peppers

For the salsa:
4 plum tomatoes
2 tablespoons diced red onion
1 lime (zest and juice)
2 cloves garlic, minced
1 tablespoon coarsely chopped cilantro
2 green onions, sliced on bias
Salt and pepper, to taste

To make the crab salad: Combine all ingredients in a large bowl and set aside.

To make the avocado puree: Mash avocado with a fork until smooth; combine it with the remaining ingredients and set aside.

To make the salsa: Combine all ingredients in a medium-size bowl and set aside.

To assemble the dish: Place crab salad in small salad bowls, top with salsa, and garnish with the avocado puree. (Note: Another serving option is to spread the crab salad over fried flour tortillas and top with the salsa and avocado puree.)

Cream of Crab Soup

Recipe courtesy of The Narrows, Grasonville, MD

SERVES 4-6

- 1 pound jumbo lump crabmeat
- 1 small carrot, grated
- 2 cups half-and-half
- 2 cups heavy cream
- 1 tablespoon dry sherry
- 1 tablespoon chicken base
- ½ teaspoon white pepper
- ½ teaspoon Old Bay Seasoning
- 3 tablespoons unsalted butter
- 3 tablespoons all-purpose flour
- Chopped parsley
- Additional sherry, to serve

Carefully pick over crabmeat to remove any cartilage or bits of shell. Set aside.

In a heavy saucepan over low heat, combine carrot, half-and-half, heavy cream, sherry, chicken base, white pepper, and Old Bay and bring to a slow simmer.

In a separate saucepan, make a roux by combining the butter and flour and cooking over low heat until it forms a thick, brown paste (do not burn).

Add the roux to the cream mixture and bring back to a simmer. Whisk until smooth. Add the crabmeat and stir gently until combined.

Serve garnished with chopped parsley and pass a cruet of sherry.

Grilled Crabmeat Sandwich

Recipe courtesy of Rod 'N' Reel Restaurant, Chesapeake Beach, MD

SERVES 4

"A decadent grilled cheese with jumbo lump crab imperial on toasted rye bread with American cheese."

For the crab imperial:
1 pound Maryland jumbo
   lump crabmeat
1 cup mayonnaise
¼ cup diced red pepper
¼ cup diced green pepper

For the sandwiches:
8 slices rye bread
12 slices American cheese
Butter, softened

To make the crab imperial: Carefully pick through the crabmeat to remove any bits of shell.

Combine crabmeat with the mayonnaise, red peppers, and green peppers. Mix until well blended.

To make the sandwiches: Heat the crab imperial mixture in a skillet until it begins to brown. Meanwhile, heat a second skillet on medium-low.

Butter one side of each slice of bread. Working in batches, place 4 slices of the bread butter-side down in the second skillet and cover each slice completely with American cheese (as if you were making a grilled cheese sandwich).

When the crab mixture is browned and warm, spoon it onto 2 of the slices of bread. Top, cheese-side down, with the remaining two slices. Repeat the procedure with the rest of the bread and crab imperial.

Cut each sandwich in half and serve with your favorite side dish.

Seafood Lover's Chesapeake Bay

Lobster Bisque with Cheesy Croutons
Recipe courtesy of Chef Leo D'Aleo, Drummers' Cafe, Berlin, MD

SERVES 4-6

    Kosher salt
    2 live lobsters
    2 cups diced onions
    2 cups diced celery
    1 cup diced carrot
    2 tablespoons minced garlic
    2 cups sherry
    8 parsley stems
    4 sprigs fresh thyme
    2 bay leaves
    ½ pound butter (reserve 2 tablespoons for sautéing)
    1 cup flour
    1 cup heavy cream
    ¼ cup tomato paste
    Salt and white pepper, to taste
    Seafood seasoning, optional
    Additional sherry, optional

For the stock: Bring a gallon of water and a few pinches of kosher salt to a boil in a lobster pot or extra-large stockpot. Put the live lobsters in the boiling water, cover, and cook for 8 minutes.

Using tongs, remove cooked lobsters and plunge them into a bowl of ice water for a few minutes. (Leave the boiling water on the burner.)

Remove and separate the lobsters' claws and tail, reserving the bodies. Crack the claws and split the tails with a chef's knife. Extract the meat and set aside. Reserve all shells, including the bodies and any internal parts or juice, for the next step.

To the boiling water, add 1 cup diced onion, 1 cup diced celery, ½ cup diced carrot, 1 tablespoon garlic, 1 cup sherry, parsley stems, thyme, bay leaves, and all the lobster shells. Bring to a boil and simmer for 25 minutes. Strain liquid into a second large pot and continue simmering, while skimming the "scum" that collects on the surface, until the liquid is reduced by half.

Make a roux by melting the butter in a saucepan and then adding the flour. Cook, stirring constantly, until a slightly nutty aroma rises, about 3 minutes. Set aside.

For the soup: Sauté the remaining onion, celery, carrot, and garlic in the remaining 2 tablespoons butter until the vegetables are slightly softened.

Stir in the remaining sherry, lobster stock, and cream. Bring to a simmer and whisk in tomato paste and roux. (Depending on how much stock you have, you may need more roux as a thickening agent. After making the soup, you will have an idea of how thick you prefer it.)

Add salt and white pepper or seafood seasoning to taste and puree with a hand mixer or (with extreme care) in a blender.

Chop the reserved lobster meat and add to the soup.

Serve with 3–4 cheesy croutons (recipe below) and a few splashes of sherry (optional) on top.

For the cheesy croutons:
1 baguette
Extra-virgin olive oil
Shaved Parmesan cheese
Chopped parsley

Preheat oven to 350°F.

Slice bread on an angle into ¼-inch slices and place on a baking sheet.

Drizzle with olive oil, sprinkle with Parmesan cheese and parsley, and bake until golden brown, about 5 minutes.

Cut into croutons for the soup, reserving the remainder to use in salads.

Maryland Blue Crab Marmalade Salad

Recipe created by Tess Klim of Middleton, VA, Grand Prize Winner, National Hard Crab Derby, Crisfield, MD

SERVES 4

⅔ cup sour cream
1 tablespoon finely chopped fresh ginger
⅓ cup orange marmalade
½ cup chopped green scallions
4–6 slices bacon, cooked and crumbled
1 pound Maryland crabmeat
Mixed greens or romaine lettuce
½ cup sliced almonds, lightly toasted

Mix sour cream, ginger, and marmalade until well blended. Stir in chopped scallions and crumbled bacon.

Gently fold in Maryland crabmeat and place a scoop of the mixture on the greens. Sprinkle with toasted almonds before serving.

Maryland Crab Soup

Recipe courtesy of Traders Seafood, Steak & Ale, Chesapeake Beach, MD

SERVES 6-8

1 (16-ounce) bag mixed
vegetables
6 strips bacon, chopped
1 onion, chopped
3 stalks celery, chopped
1 (28-ounce) can whole peeled
tomatoes
1 tablespoon hot sauce
1 clove garlic, minced

1½ gallons water
¼ cup chicken base
8 potatoes, diced
¾ cup Worcestershire sauce
1 tablespoon Old Bay Seasoning
2 tablespoons lemon juice
Salt and pepper, to taste
2 pounds crabmeat

Sauté first 5 ingredients in a large stockpot for a few minutes, until partially cooked.

Gradually add the rest of ingredients (crabmeat last) and cook, stirring, until well combined and hot. If the soup is too thick, add more water as needed to get the desired consistency.

PHOTO COURTESY OF TRADERS SEAFOOD, STEAK & ALE

Maryland Cream of Crab Soup

Recipe courtesy of Ken Upton, Ken's Creative Kitchen, Annapolis, MD

SERVES 6

- 2 tablespoons butter
- 2 tablespoons flour
- 1 cup chicken stock
- 2 cups half-and-half
- 2 cups heavy whipping cream
- Salt and white pepper, to taste
- 1 pound jumbo lump Maryland crabmeat
- Sherry, optional

Make a roux by combining the butter and flour in a saucepan and cooking over medium heat, stirring constantly, until the mixture is light brown and has a slightly nutty aroma. Set aside.

To make the soup, heat the chicken stock in a large pot. Add the roux and mix until well combined.

Add the half-and-half, cream, and salt and pepper, and mix well. Carefully fold in the crabmeat.

Cook for a few minutes until the crabmeat is heated through. Serve with sherry, if desired.

Maryland Oyster Stew

Recipe courtesy of Ken Upton, Ken's Creative Kitchen, Annapolis, MD

SERVES 4

- 1 pint oysters
- ¼ cup butter
- 1 quart half-and-half
- Salt and pepper, to taste
- Oyster crackers, optional

Sauté the oysters in their liquor and the butter until their edges curl. Add the half-and-half and seasonings, heat through, and serve immediately. Serve with oyster crackers, if desired.

Mom-Mom's Maryland Crab Soup

Recipe courtesy of Chef Bobby Jones, The Point Crab House and Grill, Arnold, MD

20 SERVINGS

This recipe was inspired by Chef Bobby Jones's grandmother, who used to make this robust soup for family gatherings at her Eastern Shore home.

- 1 gallon chicken stock
- 1 gallon beef stock
- ½ cup House Crab Seasoning (may use J.O. or Old Bay)
- ½ cup Worcestershire sauce
- 5 bay leaves
- ½ cup sugar
- 10 live crabs, cleaned and halved
- 1 gallon diced peeled tomatoes (may use canned)
- 1 tablespoon Tabasco sauce
- ½ pound Smithfield ham, finely diced
- 6 carrots, medium diced
- 12 ears fresh corn, kernels shaved
- 1 pound green beans, stemmed and chopped
- 1 pound green peas
- 2 cups diced cabbage
- 4 cups diced celery
- 2 medium yellow onions, chopped
- 2 pounds jumbo lump crabmeat
- Fresh chopped parsley, for garnish

Clean and prep all the vegetables and crabs.

Bring the stock to a boil in a large stockpot, then add all the ingredients except for the jumbo lump crabmeat and parsley.

Bring mixture back to a boil, and then reduce heat and simmer for 1 hour. Skim excess froth off top.

PHOTO COURTESY OF THE POINT CRAB HOUSE AND GRILL

Serve each bowl garnished with fresh chopped parsley, jumbo lump crabmeat, and one of the crab halves.

Quahog "Chowdah"

Recipe courtesy of Chef-Owner David Twining, Nantuckets, Fenwick Island, DE

SERVES 4

- 1 pound butter
- 1 cup scallops
- 3 cups white corn
- 1 cup diced onion
- 1 cup diced celery
- 1 pound diced red potatoes
- 1 teaspoon dried thyme
- ¼ cup diced parsley
- 1 quart clam juice
- 3 cups shucked top neck clams
- 3 ounces Worcestershire sauce
- 1 cup heavy cream

Melt butter in large pan and lightly sauté scallops, corn, onion, celery, potatoes, thyme, and parsley.

Add clam juice and bring to a boil. Lower heat and simmer 15 minutes.

Add clams and Worcestershire sauce and simmer 5 minutes.

Remove from heat, add cream, and stir until heated through. Serve in soup bowls.

Red Drum Chowder

Recipe courtesy of Executive Chef Nathan Ebersole, Bridges Restaurant, Grasonville, MD

MAKES 12 CUPS

This recipe is gluten-free.

    5 strips bacon, diced
    1 medium onion, small dice
    1 teaspoon salt
    1 teaspoon chopped fresh garlic
    3 stalks celery, small dice
    1 large red potato, medium dice
    ¼ teaspoon cayenne pepper
    1 teaspoon black pepper
    2 teaspoons Old Bay Seasoning
    1 tablespoon chopped fresh parsley
    1 cup dry white wine
    1 quart milk
    1 quart heavy cream
    1 pound red drum (also called channel bass), cut into ½-inch cubes

In a large pot, sauté the diced bacon over medium heat until brown and crispy.

Add the onions and salt, sauté for 2 more minutes, and then add the garlic, celery, potato, cayenne and black peppers, Old Bay, and parsley. Sauté for another minute.

Add the wine, stir to deglaze the pot, and cook until the liquid is reduced by half.

Add the milk and cream and bring to a boil, uncovered.

Reduce heat and simmer for about 10 minutes, or until the potatoes are barely cooked.

Add the cubes of red drum and simmer another 5 minutes until the fish is cooked through.

PHOTO COURTESY OF BRIDGES RESTAURANT

Rockfish Gyro

Recipe courtesy of Vincent Arrunategui, Stoney's Kingfishers,
Solomons Island, MD

SERVES 2

For the cucumber-wasabi sauce:
1 cucumber, peeled, seeded, and finely chopped
4 garlic cloves, pressed
4 tablespoons chopped chives
2 cups sour cream
Olive oil
Juice of 1 lemon
Salt and pepper, to taste
2 tablespoons wasabi powder, or to taste

Combine cucumber, garlic, chives, and sour cream in a large bowl.

Drizzle in a little olive oil, add lemon juice, and stir.

Season with salt and pepper, to taste.

Add wasabi to taste (the more you add, the spicier it will be), and blend well.

For the gyro:
1 (8–10 ounce) fresh rockfish fillet, halved horizontally
1 teaspoon blackened seasoning
2 slices pita bread
4 ounces white wine
4 ounces Romaine lettuce, sliced thin
2 ounces coarsely diced tomato
2 ounces diced red onion
2 ounces crumbled feta cheese

Preheat oven to 500°F.

Spray an oven-safe skillet or metal pan with cooking spray or olive oil.

Place sliced rockfish in the pan; season both sides of the fillets well with blackened seasoning.

Place in the oven for 4–5 minutes. Fish is ready when you can flake it with a fork.

While the fish is cooking, throw the pita slices into the oven to toast.

When the fish is done, pour the white wine into the pan. (Be careful—this will let out a good amount of smoke.)

To assemble the dish: Put a handful of lettuce on each toasted pita, sprinkle with tomato, red onion, and feta cheese. Place fish fillets on top and drizzle with a healthy dollop of the cucumber-wasabi sauce.

Seafood Rolls
Recipe courtesy of Severn Inn, Annapolis, MD

SERVES 5-6

    1 pound shrimp (31/40 count)
    2 lobster tails
    2 tablespoons Old Bay Seasoning, plus additional for steaming shrimp
    1 pound jumbo lump crabmeat
    1 cup mayonnaise
    ½ teaspoon Tabasco sauce
    1 teaspoon Worcestershire sauce
    2 tablespoons fresh lemon juice
    3 stalks celery, finely diced
    5–6 top-cut hot dog buns, to serve
    Mixed greens, for garnish

Steam the shrimp and lobster with a few shakes of Old Bay for 7 minutes. Cover with ice when done and set aside to cool.

Remove the meat from the lobster shells and cut it into cubes. Shell the shrimp and pick over the crabmeat to remove any bits of shell or cartilage.

Mix lobster, shrimp, and crabmeat with 2 tablespoons Old Bay, mayonnaise, Tabasco, Worcestershire, lemon juice, and diced celery. Combine and refrigerate until chilled.

Toast buns under the broiler, fill with the seafood mixture, and garnish with mixed greens.

Three Sisters Seafood & Succotash Chowder

Recipe courtesy of Chef John Shields, Gertrude's, Baltimore, MD

SERVES 4

Legend has it that Native Americans planted corn, squash, and beans together because they grow best when teamed up. There was science behind this theory: Corn leaches nitrogen from the soil, beans put it back, and squash planted in between the two seals in moisture and discourages weeds. John Shields first learned about this technique from his assistant Bonnie North, who grew them in her tiny backyard garden in Baltimore City. This chowder blends them with Maryland rockfish and crab to create a hearty dinner dish.

For the fish stock:

1 whole rockfish (4–6 pounds), cleaned and filleted, bones and head reserved
2 carrots, peeled and chopped
1 onion, sliced
1 bunch parsley, with stems
1 teaspoon dried whole thyme leaves
1 bay leaf

To make the stock, place fish head and bones in an 8-quart stockpot and add water to cover (about 12 cups). Reserve fillets.

Add carrots, onion, parsley, thyme, and bay leaf. Bring to a boil, reduce heat to low, and simmer 45 minutes, skimming off foam occasionally.

For the chowder:

6 ears sweet corn
4 tablespoons butter or olive oil
1 large onion, finely diced
3 large potatoes, cut into ½-inch dice
½ cup flour
2 cups heavy cream or half-and-half
1 pound lump crabmeat (fresh or pasteurized)
1 cup lima beans (fresh or frozen)
2 cups medium-diced yellow or green squash
Salt and pepper, to taste
2 tablespoons minced chives or parsley, optional

Husk corn and cut kernels off the ears with sharp knife, collecting kernels and "corn milk" in a bowl. Set aside and add corn cobs to the simmering fish stock.

In a large, heavy-bottomed pot, heat butter or olive oil. Add onion and sauté until translucent.

Add potatoes and continue sautéing for 4–5 minutes. Stir in the flour and cook, stirring constantly, for 2–3 minutes.

Whisk in about 8 cups of strained stock and bring almost to a boil. Reduce heat to a simmer and cook for 45 minutes. Add cream or half-and-half and bring almost to a boil. Reduce to medium heat.

Cut rockfish fillets into 1-inch cubes. Add to pot, along with crabmeat, lima beans, squash, corn kernels, and corn milk.

Simmer for an additional 20 minutes; season to taste with salt and pepper.

To serve: Ladle into chowder bowls and garnish with minced chives or parsley.

Entrees

Asian-Style Tuna

Recipe courtesy of Chef John McDonald, The Grove Market Smokehouse Restaurant, Bishopville, MD

SERVES 6

Chef's note: I prefer very rare tuna, but don't be cowed by those who say it will be ruined if it's well-done. Tuna is notoriously dry when well-done because it is very low in fat. However, if you normally eat your protein cooked well, have it your way. Please don't be offended if a server recommends "rare"—just say thanks, but I know how I prefer it.

¼ cup top-grade soy sauce
¼ cup rice wine vinegar
1 teaspoon sugar
1 teaspoon sesame oil
1 teaspoon fresh peeled and grated ginger
3 bundles green tea soba noodles
½ mango, julienned
½ red bell pepper, julienned
4 green onions, bias cut
¼ cup finely diced red onion
¼ cup cooked edamame (green soybeans)

For the tuna marinade:
¼ cup soy sauce
1 tablespoon mirin (Japanese sweet wine)
1 tablespoon honey
2 tablespoons sesame oil
2 tablespoons rice wine vinegar
6 (6-ounce) thick-cut ahi tuna steaks

For topping:
¼ teaspoon black sesame seeds
¼ teaspoon white sesame seeds

Combine the soy sauce, rice wine vinegar, sugar, sesame oil, and grated ginger in a small bowl; set aside.

Cook soba noodles according to package instructions, strain, and rinse briefly with water.

Combine the noodles with the soy dressing, mango, vegetables, and edamame. Let stand about an hour (no longer, or else the acids will soften the solid ingredients).

To prepare the marinade: Emulsify all ingredients except tuna. Dredge tuna in the marinade for a few minutes only.

To prepare the dish: Remove tuna from the marinade and pat dry with paper towels.

Heat a cast-iron skillet over high heat, and then sear the fish in the dry skillet to desired doneness, turning once to sear each side.

Meanwhile, heap noodles and vegetables in a large bowl or on individual serving plates.

Remove tuna from the skillet, slice thinly on the bias, and arrange on top of noodles. Wipe skillet clean.

Toast the black and white sesame seeds in the skillet until fragrant, and sprinkle over the plated dish.

Baked Rockfish with Lemon & Tarragon Butter

Recipe courtesy of Chef Craig Sewall, A Cook's Cafe, Annapolis, MD

SERVES 6

- 1 whole lemon
- 10 sprigs tarragon
- 1 shallot, peeled and finely chopped
- Salt and pepper
- 6 tablespoons butter, softened
- Olive oil
- 4 (6-ounce) fresh rockfish fillets
- Additional tarragon sprigs and lemon wedges, for serving

Preheat oven to 350°F.

Zest and juice the lemon and chop the tarragon.

Place the shallot in a bowl and add enough lemon juice just to cover. Let the shallot macerate in the juice for a few minutes.

Add the lemon zest and tarragon to the shallot, and season with salt and a generous amount of pepper. Add the butter and mash everything together until well mixed.

Lightly oil (or line with parchment paper) a baking dish or roasting pan.

Place the fish in the prepared pan, season with salt and pepper, and moisten lightly with olive oil.

Bake for 7–10 minutes (depending on thickness) until just cooked through.

Serve with a spoonful of the tarragon butter on top and garnish with a sprig of fresh tarragon and a lemon wedge.

BBQ Rockfish

Recipe courtesy of Chef Bruce Allen, Abner's Crab House, Chesapeake Beach, MD

SERVES 4

For the raspberry-chipotle barbecue sauce:
⅓ cup diced onion
2 teaspoons minced garlic
2½ ounces (by weight, about ⅓ can) chopped chipotle chilies in adobo
⅔ cup raspberry vinegar
1 teaspoon kosher salt
2 cups raspberry preserves
⅔ cup store-bought barbecue sauce

4 (6-ounce) thick rockfish fillets, seasoned with salt and pepper
8–12 slices applewood bacon
Raspberry-chipotle barbecue sauce
Sweet corn griddle cakes (recipe follows)
Mexican street corn with citrus aioli (recipe follows)

In a saucepan over medium heat, combine onions, garlic, chipotles, vinegar, and salt. Cook, stirring frequently, until liquid is reduced by half.

Add the raspberry preserves, bring to a boil, and then remove from heat. Stir in the barbecue sauce and puree the mixture until smooth. Set aside until ready to use.

To prepare the fish: Heat the grill (or a griddle plate or skillet, if preparing indoors) to medium-high.

Wrap each rockfish fillet in some of the bacon. Sear until the bacon begins to crisp.

Baste the fish with the raspberry-chipotle barbecue sauce and finish over indirect heat on the grill (or in a 350°F oven) for 4–6 minutes per side, depending on fillet thickness.

PHOTO COURTESY OF ABNER'S CRAB HOUSE

Serve with sweet corn cakes and Mexican street corn.

For the sweet corn griddle cakes:
1 cup grilled corn kernels
¾ cup half-and-half
1 tablespoon maple syrup
1 egg
1 cup flour
1 tablespoon butter, melted
⅓ cup cornmeal
1½ teaspoons baking powder
¾ teaspoon salt

Combine all ingredients until well mixed, and cook on a greased griddle like you would a pancake. Set aside and keep warm.

For the Mexican street corn:
8 ears fresh corn, shucked
Citrus aioli
¼ cup grated Parmesan cheese

For the citrus aioli:
2–3 roasted garlic cloves
Large pinch of coarse sea or kosher salt
2 egg yolks, at room temperature
1 tablespoon Dijon mustard
1 tablespoon lemon juice
⅔ cup pure olive oil (not extra-virgin)
⅓ cup extra-virgin olive oil
1 teaspoon pureed chipotles
2 tablespoons orange juice
1 tablespoon lime juice
2 tablespoons buttermilk
2 tablespoons sour cream
¼ cup chopped cilantro

Place garlic and salt in a food processor fitted with a metal blade, or in a blender. Pulse for 2 seconds.

Add the egg yolks, Dijon mustard, and lemon juice, and pulse on and off until blended.

Turn on food processor and begin adding the olive oil (pure first, then extra-virgin) in a thin stream. If it becomes too thick, thin it out with some of the citrus juices and buttermilk, and continue adding oil until you've used it all.

Add the chipotle puree, remaining citrus juices, buttermilk, sour cream, cilantro, and (if necessary) a bit more salt.

To prepare the corn: Preheat oven to broil.

Grill corn on an outdoor grill until slightly charred.

Remove corn from grill and place in a baking dish.

Top the corn with some of the citrus aioli and sprinkle with Parmesan cheese.

Broil until browned.

Camarones Cava (Shrimp in Lobster Sauce)

Recipe courtesy of Chef Gonzalez Rodriguez, Jalapeños, Annapolis, MD

SERVES 4

   1 pound large shrimp, peeled and deveined
   Flour for dusting
   2 tablespoons olive oil
   ½ ounce chopped garlic
   2–3 ounces lobster broth (see recipe below)
   2 ounces Spanish cava (or other dry white sparkling wine)
   2 ounces heavy cream
   Salt and pepper, to taste
   Lemon slices, for garnish

Dust the shrimp with flour, shaking off excess.

Heat olive oil in a sauté pan over high heat. Add shrimp and garlic and fry for about 2 minutes, turning constantly.

Add the lobster broth, cava, and cream, and stir gently to coat shrimp completely.

Keep stirring and reducing sauce for 3–5 minutes, add salt and pepper, and serve on a platter garnished with lemon slices.

   For the lobster broth:
   1 lobster body
   Vegetable oil
   1 tomato, chopped
   1 tablespoon chopped fresh tarragon

Clean the lobster cavity well (removing the gills) and cut lobster body into fourths.

Heat oil in a large pot and sear shells until they start to color. Add enough cold water to cover, bring to a simmer, and skim off impurities. Add tomatoes and tarragon and continue to simmer gently for 45 minutes, skimming off impurities as they appear.

Strain through a fine sieve and return strained liquid to pan. Simmer over high heat to develop a rich flavor. Leftover broth may be frozen in ice cube trays for future use.

Cioppino

Recipe courtesy of Fish Whistle, Chestertown, MD

SERVES 12

"A classic seafood stew with a little bit of everything from the sea: shrimp, scallops, clams, mussels, and fresh fish in a tomato-garlic broth served with a seasoned, toasted baguette."

¾ cup butter
2 onions, chopped
2 garlic cloves, minced
1 bunch fresh parsley, chopped
2 cups stewed tomatoes
2 cups chicken broth
2 bay leaves
1 teaspoon chopped fresh basil
1 teaspoon dried thyme
½ teaspoon dried oregano
1 cup water
1½ cups dry white wine
1½ pounds large shrimp, peeled and deveined
1½ pound bay scallops
18 small clams
1½ pounds mussels
1½ pounds crabmeat
1½ pounds cod fillets, cubed

Melt butter over medium-low heat in a large stockpot.

Add onions, garlic, and parsley. Cook slowly, occasionally stirring, until onions are soft.

Add tomatoes, chicken broth, bay leaves, basil, thyme, oregano, water, and wine. Mix well. Cover and simmer for 30 minutes.

Stir in the shrimp, scallops, clams, mussels, crabmeat, and fish. Bring to a boil, lower heat, and cover and simmer 5–7 minutes until clams and mussels open.

Serve with warm, crusty bread.

Coquilles St. Jacques

Recipe courtesy of Chef Jose Barrientos, Harry Browne's Restaurant, Annapolis, MD

SERVES 4

The chef suggests serving the dish with a glass of sauvignon blanc.

2 tablespoons butter
1 onion, finely minced
½ teaspoon minced garlic
2 tablespoons flour
½ cup sauvignon blanc or other dry white wine
½ cup water
½ cup milk
½ cup heavy cream
16 large scallops
Salt and pepper, to taste
2 tablespoons oil
4 tablespoons freshly grated Parmesan cheese

Heat pan and add butter, onion, and garlic. Cook for several minutes, but do not brown.

Stir in flour and cook for another 2–3 minutes.

Add white wine and water and reduce liquid by half over medium heat.

Stir in the milk and heavy cream, cooking until thick enough to coat the back of a spoon.

Heat oil in a large sauté pan, season scallops with salt and pepper, and then add the scallops to the hot oil and cook for several minutes or until golden brown. Flip, and cook another 2 minutes.

Place scallops in an oven-safe dish, cover with the sauce, sprinkle with Parmesan cheese, and broil until golden. (Alternatively, divide scallops into 4 portions and place in oven-safe shells. Cover with sauce, sprinkle with Parmesan, and broil briefly until tops are golden brown.)

Crab & Asparagus

Recipe courtesy of The River Shack at the Wellwood, Charlestown, MD

SERVES 1

10 asparagus spears
1 tablespoon plus 2 ounces unsalted butter
1 tablespoon minced fresh shallot
1 tablespoon minced fresh garlic
4 ounces white wine (chablis or chardonnay)
6 ounces fresh jumbo lump crabmeat
2 ounces diced ripe local tomatoes
1 tablespoon fresh chopped basil
1 teaspoon capers
1 tablespoon fresh lemon juice
Salt and pepper, to taste
Lemon wedge, for garnish

Rinse and dry asparagus. Trim off butt end by holding the end with one hand and halfway up the stalk with the other hand. Bend until asparagus snaps in two. Discard butt end or use for stock. Set cleaned asparagus aside.

Warm a medium-size skillet over medium heat. Add 1 tablespoon butter, shallots, and garlic. Sweat gently while stirring until translucent, about 5 minutes.

Deglaze the pan with white wine, reduce for 2 minutes, and then add the asparagus. Turn up the heat and cook for 3–4 minutes until the asparagus is al dente (tender, but not soft).

Place asparagus spears on a warmed plate and set aside. Add crabmeat and remaining ingredients (except the remaining 2 ounces butter and lemon wedge) to the pan. Warm the crabmeat through, scoop it from the pan, and place it on top of the asparagus.

Simmer the remaining sauce over medium to high heat until reduced by half. Add the butter and incorporate it thoroughly. Taste the sauce and add salt and pepper, as needed.

To serve: Pour the sauce over the crab-topped asparagus and garnish with a lemon wedge.

Crab Au Gratin

Recipe created by Ken Wilmer of Crisfield, MD, Second Place Winner, National Hard Crab Derby, Crisfield, MD

SERVES 4

- 1 (15-ounce) jar Cheez Whiz
- 2 tablespoons mayonnaise
- 1 teaspoon Worcestershire sauce
- 1 pound Maryland lump crabmeat
- 1 (5-ounce) jar Old English sharp cheese
- Old Bay Seasoning

Preheat oven to 375°F. Mix ¼ jar Cheez Whiz (reserve remainder for future use) with mayonnaise and Worcestershire sauce and fold into crabmeat.

Scoop mixture into four small buttered casserole dishes and spread tops with Old English cheese.

Sprinkle with Old Bay Seasoning and bake for 20–25 minutes or until bubbling.

Crabbie Eggs Benedict

Recipe courtesy of Two If By Sea, Tilghman, MD

SERVES 4

For Hollandaise sauce:
- 3 egg yolks
- 1 tablespoon cold water
- 16 tablespoons chilled butter, finely diced
- Salt, to taste
- Cayenne pepper, to taste
- Freshly ground white pepper, to taste
- Fresh lemon juice

- 1 cup crabmeat
- 1 cup shredded mozzarella, plus extra for topping
- ½ cup mayonnaise
- 1 tablespoon Old Bay Seasoning
- 1 tablespoon chopped fresh parsley
- 1 tablespoon chopped fresh chives
- 4 English muffins
- 8 eggs

Lemon wedges, for garnish (optional)
Fresh fruit, for garnish (optional)

To prepare the Hollandaise sauce: In the bottom of a double boiler, bring water to a boil and then reduce the heat to keep it just below the simmering point.

In the top of the double boiler, add egg yolks and 1 tablespoon cold water. With a whisk, beat the egg yolks to combine them thoroughly with the water, whisking until creamy.

Add a handful of chilled butter cubes to the pan and whisk until the butter is absorbed into the egg mixture.

Add remaining cubes of butter, a few at a time, until all the butter is absorbed into the mixture. Continue whisking the sauce until it is thick and creamy, about 10 minutes.

Season to taste with salt, cayenne, and white pepper. Finish the sauce with a few drops of fresh lemon juice.

Keep warm over double boiler until ready to use.

To prepare the English muffins: Preheat oven to broil.

In a medium bowl, combine the crabmeat, mozzarella, mayonnaise, Old Bay, parsley, and chives. Mix well.

Toast English muffin halves in a toaster and then spread with crabmeat mixture.

Place open-faced English muffins on a baking sheet and top with remaining cheese. Briefly place under the broiler until cheese is melted. (Be careful not to let it burn.) Place English muffins on a serving plate.

To prepare the poached eggs: Bring 2 tablespoons vinegar and a quart of water to a simmer in a skillet over medium heat. Crack eggs and gently slide them into the simmering water. Simmer for 3 minutes or until desired firmness is reached.

To assemble the dish: Remove eggs from the skillet with a slotted spoon and place one atop each prepared English muffin half. Top eggs with Hollandaise sauce and sprinkle with Old Bay Seasoning.

Serve 2 to a plate, garnished with a lemon wedge or fresh fruit, if desired.

Crab Cakes

Recipe courtesy of The Narrows, Grasonville, MD

MAKES 4

 1 pound jumbo lump crabmeat

 1 tablespoon fine cracker meal

 1 dash Worcestershire sauce

 1 dash Tabasco sauce

 1 egg

 1 tablespoon dry mustard

 1 teaspoon Old Bay Seasoning

 3–4 tablespoons mayonnaise, the creamiest available

 Juice of 1 lemon

Preheat oven to 450°F.

Place crabmeat in a large bowl and pick through to remove all loose shells and bits of cartilage. Add cracker meal and combine gently.

Mix remaining ingredients together in a separate bowl and fold into the crabmeat mixture.

Using an ice-cream scoop, scoop even portions of the crab mixture onto a nonstick baking sheet. Bake in a very hot oven until lightly browned, approximately 5–7 minutes.

Cranberry Crab Cakes
Recipe courtesy of Two If By Sea, Tilghman, MD

SERVES 6

    1 pound fresh crabmeat, picked over and flaked
    ¾ cup bread crumbs
    1 cup shredded Swiss cheese
    ¼ cup plain yogurt
    ¼ cup finely chopped scallions
    ¼ cup finely minced parsley
    2 tablespoons fresh lemon juice
    1 teaspoon minced garlic
    ½ cup finely chopped fresh cranberries
    1 egg, lightly beaten
    Lettuce
    Lemon wedges
    Fresh fruit of your choice, diced

In a medium bowl, toss crab with ¼ cup bread crumbs and cheese, yogurt, scallions, parsley, lemon juice, garlic, and cranberries.

Gently stir in beaten egg. Form mixture into a dozen 3-inch patties.

Spread remaining bread crumbs on a cookie sheet lined with waxed paper and place patties on top.

Refrigerate for 1 hour.

Pan-sear patties until crispy, turning over halfway through to brown on both sides.

Serve hot on a bed of lettuce garnished with lemon wedges and the diced fresh fruit of your choice.

Crispy Skin Bass with Piperade

Recipe courtesy of Executive Chef Jordan Lloyd, Bartlett Pear Inn, Easton, MD

SERVES 4

- 3 tablespoons canola oil
- 1 yellow Spanish onion, julienned
- 4 cloves fresh garlic, minced
- 2 ounces fresh thyme leaves
- 1 red bell pepper, finely diced
- 1 yellow bell pepper, finely diced
- 1 green bell pepper, finely diced
- 2 tablespoons tomato paste
- 3 medium ripe tomatoes, medium dice
- 1 bunch parsley, leaves picked and chopped fine, stems discarded
- 4 (6-ounce) portions fresh bass (wild striped bass, black bass, Mediterranean sea bass, etc.)
- Salt, to taste

For the piperade: Over medium heat, heat oil in a large sauté pan. When hot, add the julienned onions and begin to sweat. Allow very little color to develop.

When the onions are sweated and translucent, add the minced garlic and fresh thyme leaves. Continue to sweat on medium heat until garlic is soft.

Then add all of the bell peppers and continue sweating. When bell peppers are soft and cooked through, add the tomato paste. Continue to cook and mix tomato paste throughout ragout.

Once all is well incorporated and cooked through, add the fresh medium-dice tomato and pull the pan off the stove.

The chopped parsley should be added at the last minute, just before serving.

Searing the fish: Pull the fish out of the refrigerator 30 minutes before beginning the cooking process. Dab the skin side with a paper towel to make sure there is no excessive moisture. Searing room-temperature fish will prevent the fish from sticking to the skillet and aid in crisping the skin.

Heat a large skillet with a mask of canola oil on the bottom of the pan. Season the fish with salt, to taste. When the oil just begins to smoke, add the fish skin side down. The fish may begin to buckle a bit. Force the skin against the hot pan with a spatula and turn the heat to just below a medium flame. When the fish gives up resistance, turn the heat down a touch more and let the fish go 1–2 minutes until the skin has become crispy.

Flip the fish to the flesh side and finishing cooking the fish in the pan (if it is a thin fillet). If it is a bit thicker, put the fish in a 350°F oven for just a few minutes until the fish is cooked just through. Pull off the pan and let rest on a paper towel to absorb any residual pan juices.

To serve: Heat up the piperade and add the chopped parsley. On a serving platter, mound the piperade and place the fish right on top. Garnish with some fresh organic crisp greens (baby kale, tatsoi, frisee, crisp baby spinach, arugula, etc.).

Duck Breast with Crab Hash

Recipe courtesy of Sous Chef David Fitzhugh, The Tidewater Inn, Easton, MD

SERVES 6

  6 skin-on duck breasts
  Sea salt and pepper, to taste
  2 tablespoons olive oil
  1 medium butternut squash, peeled and diced
  1 bell pepper, julienned
  1 carrot, julienned
  2 scallions, chopped
  8 ounces jumbo lump crabmeat
  ¾ cup honey
  ¼ cup sriracha*

Preheat oven to 350°F.

Salt and pepper duck breasts and sear in an oven-proof skillet skin-side down over medium heat for 8–10 minutes until crispy and golden brown.

Turn duck breasts over and then place skillet in the oven. Bake for 10–15 minutes or until desired doneness.

In another skillet, heat olive oil over medium heat, add the squash, and sauté about 10 minutes, or until tender.

Add the peppers, carrots, scallions, and crab and sauté for 5 more minutes.

In a mixing bowl, whisk together the honey and sriracha. Set aside.

To serve, place duck breasts on plates, top with crab-vegetable mix, and drizzle with sriracha-honey sauce.

*Note: Sriracha is a hot sauce made with Chilean peppers and is widely available at grocery stores and in specialty markets. Another hot sauce may be substituted.

Fried & Stuffed Hard-Shell Crab

Recipe courtesy of Bo Brooks Restaurant & Catering, Baltimore, MD

SERVES 1

This is an old Baltimore-style recipe seldom seen on modern menus. You'll need a deep fat fryer and a basket to re-create this Bo Brooks special.

1 hard-shell blue crab, claws intact
1 jumbo lump crab cake
1½ cups prepared beer batter
1 lemon crown
¼ cup tartar sauce

Steam crab and remove exterior shell. Clean out interior, removing lungs.

Insert crab cake into cavity and press down firmly to embed crab cake in crab.

Dip entire assembly in beer batter, lift out, and let drip for 5 seconds.

Immediately immerse in hot oil in deep fat fryer and cover with metal grate.

Cook 6–8 minutes, remove from fat, and let sit in empty basket for about a minute while excess fat drips off. Insert a meat thermometer at thickest part to see if temperature has reached 135°F.

To serve, top with lemon crown and a container of tartar sauce.

PHOTO COURTESY OF BO BROOKS

"Harbor of Mercy" Award-Winning Rockfish Dinner

Recipe courtesy of MacGregor's Restaurant, Havre de Grace, MD

SERVES 1

1 tomato, chopped
1 tablespoon
    prepared vinaigrette
    dressing
4 tablespoons butter
1 shallot, minced
½ cup dry white wine
Juice of 1 lemon
2 teaspoons chopped
    parsley
Pinch each dried
    oregano and basil
2 cups panko (Japanese bread crumbs)
1 (8-ounce) rockfish fillet
1 tablespoon Dijon mustard
1 cup sweet corn off the cob
4 asparagus stalks
Salt and pepper, to taste
4 ounces garlic Yukon Gold mashed potatoes

Preheat oven to 500°F.

Marinate tomatoes in vinaigrette dressing. Set aside.

Make a beurre blanc sauce by sautéing shallots in butter until soft. Add the white wine and boil briefly until reduced by half. Add lemon juice and set aside.

Mix herbs and panko together. Brush rockfish fillet with mustard and coat with panko, shaking off excess.

Place breaded rockfish in 500°F oven and broil until fish is at least 160°F in the center and bread crumbs become a nice golden brown.

Meanwhile, cook corn and asparagus in boiling water for 3–5 minutes. Drain. Put vegetables into a sauté pan and season with salt and pepper. Lay the fish over mashed potatoes and surround with vegetables. Top with marinated tomatoes and drizzle with lemon beurre-blanc sauce.

I Can't Believe It's Not Crab Cakes (Mock Crab Cakes)
Recipe courtesy of Chef John Shields, Gertrude's, Baltimore, MD

MAKES 4

- 2 cups coarsely grated zucchini, drained in a colander for 30 minutes
- 1 cup bread crumbs, plus additional for coating
- 2 eggs
- 1 teaspoon Old Bay Seasoning
- 1 teaspoon Dijon mustard
- 1 tablespoon mayonnaise
- Juice of ½ lemon
- ¼ cup chopped fresh parsley
- Vegetable oil for frying

Mix the drained zucchini and 1 cup of bread crumbs together in a bowl. In another bowl, combine the eggs, Old Bay, mustard, mayo, lemon juice, and parsley. Beat well.

Combine both mixtures and fold together until mixed.

Heat oil in a skillet over medium-high heat. Form mixture into patties, dust in bread crumbs, and pan fry in hot oil until well browned on both sides.

Jumbo Lump Maryland Crab Cakes
Recipe courtesy of Ken Upton, Ken's Creative Kitchen, Annapolis, MD

SERVES 4

- 1 pound jumbo lump Maryland crabmeat
- 1 egg
- 1 tablespoon Dijon mustard
- ¼ cup mayonnaise (homemade with lemon would be great)
- ½ teaspoon salt
- ¼ teaspoon pepper
- ¼–½ cup fresh bread crumbs

Carefully pick over crabmeat to remove cartilage and bits of shell. Set aside.

Combine egg, mustard, mayonnaise, salt, and pepper in a large bowl and mix well.

Add the crabmeat to the mayonnaise mixture and stir until combined. Add enough bread crumbs to form a sticky mixture.

Shape the mixture into 4 crab cakes and sauté in a buttered skillet over medium heat until golden brown.

The Kitchen's Trout

Recipe courtesy of Chef-Owner Steve Quigg, The Kitchen at Rock Hall, Rock Hall, MD

SERVES 4

 3 red-skinned potatoes
 4 skinned rainbow trout fillets
 2 tablespoons canola oil
 4 cups mixed greens
 Salad dressing of your choice (a citrusy vinaigrette is ideal)
 Kosher salt, to serve
 Extra-virgin olive oil, to serve

Using a mandoline, thinly slice potatoes.

Place the trout fillets on a cutting board, skinned side up. Starting at the tail, place potato slices on the fillets, overlapping them to form a fish-scale pattern.

Heat canola oil over medium-high heat in a nonstick skillet large enough to hold 4 fillets, or use two skillets that can hold 2 fillets each.

Gently lay each crusted fillet, potato side down, into the skillet, being careful not to let the hot oil splash you.

Sauté each fillet for several minutes, until the potatoes start to brown (like a potato chip). Using a fish spatula, very carefully flip each fillet. Sauté for 1 more minute, then remove pan from heat and cover (fish will continue to cook).

Meanwhile, toss mixed greens with the salad dressing and place off-center on four plates. After 5 minutes, uncover the fillets and place one on each plate, leaning it on the greens. Sprinkle with a bit of kosher salt and drizzle in a "Z" pattern with a little high-quality extra-virgin olive oil to finish.

Les Moules Bistro (Mussels "Bistro-Style")

Recipe courtesy of Chef Loïc Jaffres, Cafe des Artistes, Leonardtown, MD

SERVES 2

For the mussels:
5 pounds mussels, cleaned
½ onion, diced
½ cup white wine
1 sprig fresh thyme
3 bay leaves

For the garlic butter:
1 pound butter
1 ounce Pernod

1 tablespoon chopped parsley
1 tablespoon chopped garlic

For the Provençale sauce:
Clarified butter
1 onion, diced
2 tomatoes, diced
½ tablespoon dried thyme
2 tablespoons capers
Salt and pepper, to taste

To prepare the mussels: Combine all ingredients in a large pot over medium heat. Steam until the mussels open. Allow the mussels to cool, and then remove them from their shells.

To make the garlic butter: Combine all ingredients in a bowl and blend well with an electric mixer.

To make the Provençale sauce: Melt clarified butter in a saucepan over medium heat. Add the onions and sauté until translucent. Add the tomatoes and cook for 8 minutes. Remove pan from heat and add thyme, capers, and salt and pepper.

To assemble the dish: Preheat oven to 350°F.

Place 6 cooked, cooled mussels in each of two escargot dishes and cover completely with garlic butter. Bake for 7–8 minutes.

Remove mussels from the oven and top each dish with 1 full tablespoon of Provençale sauce.

Finish under a broiler or salamander for 2 minutes. Serve with toasted croutons. Bon appétit!

PHOTO COURTESY OF CAFE DES ARTISTES

Mussels Arugula

Recipe courtesy of Chef Bill Vincent, Characters Bridge Restaurant, Tilghman Island, MD

SERVES 2

3 ounces extra-virgin olive oil
1 teaspoon chopped fresh garlic
Pinches kosher salt and black pepper
1 teaspoon dried oregano (or 1 tablespoon fresh)
6 ounces dry white wine

4 ounces chicken broth
24 Prince Edward Island mussels
6 ounces blue cheese crumbles
Handful of arugula
Lemon wedges
1 baguette

Heat olive oil in a saucepan. Add garlic, salt, pepper, oregano, wine, and broth.

Add mussels, cover, and simmer until mussels open.

Add blue cheese crumbles and place arugula on top.

Cover again for a few minutes until arugula wilts.

Uncover and pour all ingredients into a serving bowl. Garnish with lemon wedges and serve with a hot baguette for dipping.

PHOTO COURTESY OF CHARACTERS BRIDGE RESTAURANT

Osprey Point Rockfish

Recipe courtesy of Chef John Evans, Osprey Point Inn, Rock Hall, MD

SERVES 6

2 ounces diced bacon
1 shallot, minced
¼ cup Pernod
¾ cup heavy cream
12 ounces chopped fresh spinach
¼ cup Parmigiano-Reggiano

Salt
White pepper
4 (6-ounce) rockfish fillets
2 tablespoons unsalted butter
1 tablespoon olive oil

To make the sauce: Heat a skillet on medium-high and cook bacon bits until brown.

Add the shallots and cook, stirring constantly, for about 2 minutes.

Pour in Pernod and stir to deglaze the pan.

Add the cream and simmer, stirring constantly, until reduced by a third.

Add the spinach and stir until it just starts to wilt.

Add the cheese and stir until melted and mixed through.

Season to taste with salt and pepper and set aside.

To make the fish: Preheat oven to 350°F.

With a sharp knife, make a few incisions on the skin of the fish, making sure not to cut into the flesh. Salt and pepper the fish.

Add butter and oil to a skillet and turn heat up to high. Add the fish fillets, flesh side down, to the pan. Cook for 3–4 minutes until nicely browned, turn fish over to the skin side, and sear to a crispy finish.

While the fillets are cooking, add 1 tablespoon of the sauce to the top of each one. Once the fish is nearly cooked, put it in the oven to finish the cooking process and to meld the sauce and the fish.

Remove the fish from the oven and allow it to rest for a few moments before plating.

Paella Valenciana

Recipe courtesy of Executive Chef Emiliano Sanz, Tio Pepe, Baltimore, MD

SERVES 4

- ½ cup olive oil
- 1 whole chicken, cut into 8 pieces
- ½ pound cubed veal
- 2 garlic cloves, minced
- 1 large onion, chopped
- 1 fresh red pepper, chopped
- 1 squid, cleaned and sliced
- 2 cups rice
- 5 cups chicken broth or water
- Pinch saffron
- ½ cup string beans
- ½ cup green peas
- 1 pound large shrimp
- 12 mussels
- 8 clams
- Meat from whole cooked lobster, cut into chunks
- Salt, to taste
- 3 canned red pimentos, sliced into 1-inch-thick pieces
- Lemon wedges, to serve

Preheat oven to 425°F.

In a paella pan, heat olive oil over high flame. Add the chicken and veal and brown, turning to color all sides.

Add garlic, onion, red pepper, and squid. Cook, stirring, until they are lightly browned.

Stir in rice, mixing well with other ingredients. Add broth (or water) and saffron and heat until boiling.

Add string beans and green peas and cook to desired doneness.

Add shrimp, mussels, clams, and lobster and allow to boil until liquid is absorbed. Salt to taste.

Place sliced pimentos on top, remove from stove, and bake for 25 minutes.

Remove from oven, garnish with fresh lemon wedges, and bring the paella pan to the table to serve.

Pan-Seared Sea Scallops

Recipe courtesy of Chef Christopher Lawrence and his talented kitchen staff, Port Tobacco Restaurant, Port Tobacco, MD

MAKES 20 PORTIONS

For the vinaigrette:
¼ cup olive oil
¾ cup red wine vinegar
1 tablespoon garlic, minced
Salt and pepper, to taste

1 red beet
1 golden beet
1 candy-striped beet
Olive oil
Salt and pepper, to taste
20–30 diver scallops
Fresh arugula

To prepare the vinaigrette: Mix all ingredients until well combined; set aside.

To prepare the dish: Preheat oven to 350°F. Spread the beets out on a sheet pan. Drizzle with olive oil and sprinkle with salt and pepper. Roast beets until fork-tender, about 30–40 minutes.

Under cool water, wash diver scallops. Pat dry with a paper towel. Once dry, look for the side muscle attached to each scallop and remove it. Spreading the scallops out evenly, lightly sprinkle with salt and pepper on both sides.

Once the beets have become fork-tender, peel them, and then dice them into ¼-inch-thick pieces.

Heat a sauté pan over medium to high heat until hot. Drizzle the pan with olive oil. Place each scallop down flat in the pan. Once the scallops have become golden brown, flip them and sear off the other side. (The scallops' thickness will determine the cooking time.) If the scallops don't reach an internal temperature of 120–125°F, put them in the oven until they do.

Rinse the arugula to remove any debris, and then lightly dry the leaves. Gently toss the arugula in the vinaigrette; add salt and pepper, to taste.

To serve: Layer the arugula with some of the beets and then top with a seared scallop.

Pan-Seared Striped Bass with a Spring Salad of Peas & Carrots

Recipe courtesy of Chef Douglas Potts, Peacock Restaurant & Lounge, Easton, MD

SERVES 1

For the ginger-carrot vinaigrette:
Juice of 6 carrots
4 tablespoons pickled ginger
¼ cup canola oil
Juice of 2 lemons
Salt and pepper, to taste

For the striped bass:
Canola oil
1 striped bass (aka rockfish) fillet

For the salad:
Pea tendrils
10 to 12 peeled baby carrots with tops, halved lengthwise
    and blanched for 4 minutes

To make the vinaigrette: Combine all ingredients in a blender and mix until well blended. Set aside.

To make the striped bass: Heat canola oil in a large skillet over medium-high heat. Pan-sear striped bass until golden brown.

To serve: Place pea tendrils and baby carrots next to one another on a serving plate. Carefully place the striped bass fillet on top of the pea tendrils. Liberally spoon ginger-carrot vinaigrette over the fish and carrots.

PHOTO COURTESY OF INN AT 202 DOVER

Pasta Pescatore
Recipe courtesy of Tidewater Grille, Havre de Grace, MD

SERVES 4

    1 tablespoon olive oil
    1 small red pepper, chopped
    1 small onion, chopped
    3 littleneck clams
    4 large scallops
    4 large shrimp, peeled and deveined
    1 (3-ounce) lobster tail, chopped
    8–10 mussels
    ½ teaspoon chopped garlic
    ¼ cup dry white wine
    6 ounces marinara sauce
    4 ounces heavy cream
    7 ounces pasta, cooked
    Lemon wedges, for garnish

Heat oil in a large sauté pan and sauté red peppers and onions until soft.

Add clams and scallops. When scallops are halfway done, flip and add shrimp, lobster, and mussels. Sauté until mussels and clams open and the seafood is almost done.

Add garlic and deglaze the pan with the white wine.

Add the marinara sauce and heavy cream and stir gently until well combined with the seafood.

To serve: Ladle the seafood sauce over cooked pasta and garnish with lemon wedges.

Rockfish Love Point

Recipe courtesy of Chef George Betz, Boatyard Bar & Grill, Annapolis, MD

SERVES 1

This is an original recipe the chef often prepares by special request.

For the lemon herb butter:
1 cup butter, softened
1 tablespoon grated lemon rind
¼ cup fresh lemon juice
2 tablespoons chopped fresh
  parsley
2 tablespoons chopped fresh
  basil
1 tablespoon minced shallots
1 tablespoon chopped fresh
  chives

¼ teaspoon freshly ground
  pepper

1 (8-ounce) fresh rockfish fillet
Olive oil to rub fillets
Sea salt and pepper, to taste
2–3 ounces jumbo lump
  crabmeat (Maryland is best)
2–3 heirloom cherry tomatoes
2–3 fresh asparagus spears,
  blanched
4 ounces cooked rice

To prepare the lemon herb butter: Combine all ingredients and refrigerate until ready to use in this recipe. Freeze the remainder for future use on fish, chicken, steaks, or vegetables.

To prepare the fish: Rub each fillet with a touch of olive oil, sea salt, and pepper.

Place fillet on a medium-hot grill and cook 3–4 minutes, making sure you switch angles so you get those sexy grill marks on the fish. (Do not overcook the fish; you can always cook it more, but once it's overcooked, there's no taking it back.)

In a saucepan, either over a burner or on the grill, melt half or all of the lemon butter (according to taste) and gently toss it with the crab and tomatoes until everything is warm.

Just before the fish is done, throw the blanched asparagus on the grill to heat.

To serve: Mound the rice on a plate. When the fish is done, place it on top of the cooked rice. Arrange crab, tomatoes, and butter sauce over the fish and top with asparagus spears.

Rock & Crab

Recipe courtesy of Chef James Hughes, Restaurant 213, Fruitland, MD

SERVES 2

½ cup minced shallots
1 cup dry white wine
2 tablespoons minced fresh tarragon
¼ cup sun-dried tomatoes
Salt and pepper, to taste
1 cup jumbo lump crabmeat
3 cups heavy cream
Salt and pepper, to taste
2 (8-ounce) fresh rockfish fillets
¼ cup sweet butter, melted
Enough wine or stock to moisten surface of fish
2 cups sautéed spinach
Fresh tarragon sprigs for garnish, optional
Lemon wedges for garnish, optional

Preheat oven to 375°F.

Combine first 6 ingredients in a large saucepan over medium heat.

Simmer until the wine is almost evaporated.

Add the heavy cream and reduce the mixture by half. Season with salt and pepper, to taste.

Place the rockfish on an oiled cookie sheet and top with melted butter. Add small amount of wine or stock to the surface of the fish.

Bake rockfish in the oven for 6–7 minutes or until done.

To serve: Place the rockfish on a bed of sautéed spinach and top with the crab-cream sauce. Garnish with fresh tarragon sprigs and/or lemon wedges.

Salt-Crusted Rockfish with Crab Cream Sauce
Recipe courtesy of Chef Brian Julian, Watermen's Inn, Crisfield, MD
SERVES 4

For the fish:
6 egg whites
2 tablespoons chopped herbs
(parsley/dill/thyme/chives/
rosemary)
2 pounds kosher salt
2 tablespoons black pepper
1 (2-pound) fresh rockfish,
cleaned and deboned, skin on

For the crab cream sauce:
1 tablespoon butter
2 tablespoons finely chopped
shallots
1 cup dry white wine
2 cups heavy cream
Salt and pepper, to taste
8 ounces lump crabmeat
Chopped parsley
Lemon juice

To make the fish: Preheat oven to 350°F. In a small bowl, whip egg whites for approximately 1 minute. Add herbs, salt, and pepper and mix with a spoon to make a slurry, like wet snow.

Apply a small amount of the salt mixture, approximately the size of the fish, to a baking sheet. Lay fish on salt bed and apply remaining mixture on top of and around fish to seal it. Do not put mixture in cavity.

Once fish is encased in salt mixture, bake for approximately 30 minutes. The salt will harden around the fish, thus steaming the flesh inside.

To check for doneness, chip off a piece of salt and test the fish to see if it flakes easily. Remove from oven and let rest.

To make the sauce: Heat saucepan or skillet over medium heat, add butter and shallots, and cook until translucent.

Stir in wine and heavy cream, season with salt and pepper, and simmer until reduced.

Add crabmeat, a little chopped parsley, and a squeeze of lemon juice.

To serve: Carefully remove salt crust from around fish and brush off any remaining chunks. Peel off skin, divide into four portions, transfer to four plates, and ladle sauce over fish.

Scallops a la Bistro St. Michaels
(Scallops with Pork Belly)
**Recipe courtesy of Chef David Hayes, Bistro St. Michaels,
St. Michaels, MD**

SERVES 2-4

Chef's note: Using fresh day-boat scallops is a must for this dish. Go to
your local seafood market and ask for them; if you see them swimming in
something that looks like milk, walk away.

Note: This recipe requires 3 days of advance prep work.

For the cured pork belly:
1 cup salt
1 cup sugar
6 sprigs fresh thyme
3 pounds fresh pork belly
½ gallon orange juice
2 tablespoons freshly ground black pepper

Mix salt, sugar, and thyme together and rub mixture on both sides of pork
belly, leaving a heavy layer on each side. Refrigerate in a large storage
container for 2 days.

Remove pork belly from container, rinse well, and soak in orange juice (using
the same container is fine) for one more day.

Preheat oven to 300°F. Place pork belly on baking rack, pat dry, and dust with
black pepper.

Bake for 3½ hours and then set aside to cool.

Once cooled, cut the pork belly into big slices.

Fry the slices in an oiled skillet over medium heat until browned. Drain on
paper towels.

For the sherried white corn rogue:
2 tablespoons olive oil
4 shallots, sliced
2 cloves garlic, minced
1 cup fresh white corn kernels
1 cup dry sherry
1 cup heavy cream

¼ cup fresh green peas

½ bunch parsley, finely chopped

½ cup heirloom cherry tomatoes

Heat olive oil in a deep-bottomed pan and cook shallots and garlic until soft.

Add corn and cook for several minutes until tender. Add sherry and reduce by a little over a half.

Add heavy cream and reduce by half again, adding peas halfway through. You will know it is ready when the cream thickens and binds everything together.

Keep warm until ready to serve. Just before serving, stir in the parsley and cherry tomatoes.

For the scallops:

Vegetable oil

1 pound day-boat scallops

Salt and pepper, to taste

2 ounces butter

1 tablespoon lemon juice

Add a little oil to a thick-bottomed sauté pan and heat on high until you see some smoke coming from the pan.

Season scallops with salt and pepper and very carefully place scallops in the pan. Let cook for 1 minute, turn over, and cook for another minute until golden brown.

Add the butter and lemon juice to the pan, remove the pan from the heat, and with a spoon, ladle the butter and lemon mixture over the scallops again and again until they shine. (The butter will start turning golden brown, but you want that!)

To serve: Mound the sherried corn mixture on a plate, top with sauced scallops, and surround with crisp pork belly slices.

Seafood Alfredo

Recipe courtesy of G&M Restaurant, Linthicum, MD

SERVES 4

For the Alfredo sauce:
8 ounces heavy cream
2 ounces sweet butter
Fresh ground pepper
2 ounces freshly grated
Parmigiano-Reggiano
cheese

For the seafood:
2 tablespoons butter,
melted
8 medium shrimp, peeled
and deveined
4 jumbo sea scallops
½ cup dry white wine
3 ounces jumbo lump crabmeat

PHOTO COURTESY OF G&M RESTAURANT

12 ounces linguini, prepared according to package directions
Fresh Italian parsley, chopped

To make the Alfredo sauce: Pour heavy cream in a saucepan over medium heat and cook until reduced, stirring constantly.

Add sweet butter, pepper, and grated Parmigiano-Reggiano cheese and stir until thick and smooth. Remove from heat and set aside.

To prepare the seafood: Heat butter in a skillet over medium heat. Add the shrimp and scallops and sauté for approximately 2 minutes.

Pour in the white wine to deglaze the skillet. Stir.

Add the lump crabmeat and stir gently until combined.

Add the Alfredo sauce to the skillet, stir, and simmer mixture for another minute.

To serve: Toss the seafood Alfredo with linguini and divide among four bowls. Sprinkle each serving of pasta with chopped Italian parsley.

Seafood Fra Diavolo

Recipe courtesy of Rustico Restaurant & Wine Bar, Stevensville MD

SERVES 6

- 3 cups diced tomatoes
- 8 ounces tomato sauce
- 2 teaspoons crushed red pepper flakes
- 1 tablespoon fresh chopped parsley
- 1 tablespoon fresh chopped basil
- ¾ cup dry red wine
- 1 pound linguini
- 4 tablespoons olive oil
- 8 garlic cloves, minced
- 24 littleneck clams
- 24 mussels
- 8 ounces bay scallops
- 8 ounces calamari
- 4 ounces shrimp (peeled and tails removed)
- 8 ounces fresh lobster meat
- Salt and pepper, to taste

In a saucepan, combine the tomatoes, tomato sauce, red pepper flakes, parsley, and basil and bring to a boil. Lower the heat, add the red wine, and let simmer for 10–15 minutes, stirring as needed.

Meanwhile, bring another large pot of lightly salted water to a boil. Add the linguini and boil for 8–10 minutes, or until al dente. Drain and set aside.

While the sauce is simmering and the pasta is cooking, in another large skillet, heat the olive oil with the garlic over medium heat.

When the garlic starts to sizzle, add the clams and mussels. Once the shells have opened, add the rest of the seafood and cook for about 5 minutes.

Once the seafood is ready, add it to the pan full of sauce and then toss with the pasta until well combined. Season with salt and pepper, to taste, and serve immediately.

Seafood Tourte

Recipe courtesy of Chef-Owner Alain Matrat, Les Folies Brasserie, Annapolis, MD

SERVES 1-2

This recipe was shared by Owner Alain Matrat in memory of his dear friend and longtime chef at Les Folies, Jean Claude Galan, who died in 2009. While it is too intricate for the average cook, it may be an inspiration to many readers.

For the garnish:

8 sea scallops
16 Prince Edward Island mussels
4 jumbo shrimp
4 clams
4 button mushrooms
2 tablespoons chopped shallots
1 tablespoon chopped garlic
1 teaspoon chopped fresh thyme
1 cup dry white wine
½ cup dry vermouth
2 bay leaves

Steam seafood for 5 minutes in a casserole with mushrooms, shallots, garlic, thyme, white wine, dry vermouth, and bay leaves. Set aside to cool.

For the fish stock:

Vegetable oil
2 carrots, sliced
2 leeks, sliced
1 whole onion, sliced
½ celery stalk
2 bay leaves
½ pound fish bones
1 gallon water

Coat a large pot with a film of oil and add sliced vegetables and bay leaves. Cover and let sweat until tender.

Add fish bones, stir, and let cook for a few minutes.

Add water and bring to a boil. Simmer 20 minutes, strain, and reserve liquid fish stock.

For the fish veloute:
2 onions, sliced
2 cups dry white wine
5 ounces dry vermouth
Reserved broth from steamed seafood
Reserved fish stock
1 quart heavy cream
5 ounces butter
6 ounces flour
Salt and pepper to taste

To a casserole, add sliced onions, white wine, vermouth, seafood broth, and fish stock. Bring to a boil and simmer over medium heat for 10 minutes.

Add heavy cream and cook until reduced by half.

In a small saucepan, melt butter and add flour to make a roux. Cook for 4 minutes on low heat.

Stir roux into the fish veloute and cook on low for 5 minutes to thicken, stirring often. Add salt and pepper, to taste.

Pastry shell for tourte:
2 frozen puff pastry sheets
Melted butter

Preheat oven to 400°F. Place puff pastry sheets on flat cutting surface to soften for 5 minutes. Use an 8-inch round plate and a 6-inch round plate as cutting templates, placing them upside down on pastry sheets as your cutting guide.

On one sheet, use a sharp knife to cut two 8-inch circles. Repeat on second pastry sheet.

Cover a cookie pan with wax paper, place two of the circles several inches apart on the pan, and brush with melted butter.

On the remaining two 8-inch circles, center a 6-inch plate on each and cut around them to form two rings.

Remove rings, press on top of first circles (now on the cookie sheet), and score the outer edges.

Remove remaining 6-inch circles and layer on top of pastry shell (forming a lid), making sure you brush the dough before doing so.

Prick the dough with a fork and drag a fork over the top circle to make a pattern.

Bake at 400°F until puffy and golden brown, about 20 minutes. Let cool.

Use a sharp paring knife to remove the top "lid" without cutting the bottom pastry.

To serve: Fill the tourte with the shellfish mixture, including mushrooms, top with the pastry lid, and place the tourte back in the oven for 3 minutes. Ladle fish veloute over the tourte and serve.

Note: This dish is not on the regular menu at Les Folies, but may be ordered in advance.

Seared Diver Scallops

Recipe courtesy of Chef Jeff Burress, The Granary, Georgetown, MD

SERVES 1

- 4 large sea scallops
- Kosher salt and fresh cracked pepper, to taste
- 2 tablespoons extra-virgin olive oil
- 1 teaspoon unsalted butter
- ½ cup diced watermelon
- 1 teaspoon pickled red onion
- 1 teaspoon chopped pickled jalapeño
- 1 ounce crumbled feta cheese
- 1 cup baby arugula
- ½ orange, juiced
- ½ lemon, juiced
- 1 tablespoon balsamic reduction
- Thin slices lemon and orange, for garnish

Heat a sauté pan over medium-high heat.

Pat scallops dry and season with salt and pepper.

Add 1 tablespoon of the olive oil to the pan and sear scallops on one side until golden brown; flip scallops over and turn heat down to very low.

Add butter to pan and baste scallops as butter melts. Turn off heat and let scallops rest while making the salad.

Combine watermelon, pickled onion, jalapeño, feta, and arugula in a small mixing bowl.

Blend the remaining olive oil and citrus juices, add salt and pepper to taste, and add to salad, tossing gently to coat.

To serve: Arrange salad on a plate and place scallops on top. Drizzle with balsamic reduction and serve garnished with thin slices of lemon and orange.

Shad Roe

Recipe courtesy of Faidley Seafood at Lexington Market, Baltimore, MD

SERVES 1–2

    1 large set or 2 medium sets shad roe (fish eggs)
    3 tablespoons butter
    1 tablespoon olive oil
    1 garlic clove, minced
    2 chopped green onions
    Salt and pepper, to taste
    ¼ cup dry white wine
    2 strips bacon, cooked and crumbled
    Lemon wedges, for garnish

Place roe in a sauté pan with just enough water to cover.

Bring water to a simmer over medium heat and poach the roe until it is gray and firm, about 5 minutes. Do not allow the water to boil. Poaching seals the membrane and reduces the chance of the tiny eggs popping during the browning process.

Carefully pour off all the water and add 1 tablespoon of the butter, along with the olive oil, garlic, and onions, to the pan.

Gently brown everything over medium-low heat until a light golden crust forms on the roe. Add salt and pepper to taste.

When the roe is browned and firm throughout (3–5 minutes), transfer it to a serving plate.

Add wine to the pan and cook over high heat until the wine is reduced by half. Whisk in the remaining butter until well combined, and then pour the butter-wine mixture over the roe.

To serve, top the roe with crumbled bacon and garnish with lemon wedges.

Note: Each spring, shad migrate from ocean waters to the Chesapeake Bay, where they spawn in its rivers and streams. Its roe, or eggs, are considered a delicacy.

Shirley Phillips' Signature Crab Cakes

Recipe courtesy of Phillips Seafood Restaurant, Annapolis, MD

MAKES 6

- 1 egg
- 2 teaspoons Worcestershire sauce
- ½ teaspoon dry mustard
- 2 tablespoons mayonnaise
- 1 teaspoon lemon juice
- 1 tablespoon mustard
- 1 tablespoon melted butter
- 1 teaspoon parsley flakes
- 1 teaspoon Phillips Seafood Seasoning
- ½ cup bread crumbs
- 1 pound Phillips crabmeat, picked over

In a large mixing bowl, combine all ingredients except for crabmeat. Gently fold in the crabmeat, being careful not to break up the lumps.

Shape into 6 cakes. Pan-fry or bake at 375°F for 12–15 minutes or until evenly browned on each side and internal temperature reaches 165°F.

Shrimp & Grits
Recipe courtesy of Sascha's 527 Cafe, Baltimore, MD

MAKES 4 APPETIZER SERVINGS

    12 large shrimp
    ¼ cup olive oil
    Juice of 1 lemon
    1 teaspoon Cajun seasoning or herb/spice of your choice
    1 link andouille sausage, diced
    ½ red pepper, diced
    1 jalapeño pepper, cleaned and diced
    2 tablespoons cooking oil
    2 cups water
    2 cups heavy cream
    1 cup stone-ground grits
    ¼ cup freshly grated Parmesan cheese
    ½ tablespoon salt
    1 teaspoon pepper
    Lemon slices, for garnish

Marinate the shrimp in olive oil, lemon juice, and Cajun spices for 30 minutes.

Remove shrimp from marinade and grill on a hot grill for about 2 minutes per side.

In a 2-quart saucepan, sauté the sausage, red peppers, and jalapeños in oil for 2–3 minutes, or until sausage starts to brown.

Add water and cream, bring to a boil, and slowly add grits.

Cook on low for about 25–30 minutes, stirring occasionally. If you want creamier grits, add more water.

Stir in Parmesan cheese, salt, and pepper when grits are done. Adjust with additional salt and pepper, as needed.

To serve, divide grits among four small plates and top with 3 grilled shrimp each. Garnish with lemon slices and serve warm.

Shrimp Sauté alla Scossa

Recipe courtesy of Chef-Owner Giancarlo Tondon, Scossa Restaurant, Easton, MD

SERVES 6

  2½ pounds large shrimp, peeled and deveined
  Salt
  Freshly ground pepper
  Flour for dredging
  4–6 tablespoons olive oil
  ¼ cup unsalted butter, cut into bits
  ¼ cup chopped flat-leaf parsley
  1 tablespoon chopped, drained capers
  2 tablespoons chopped unsweetened gherkins or cornichons
  Dash of Worcestershire sauce
  ¼ cup tomato sauce
  Juice of ½ lemon

Wash the shrimp and dry them well with paper towels. Season with salt and pepper, dredge them in flour, and shake them in a sieve to remove excess flour.

Heat the olive oil in a large skillet over medium-high heat. Add the shrimp and cook them in batches, tossing constantly, for 4–5 minutes, until they are slightly browned and crisp.

Remove the shrimp from the pan with a slotted spoon and arrange them in one layer in a shallow ovenproof dish. Pour off the oil from the skillet, add the butter and parsley, and cook for 30 seconds or so, until the butter just starts to brown.

Sprinkle the capers and gherkins over the shrimp, sprinkle on a few drops of Worcestershire sauce, and dot with tomato sauce. Squeeze on some lemon juice and pour the butter and parsley over all. Serve immediately.

Soft Crab with Chipotle Sauce & Fried Green Tomatoes

Recipe courtesy of Cantler's Riverside Inn, Annapolis, MD

SERVES 1

- 2 tablespoons olive oil
- ¼ cup roasted corn kernels
- ¼ cup canned black beans
- 2 tablespoons chopped red onion
- 2 tablespoons chopped cilantro
- ½ cup heavy cream
- 2 tablespoons chipotle sauce
- ½ teaspoon Montreal seafood seasoning
- 2 ounces jumbo crabmeat
- 1 large soft-shelled crab
- 3 slices fried green tomatoes

Heat olive oil in a small skillet over medium heat. Add corn, black beans, onion, and cilantro and sauté until onions soften and the mixture is fragrant.

In another skillet, heat the heavy cream, chipotle sauce, seafood seasoning, and crabmeat. Gently mix together.

Meanwhile, coat the soft crab with cornmeal and fry in an oiled skillet until crusty and golden brown.

To serve, arrange the fried green tomatoes in a triangular pattern, place soft crab in the center, and top with the chipotle-cream sauce.

Tournedos Baltimore

Recipe courtesy of Executive Chef Wernfried Wiesnegger, Bayard House, Chesapeake City, MD

SERVES 1

    3 ounces lump crabmeat
    3 ounces lobster meat
    3 ounces mayonnaise
    1 egg
    Salt and pepper, to taste
    1 ounce Champagne
    1 ounce tomato paste
    1 ounce Madeira wine
    4 ounces heavy cream
    2 ounces butter
    2 (4-ounce) center-cut filet mignons, sautéed or grilled
    1 ounce caviar

Put crabmeat and lobster meat in separate bowls and divide the mayonnaise equally between the two, mixing gently to combine.

Crack the egg in a small bowl, whisk it, and then divide it evenly between the two mayonnaise-seafood mixtures.

Add salt and pepper to taste and form mixtures into one crab cake and one lobster cake.

Put the Champagne and the tomato paste in one saucepan; put the Madeira in a second saucepan. Divide the heavy cream equally between the two pans.

Simmer the sauces until they're creamy and reduced. Season with salt and pepper, to taste.

Heat butter in a skillet and sauté the crab cake and lobster cake until both are golden brown and cooked through.

To assemble the dish: Place the crab cake on top of one filet mignon and the lobster cake on top of the other. Spoon the Champagne sauce over the lobster cake and the Madeira sauce over the crab cake.

Garnish with caviar and enjoy!

Tuna Tacos with Ginger Pineapple Coleslaw

Recipe courtesy of The Masthead at Pier Street Marina, Oxford, MD

SERVES 2

- 1 whole pineapple
- 12 ounces fresh ahi tuna steak
- Cajun seasoning, to taste
- 1 head green cabbage, chopped
- 1 small carrot, shredded
- 1 cup mayonnaise
- 4 ounces apple cider vinegar
- 1½ teaspoons ground ginger
- 4 small flour tortillas

Cut pineapple in half, reserving juice, and grill for 5–7 minutes. Finish off in a 350°F oven until soft. Let cool. Cut into small chunks and reserve.

Dredge tuna steaks in Cajun seasoning and sear in a hot skillet until rare. Let cool and cut into thin slices.

To make the coleslaw, mix together cabbage, carrot, mayonnaise, vinegar, pineapple chunks, reserved pineapple juice, and ginger.

To serve, grill tortillas briefly and fill with a generous amount of slaw. Add sliced tuna and serve immediately.

Whole Fish with Thai Hoisin Glaze

Recipe courtesy of Owner/Executive Chef Julius Adam Sanders, Jules Fine Dining, Ocean City, MD

SERVES 4

Note: This recipe requires a deep fryer.

Oil for deep frying
1 whole fish, such as rockfish or
   snapper (about 1½ pounds)
½ cup flour
½ cup hoisin sauce
½ cup oyster sauce
½ cup soy sauce
1 tablespoon sesame oil
1 tablespoon minced garlic
1 tablespoon minced ginger
1 teaspoon hot sauce
Toasted sesame seeds, for garnish
Microgreens, for garnish

PHOTO COURTESY OF JULES FINE DINING

Score fish with a sharp knife, cutting through skin in a crisscross pattern.

Coat fish with flour, shaking off excess. Carefully place fish in hot oil in a deep fryer for 8–10 minutes or until done.

Meanwhile, make the glaze by mixing together all the other ingredients, except sesame seeds and microgreens, in a small saucepan over medium heat until warm.

Remove fish from fryer and drain on paper towels.

To serve, drizzle glaze over fish and garnish with toasted sesame seeds and microgreens.

Sides, Sauces & Rubs

Blackened Catfish Rub

Recipe courtesy of Chef Chad Wells, formerly of Rockfish Restaurant in Annapolis, MD.

MAKES ENOUGH FOR SEVERAL DISHES

2 tablespoons cinnamon
3 tablespoons cumin
5 tablespoons sweet paprika
3 tablespoons coriander

6 tablespoons granulated garlic
5 tablespoons kosher salt
5 tablespoons brown sugar

Thoroughly mix all ingredients until well combined. Store in an airtight container. Use as a rub for catfish or other seafood.

Crab & Corn Pudding

Recipe courtesy of Wendy Palmer, Latitude 38 Bistro & Spirits, Oxford, MD

SERVES 4

4 cups milk
1 cup yellow cornmeal
2 tablespoons sugar
⅓ teaspoon salt
Pinch cayenne pepper
4 eggs

½ cup butter, melted and cooled, plus extra for pan
½ teaspoon baking powder
2 cups fresh corn (taken off the cob)
1 pound crabmeat

Preheat oven to 350°F.

In a saucepan, heat milk to a simmer. Stir in cornmeal, sugar, salt, and cayenne pepper. Bring to a boil, stir, and simmer on low for 5–6 minutes. Remove from heat and set aside to cool for 10 minutes.

In a bowl, whisk together the eggs, melted butter, and baking powder. Stir in the fresh corn.

Add the cornmeal mixture to the wet ingredients, stir to combine, and then gently fold in the crabmeat.

Pour mixture into a well-buttered 2½-quart baking dish and bake at 350°F for 45–60 minutes, or until the top is lightly browned and a knife inserted near the center comes out clean.

Oyster & Smithfield Ham Cream Sauce for Pasta

Recipe courtesy of Chef-Owner Kevin McKinney, Brooks Tavern, Chestertown, MD

SERVES 6

- 6 tablespoons butter
- ½ cup diced Smithfield ham
- 2 cups heavy cream
- 6 leaves fresh sage, finely shredded
- 1 quart shucked oysters
- Salt and fresh ground pepper, to taste
- Grated cheese, optional

Melt butter in a large pan or pot over medium heat. Add the ham and cook for 1 minute.

Turn the heat up to high and add the cream and sage.

Cook, stirring constantly, over medium heat until the cream mixture is reduced by half.

Add oysters and cook, stirring, until they slightly curl at the edges.

Remove from heat, season to taste with salt and pepper, and ladle the sauce on top of your favorite pasta.

Sprinkle with grated cheese, if desired, and serve in pasta bowls.

Tomato Pie

Recipe courtesy of Chef John Shields, Gertrude's, Baltimore, MD

SERVES 6

"The traditional tomato pie made in-season with Maryland tomatoes is a fantastic appetizer—or, as peculiar as it sounds, dessert," says Chef John Shields. "It is also a perfect lunch dish with a salad of arugula and mixed greens. You'll like the contrast of the bitter arugula with the sweetness of the pie. For dessert, top a slice with a dollop of whipped cream that is lightly sweetened with maple syrup."

6 ripe tomatoes, peeled and cut into ½-inch slices
½ cup firmly packed brown sugar
Salt and pepper, to taste
Pinch of mace or nutmeg
1 cup dry bread crumbs
1 tablespoon fresh lemon juice
4 tablespoons unsalted butter
Pastry dough for 1 single-crust pie
1 egg, beaten with 1 tablespoon water, for glaze

Preheat oven to 350°F. Butter the bottom of a 9-inch pie pan.

Place a layer of tomato slices in the pie pan and sprinkle with some of the sugar, salt, pepper, mace or nutmeg, and bread crumbs. Continue making layers, ending with bread crumbs. Sprinkle with lemon juice and dot with butter.

On a lightly floured board, roll out the dough to form a top crust, transfer to the pan, and flute the edges with a fork. Brush top with egg glaze.

Bake 30–35 minutes or until nicely browned. Remove from oven. Pie is best served warm or at room temperature.

Drinks

Harrison's Famous Oyster Shooter
Recipe courtesy of Harrison's Harbor Watch, Ocean City, MD

SERVES 1

    1 Chesapeake Bay oyster, shucked, natural liquor reserved
    2 ounces chili-infused Finlandia vodka (see note below)
    3 dashes Tabasco sauce
    1½ ounces cocktail sauce
    1 dash Worcestershire sauce
    2 dashes black pepper
    ¼ lemon wedge

Place shucked oyster, including its natural liquor, into a small rocks glass.

Pour chilled vodka over ice in a cocktail shaker.

Combine vodka and all other ingredients except the lemon wedge in the glass with the oyster. Stir well and garnish with a lemon wedge.

Note: To make chili-infused vodka, add 7 dried hot chili peppers (chile de árbol are recommended) to 1 liter of Finlandia vodka. Let infuse for 2 weeks. Vodka will naturally take on a golden amber color when ready.

Sangria
Recipe courtesy of Tio Pepe, Baltimore, MD

SERVES 4

    ⅓ cup sliced apples
    ⅓ cup sliced oranges
    ⅓ cup sliced lemons
    Ice cubes
    2 tablespoons sugar
    3 ounces triple sec
    3 ounces brandy
    1 large bottle heavy red table wine

Place sliced fruit and ice cubes in a 2-quart pitcher.

Add sugar, triple sec, and brandy. Stir with a wooden spoon and pour in enough wine to fill pitcher. Work spoon up and down hard enough to crush fruit and mix thoroughly.

Taste and add more sugar, if necessary.

Mix again just before serving to add sparkle; pour over ice in stemmed goblets.

Desserts

Smith Island Cake

Recipe courtesy of Chef Henry Miller, Two If By Sea, Tilghman, MD

SERVES 12-16

Note: You will need 7 9-inch cake pans for this recipe.

For the cake:
2 cups sugar
2 sticks unsalted butter, cut into chunks and softened
5 eggs
3 cups flour
½ teaspoon salt
1½ teaspoons baking powder
1 cup evaporated milk
Zest of 1 small orange
½ cup water
Food coloring: red, pink, orange, yellow, green, blue, and purple

Preheat oven to 350°F. Using an electric mixer, cream sugar and butter together on low speed. Add eggs and beat until smooth. Sift flour, salt, and baking powder together and add to eggs, 1 cup at a time, mixing well after each addition.

Combine milk, orange zest, and water, with mixer running, add to batter and mix just until liquids incorporated into batter.

Divide batter into 7 bowls. Add food coloring and mix till bright. Spray pans well with nonstick spray. Pour batter into pans and spread evenly.

Bake at 350°F for 8–10 minutes or until toothpick inserted in the middle comes out clean.

Tap each pan and turn out onto parchment sheets. Let cool.

Note: Begin making the frosting when the first batch of cakes goes into the oven so you'll be ready to start "building" the cake as soon as the layers cool.

For the frosting:
1 pound butter
5 cups confectioners' sugar
2 teaspoons pure vanilla extract

Whip butter till soft.

Add confectioners' sugar and vanilla.

Whip on low till sugar is combined. Then whip at medium speed till fluffy.

To assemble the cake: Place purple cooled layer on large cake plate. Spread blue layer with icing and flip onto first. Line layers up evenly.

Repeat process with green, yellow, orange, pink, and red. Generously frost top and sides of cake.

Let chill and set for 1 hour.

Don't tell anyone it's a rainbow cake. Watch their reactions when you cut it. Enjoy!

White Chocolate Mousse in a Bag with Strawberry Garnish

Recipe courtesy of The Narrows, Grasonville, MD

This recipe is Narrows Restaurant's signature dessert.

SERVES 6

For the mousse:

2 teaspoons unflavored powdered gelatin
4 large egg yolks
¼ cup sugar
3 cups heavy cream
½ cup whole milk
½ teaspoon kosher salt
10½ ounces white chocolate, chopped
2 cups whole strawberries

For the chocolate bags:

1 pound good-quality chocolate, chopped into peanut-size pieces
6 small wax-coated or cellophane bags, approximately 3 inches wide and
  4 inches tall (see note)

Note: Small popcorn bags or hot dog serving bags work best. However, some coffee bags can also be used, but due to the larger dimensions, they may need to be cut down in size. Also, a waxy pastry bag or small cellophane bags from a candy store can be used.

To prepare the mousse: In a small bowl, sprinkle the gelatin over 2 tablespoons of water and let stand for 5 minutes.

In a medium bowl, beat the egg yolks with the sugar until fluffy.

In a medium saucepan, combine ½ cup of the cream with the milk and salt and bring to a simmer.

While whisking constantly, drizzle the hot milk mixture into the egg yolks until incorporated. Transfer the mixture back to the saucepan and cook over low heat, stirring, until the custard is thickened and coats the back of a spoon, about 10 minutes. Remove from the heat.

Add the dissolved gelatin and chopped white chocolate to the custard and stir until the chocolate is melted.

Strain the custard into a medium metal bowl set in a bowl of ice water and cool to room temperature, stirring, about 2 minutes. Remove the bowl from the ice bath.

In a large bowl, beat the remaining 2½ cups heavy cream until soft peaks form. Gently fold the whipped cream into the custard. Refrigerate the mousse until chilled, about 2 hours.

To make the chocolate bags: Fold 1 to 2 inches of the top edge of each bag outward to create a lip at the desired height (approximately 4 inches tall). The lip will be used to handle the bags when removing the paper from the chocolate.

Place the bags on a flat baking sheet or plate that can fit in the refrigerator and freezer.

Heat water in the bottom of a double boiler until just simmering.

Put chocolate pieces in the top of the double boiler and cook, stirring constantly, until the chocolate reaches approximately 89°F, as measured on a candy thermometer.

Using a pastry brush, begin "painting" the inside of each bag with the melted chocolate, being careful to cover all four sides and the bottom.

Allow first coat of chocolate to harden, and then apply a second coat.

Place the coated bags in the freezer for a minimum of several hours; the longer, the better.

When chocolate is hardened, carefully peel away the paper bags, starting at the lip of each bag and tearing away strips in a circular manner. Return bags to the refrigerator or freezer until ready to use.

To prepare the dish: An hour before serving, fill each bag with some of the mousse and generously garnish with fresh strawberries. Refrigerate until ready to serve.

Appendix A: Glossary

Aquaculture. Also known as aquafarming, it is the breeding of fish, crustaceans, mollusks, and aquatic plants under controlled conditions. Because it has the potential to produce large numbers of various species, aquaculture is seen by some as a possible solution to the problem of overfishing.

Blue crab. A crustacean with bright blue claws and an olive-green shell, the blue crab is synonymous with the Chesapeake Bay. Growing up to 9 inches wide, blue crabs dwell on the bottom of the bay, hibernating in its deep trenches each winter. Male blue crabs are typically found in the fresh waters of the bay and its tributaries, while females prefer the saltier waters.

Bugeye. The predecessor of the skipjack, the bugeye is an oyster-dredging sailboat developed in the Chesapeake Bay region.

Chesapeake Bay Watershed. Covering more than 64,000 square miles, the Chesapeake Bay watershed—a large swath of land whose streams, creeks, and rivers empty into the bay—comprises parts of Maryland, Delaware, New York, Pennsylvania, Virginia, and West Virginia, as well as all of Washington DC. Over 17 million people live in the Chesapeake Bay watershed.

Crab feast. A Chesapeake Bay tradition, crab feasts are lively, communal meals where diners devour piles of freshly steamed blue crabs. Mallets, hand wipes, and beer figure heavily into the messy feasts, which usually also include corn on the cob and a can of Old Bay on the side.

Crab mallet. A small wooden hammer used to crack open crab shells.

Crab pot. Smallish wire and steel traps used to catch crabs.

Crustaceans. Any primarily aquatic arthropod belonging to the class Crustacea, including crabs, lobsters, and shrimp. Crustaceans typically have hard shells (or exoskeletons) and two-parted limbs.

Deadrise. A traditional workboat used for oystering, fishing, and crabbing on the Chesapeake Bay. These boats are traditionally made of wood and include a small cabin in front and a large work area in the rear.

Dredging. A method of harvesting oysters and other bottom-dwelling species in which a framed net-like structure (a dredge) is dragged by boat along the Chesapeake Bay's floor, snagging critters as it goes. Once the dredge is full, it is hauled back into the boat and emptied.

Estuary. A partially enclosed coastal body of brackish water (i.e., a mixture of salt and fresh water) with one or more rivers, streams, or creeks flowing into it, and with a connection to the ocean. The Chesapeake Bay is one of the largest estuaries in the US.

Finfish. A true fish. The term "finfish" is often used to distinguish between true fish and shellfish.

Jimmy. A male blue crab. Jimmies have blue-tipped claws and an inverted-T shape on their underside.

Mollusks. Invertebrates from the phylum Mollusca, mollusks include clams, snails, squid, and octopus.

Molting. The process of sloughing off or shedding a skin or shell. Immediately post molting, a crab is known as a "soft shell" crab, the kind used in Maryland's iconic sandwich.

Overfishing. The process of over-harvesting finfish and shellfish to the point where certain species become dangerously depleted. Overfishing of the Chesapeake Bay has had a devastating impact on the region's blue crab and oyster populations.

Rockfish. Also known as striped bass, rockfish are a favorite on menus throughout the Chesapeake Bay region and were declared Maryland's official state fish in 1965.

Sally. An adolescent female blue crab. Sallies (also known as she-crabs) have red-tipped claws and an inverted-V shape on their underside.

Shoal. A shallow area—such as a sand bank or sandbar—in a body of water. Many of Maryland's lighthouses are built on shoals.

Skipjack. Designated Maryland's official state boat, the skipjack is the Chesapeake Bay region's most iconic vessel. A wooden-hulled sailboat, the skipjack has been used for oyster dredging since the late 19th century.

Sook. A mature female blue crab. Sooks have red-tipped claws and an inverted-bell shape on their underside.

Tonging. A seafood-harvesting method in which watermen and women use long, rake-like tongs to drag the floor of the Chesapeake Bay, scooping up oysters and other bottom-dwelling species as they go. Still practiced in the region today, tonging is an eco-friendly—if back-breaking—way to harvest the bay's bounty.

Trawling. A method of fishing wherein a net is pulled behind a boat, snagging fish as it goes. The net used for trawling is called a trawl; the boat is known as a trawler.

Appendix B: Seafood Markets

Upper Bay

Blue Crab House, 3501 Ady St., Street, MD 21154; (410) 836-1600; bluecrabhouse.com. Part restaurant, part carryout, and part market, the Blue Crab House offers some of the most delicious crustaceans in the Upper Bay (not to mention terrific sandwiches, snacks, and sides). Visit its website to sign up for text alerts—it'll give you the lowdown on the day's bulk crab prices.

Richard's Fish and Crabs, 2201 E. Churchville Rd., Bel Air, MD 21015; (410) 734-6161; richardsfishandcrabs.com. Locally owned and operated, Richard's Fish and Crabs is "dedicated to providing [customers] with premium local crabs and seafood consistently done right!" Because Richard's is serious about supporting area watermen, many of the offerings—which include grouper, haddock, rockfish, clams, and oysters—are pulled straight from the Chesapeake.

The Seafood Stop, 1607 Belair Rd., Fallston, MD 21047; (410) 887-2900; theseafoodstop.com. A full-service carryout and seafood market boasting hot steamed crabs (voted the best in Harford County), crab cakes, premium Gulf of Mexico shrimp, hand-picked Maryland crabmeat, a wide variety of fresh oysters, and too many other undersea treasures to name.

Eastern Shore

Captain's Ketch Seafood Market, 316 Glebe Rd., Easton, MD 21601; (410) 820-7177; captainsketchseafood.com. Founded in 1982 by Keith MacPherson, Captain's Ketch is dedicated to selecting "only the freshest quality product available." With a focus on Chesapeake Bay seafood, that means you should expect decadent blue crabs, briny oysters, flaky rockfish, and more.

Chesapeake Landing Seafood Market & Carry Out, 23713 St. Michaels Rd., St. Michaels, MD 21663; (410) 745-9600; chesapeake landingrestaurant.com. Boasting one of the Eastern Shore's premium assortments of fresh fish, clams, oysters, crabs, and shrimp, the market's carryout also offers all the requisite sides—including coleslaw and potato salad—to accompany your catch. (Note: Chesapeake Landing ships fresh seafood to anywhere in the US.)

Crab Alley Restaurant & Seafood Market, 9703 Golf Course Rd., West Ocean City, MD 21842; (410) 213-7800; craballeyoc.com. Also a restaurant, it's Crab Alley's Seafood Market that lures locals in the know who want to take home some excellent cream of crab soup, raw oysters and scallops, uncooked crab cakes, fresh rockfish fillets, and other maritime delicacies. Hoping to score a huge haul of fresh crabs? Call ahead for availability.

Fisherman's Inn Seafood Market, 3116 Main St., Grasonville, MD 21638; (410) 827-7323; crabdeck.com. On the hunt for succulent oysters, crabs, shrimp, scallops, clams, and fish? You'll find it all here—not to mention a large enough assortment of spices, breading mixes, soups, and sauces to make your next seafood soiree one for the record books.

Linton's Seafood Carryout, 4500 Crisfield Hwy., Crisfield, MD 21817; (410) 968-0127; lintonseafood.com. Whether you're on the hunt for hot steamed crabs, lobster tails, spiced shrimp, scallops, or just about anything with gills, you're bound to find it here. And when you do? Have your catch bagged up to take home, or head to Linton's deck and enjoy your bounty there. (Nowhere near Crisfield? Visit Linton's website and have them ship your order to you.)

Martin Fish Company, 12929 Harbor Rd., Ocean City, MD 21842; (410) 213-2195; martinfishco.com. Known as the place "Where the Boats Unload," the family-owned Martin Fish Company is synonymous with fresh Atlantic Ocean and Chesapeake Bay goodies, including the water's choicest fish, crabs, oysters, and clams.

Western Shore

Annapolis Seafood Markets, 1300 Forest Dr., Annapolis, MD
21403; (410) 269-5380; 552-L Ritchie Hwy., Severna Park, MD
21146; (410) 544-4900; annapolisseafoodmarket.com; @Anna
SeafoodMkt. With both its locations favorites among locals, the Annapolis Seafood Market has been a go-to resource for undersea delicacies in the
state's capital for more than 40 years. Believing that every "fish has a tale,"
the market prides itself on knowing just which waters its crabs, shrimp,
fish, and other delicacies were pulled from.

Conrad's Crabs & Seafood Market, 1720 E. Joppa Rd., Parkville,
MD 21234; (410) 882-1515; conradscrabs.com; @conradscrabs.
Since opening its doors in 2007, Conrad's has prided itself on selling the
finest-quality crabs in the Mid-Atlantic. Owner Anthony Conrad, a true
waterman, catches many of the crustaceans himself—sorting and steaming them to perfection before adding a sprinkle of the market's custom
seasoning.

Cross Street Seafood, 1065 S. Charles St., Baltimore, MD 21230;
(410) 727-7575. Featuring the freshest fish this side of Atlantis, Cross
Street Seafood is Federal Hill's one-stop shop for nautical noshes, whether
you're in the mood for half a dozen oysters or a mammoth batch of king
crab legs for a Poseidon-worthy picnic.

Wild Country Seafood, 124 Bay Shore Ave., Annapolis, MD 21403;
(410) 267-6711; wildcountryseafood.com. Also a restaurant, Wild
Country Seafood sells Owner Pat Mahoney's freshest catches in its on-site
market. That means the oysters will taste of the Chesapeake, the rockfish
will glisten from the bay water it was just pulled from, and the crabs will
still be pinching. And if the opening hours are a bit late? It's because
Mahoney is out on his boat reeling in the bounty.

Southern Maryland

Captain Smith's Seafood Market, 13944 Solomons Island Rd., Solomons, MD 20688; (410) 326-1134; tinyurl.com/qbfen7z. Why waste time steaming and seasoning your own crabs? Order them from Captain Smith's Seafood Market, and your only job will be to take 'em home and eat 'em! Craving fresh fish, shrimp, and oysters? Captain Smith's has you covered there, too.

Doc's Crabs, 7105 Indian Head Hwy., Bryans Road, MD 20616; (301) 283-6733; docscrabs.com. This no-frills seafood carryout boasts a terrific assortment of Maryland crabs, spiced shrimp, scallops, oysters, and just about anything else a Chesapeake Bay sea-foodie could want. (That includes all the necessary accoutrements—from crab mallets to knives—to make digging in that much easier.)

Kellam's Seafood, 16616 Three Notch Rd., Ridge, MD 20680; (301) 872-0100; kellamsseafood.com. Like its motto says, "We have the best seafood around and bait and tackle for all your fishing needs." That means fresh fish, soft and hard crabs (in season), oysters, and more. Pick up crabbing supplies and a Maryland Fishing License while you're here, or better yet, just savor the delectable seafood Kellam's has already hauled in!

Leonard Copsey's, 29004 Three Notch Rd., Mechanicsville, MD 20659; (301) 884-9529. Stop in for a huge pile of steamed hard-shell crabs or a bushel of clams or oysters—available both raw and ready to eat—to take home. Grab a six-pack of Bud on your way out, and don't forget to pick up a quart of hot crab soup, too. You'll be glad you did!

The Market at Captain John's Crab House, 16215 Cobb Island Rd., Newburg, MD 20664; (301) 259-2315; cjcrab.com. After tucking into a spectacular seafood feast at Captain John's Crab House, step into the adjacent market for some treats to take home. Offerings include steamed shrimp, crab legs by the pound, raw or shucked oysters, rockfish fillets, and even whole rockfish for DIY fishmongers.

Index